TRANS | GENDER

Warriors

TRANS

gender WARRIORS

MAKING HISTORY

FROM JOAN OF ARC

TO DENNIS RODMAN

LESLIE FEINBERG

Beacon Press

BOSTON

BEACON PRESS

25 Beacon Street

Boston, Massachusetts

02108-2892

*Beacon Press books are published under the
auspices of the Unitarian Universalist Association
of Congregations.*

05   10 9 8

*Book Design and Formatting
by Lucinda Hitchcock*

Library of Congress Cataloging-in-Publication Data

Feinberg, Leslie, 1949–

Transgender warriors: making history from
Joan of Arc to Dennis Rodman / Leslie Feinberg.

p. cm.

Includes bibliographical references and index.

ISBN 0-8070-7940-5 (cloth)

ISBN 0-8070-7941-3 (paper)

1. Transsexualism – History. 2. Transvestism –
History. 3. Gender identity – History. I. Title

HQ77.9.F44 1997

305.3 – dc21   96-37682

EPIGRAPH CREDITS

Part One: "Before the Scales, Tomorrow," by Otto
René Castillo from *Poetry Like Bread: Poets of the
Political Imagination From Curbstone Press*, edited by
Martin Espada, Curbstone Press, 1994. Translation
copyright ©1971 by Margaret Randall. Reprinted
with permission by Curbstone Press.

Part Two: Schlipp, P. A. *Albert Einstein, Philosopher-
Scientist.* New York: Tudor, 1950.

Part Three: "Still I Rise," from *And Still I Rise*, by
Maya Angelou. Copyright ©1978 by Maya
Angelou. Reprinted by permission of Random
House, Inc.

Part Four: Written by Karl Marx in the spring of
1845. First published by Frederick Engels in
Stuttgart in the 1888 Appendix to the separate edi-
tion of his book *Ludwig Feuerbach und der Ausgang
der klassischen deutschen Philosophie.*

Part Five: From *Sister Outsider: Essays & Speeches by
Audre Lorde.* Copyright ©1984 by Audre Lorde.
The Crossing Press Feminist Series, Freedom, Cali-
fornia: 1984.

CONTENTS

Preface   ix

Acknowledgments   xv

PART 1

ONE   *The Journey Begins   3*

TWO   *My Path to Consciousness   11*

THREE   *The Give Away   21*

FOUR   *They Called Her "Hommasse"   31*

PART 2

FIVE   *Our Sacred Past   39*

SIX   *Why Bigotry Began   49*

SEVEN   *But They Had Slaves!   55*

EIGHT   *Natural Becomes "Unnatural"   61*

PART 3

NINE   *"Holy War" against Trans People   67*

TEN   *Leading the Charge   75*

ELEVEN   *Not Just Passing   83*

PART 4

TWELVE   *From Germany to Stonewall   91*

THIRTEEN   *To Be or Not to Be   101*

FOURTEEN   *Sisterhood: Make It Real!   109*

FIFTEEN   *Making History   121*

PART 5

Portrait Gallery   131

APPENDIX A.

International Gender Bill of Rights   165

APPENDIX B.

Transgender Organizations   171

APPENDIX C.

Transgender Publications   177

Notes   181

Selected Bibliography   195

Photo Credits   199

Index   205

I've heard the question all my life. The answer is not so simple, since there are no pronouns in the English language as complex as I am, and I do not want to simplify myself in order to neatly fit one or the other. There are millions more like me in the United States alone.

We have a history filled with militant hero/ines. Yet therein lies the rub! How can I tell you about their battles when the words *woman* and *man*, *feminine* and *masculine*, are almost the only words that exist in the English language to describe all the vicissitudes of bodies and styles of expression?

Living struggles accelerate changes in language. I heard language evolve during the 1960s, when I came out into the drag bars of western New York and southern Ontario. At that time, the only words used to describe us cut and seared – yelled at us from the window of a screeching car, filled with potential bashers. There were no words that we'd go out of our way to use that made us feel good about ourselves.

When we all first heard the word "gay," some of my friends vehemently opposed the word on the grounds that it made us sound happy. "No one will ever use 'gay'," my friends assured me, each offering an alternative word, none of which took root. I learned that language can't be ordered individually, as if from a Sears catalog. It is forged collectively, in the fiery heat of struggle.

Right now, much of the sensitive language that was won by the liberation movements in the United States during the sixties and seventies is bearing the brunt of a right-wing backlash against being "politically correct." Where I come from, being "politically correct" means using language that respects other peoples' oppressions and wounds. This chosen language needs to be defended.

The words I use in this book may become outdated in a very short time, because the transgender movement is still young and defining itself. But while the slogans lettered on the banners may change quickly, the struggle will rage on. Since I am writing this book as a contribution to the demand for transgender liberation, the language I'm using in this book is not aimed at *defining* but at *defending* the diverse communities that are coalescing.

I don't have a personal stake in whether the trans liberation movement results in a new third pronoun, or gender-neutral pronouns, like the ones, such as *ze* (she/he) and *hir* (her/his), being experimented with in cyberspace. It is not the words in and of themselves that are important to me – it's our lives. The struggle of trans people over the centuries is not *his*-story or *her*-story. It is *our*-story.

I've been called a he-she, butch, bulldagger, cross-dresser, passing woman, female-to-male transvestite, and drag king. The word I prefer to use to describe myself is *transgender*.

Today the word transgender has at least two colloquial meanings. It has been used as an umbrella term to include everyone who challenges the boundaries of sex and gender. It is also used to draw a distinction between those who reassign the sex they were labeled at birth, and those of us whose gender expression is considered inappropriate for our sex. Presently, many organizations – from Transgender Nation in San Francisco to Monmouth Ocean Transgender on the Jersey shore – use this term inclusively.

I asked many self-identified transgender activists who are named or pictured in this book who they believed were included under the umbrella term. Those polled named: transsexuals, transgenders, transvestites, transgenderists, bigenders, drag queens, drag kings, cross-dressers, masculine women, feminine men, intersexuals (people referred to in the past as "hermaphrodites"), androgynes, cross-genders, shape-shifters, passing women, passing men, gender-benders, gender-blenders, bearded women, and women bodybuilders who have crossed the line of what is considered socially acceptable for a female body.

But the word transgender is increasingly being used in a more specific way as well. The term *transgenderist* was first introduced into the English language by trans warrior Virginia Prince. Virginia told me, "I coined the noun *transgenderist* in 1987 or '88. There had to be some name for people like myself who trans the gender barrier – meaning somebody who lives full time in the gender opposite to their anatomy. I have not transed the sex barrier."

As the overall transgender movement has developed, more people are exploring this distinction between a person's sex – female, intersexual; male – and their gender expression – feminine, androgynous, masculine, and other variations. Many national and local gender magazines and community groups are starting to use TS/TG: transsexual and transgender.

Under Western law, doctors glance at the genitals of an infant and pronounce the baby female or male, and that's that. Trans*sexual* men and women traverse the boundary of the *sex* they were assigned at birth.

And in dominant Western cultures, the gender expression of babies is assumed at birth: pink for girls, blue for boys; girls are expected to grow up feminine, boys masculine. Trans*gender* people traverse, bridge, or blur the boundary of the *gender expression* they were assigned at birth.

However, not all transsexuals choose surgery or hormones; some transgender people do. I am trans*gender* and I have shaped myself surgically and hormonally twice in my life, and I reserve the right to do it again.

But while our movement has introduced some new terminology, all the words used to refer to our communities still suffer from limitations. For example, terms like cross-dress, cross-gender, male-to-female, and female-to-male reinforce the idea that there are only two distinct ways to be – you're either one or the other – and that's just not true. *Bigender* means people have both a feminine side and a masculine side. In the past, most bigendered individuals were lumped together under the category of cross-dressers. However, some people live their whole lives cross-dressed; others are referred to as part-time cross-dressers. Perhaps if gender oppression didn't exist, some of those part-timers would enjoy the freedom to cross-dress all the time. But bigendered people want to be able to express *both* facets of who they are.

Although I defend any person's right to use *transvestite* as a *self*-definition, I use the term sparingly in this book. Although some trans publications and organizations still use "transvestite" or the abbreviation "TV" in their titles, many people who are labeled transvestites have rejected the term because it invokes concepts of psychological pathology, sexual fetishism, and obsession, when there's really nothing at all unhealthy about this form of self-expression. And the medical and psychiatric industries have always defined transvestites as males, but there are many female cross-dressers as well.

The words cross-dresser, transvestite, and drag convey the sense that these intricate expressions of self revolve solely around clothing. This creates the impression that if you're so oppressed because of what you're wearing, you can just change your outfit! But anyone who saw *La Cage aux Folles* remembers that the drag queen never seemed more feminine than when she was crammed into a three-piece "man's" suit and taught to butter bread like a "real man." Because it is our entire spirit – the essence of who we are – that doesn't conform to narrow gender stereotypes, many people who in the past have been referred to as cross-dressers, transvestites, drag queens, and drag kings today define themselves as trans*gender.*

All together, our many communities challenge *all* sex and gender borders and restrictions. The glue that cements these diverse communities together is the defense of the right of each individual to define themselves.

As I write this book, the word *trans* is being used increasingly by the gender community as a term uniting the entire coalition. If the term had already enjoyed popular recognition, I would have titled this book *Trans Warriors*. But since the word *transgender* is still most recognizable to people all over the world, I use it in its most inclusive sense: to refer to all courageous trans warriors of every sex and gender – those who led battles and rebellions throughout history and those who today muster the courage to battle for their identities and for their very lives.

Transgender Warriors is not an exhaustive trans history, or even the history of the rise and development of the modern trans movement. Instead, it is a fresh look at sex and gender in history and the interrelationships of class, nationality, race, and sexuality. Have all societies recognized only two sexes? Have people who traversed the boundaries of sex and gender always been so demonized? Why is sex-reassignment or cross-dressing a matter of law?

But how could I find the answers to these questions when it means wending my way through diverse societies in which the concepts of sex and gender shift like sand dunes over the ages? And as a white, transgender researcher, how can I avoid foisting my own interpretations on the cultures of oppressed peoples' nationalities?

I tackled this problem in several ways. First, I focused a great deal of attention on Western Europe, not out of unexamined Eurocentrism, but because I hold the powers that ruled there for centuries responsible for campaigns of hatred and bigotry that are today woven into the fabric of Western cultures and have been imposed upon colonized peoples all over the world. Setting the blame for these attitudes squarely on the shoulders of the European ruling classes is part of my contribution to the anti-imperialist movements.

I've also included photos from cultures all over the world, and I've sought out people from those countries and nationalities to help me create short, factual captions. I tried very hard not to interpret or compare these different cultural expressions. These photographs are not meant to imply that the individuals pictured identify themselves as transgender in the modern, Western sense of the word. Instead, I've presented their images as a challenge to the currently accepted Western dominant view that woman and man are all that exist, and that there is only one way to be a woman or a man.

I don't take a view that an individual's gender expression is exclusively a product of either biology or culture. If gender is solely biologically determined, why do rural women, for example, tend to be more "masculine" than urban women? On the other hand, if gender expression is simply something we are taught, why has such a huge trans segment of the population not learned it? If two sexes are an immutable biological fact, why have so many societies recognized more than two? Yet while biology is not destiny, there *are* some biological markers on the human anatomical spectrum. So is sex a social construct, or is the rigid categorization of sexes the cultural component? Clearly there must be a complex interaction between individuals and their societies.

My interest in this subject is not merely theoretical. You probably already know that those of us who cross the cultural boundaries of sex and gender are paying a terrible price. We face discrimination and physical violence. We are denied the right to live and work with dignity and respect. It takes so much courage to live our lives that sometimes just leaving our homes in the morning and facing the world as who we really are is in itself an act of resistance. But perhaps you didn't know that we have a history of fighting against such injustice, and that today we are forging a movement for liberation. Since I couldn't include photos of all the hard-working leading activists who make up our movement, I have included a collection of photos that begins to illustrate the depth and breadth of sex and gender identities, balanced by race, nationality, and region. No one book could include all the sundry identities of trans individuals and organizations, which range from the Short Mountain Fairies from Tennessee to the Sisters of Perpetual Indulgence in San Francisco.

It is time for us to write as experts on our own histories. For too long our light has been refracted through other people's prisms. My goal in this book is to fashion history, politics, and theory into a steely weapon with which to defend a very oppressed segment of the population.

I grew up thinking that the hatred I faced because of my gender expression was simply a by-product of human nature, and that it must be my fault that I was a target for such outrage. I don't want any young person to ever believe that's true again, and so I wrote this book to lay bare the roots and tendrils of sex and gender oppression.

Today, a great deal of "gender theory" is abstracted from human experience. But if theory is not the crystallized resin of experience, it ceases to be a guide to action. I offer history, politics, and theory that live and breathe because they are rooted in the experience of real people who fought flesh-and-blood battles for freedom. And my work is not solely devoted to chronicling the past, but is a component of my organizing to help shape the future.

This is the *heart* of my life's work. When I clenched my fists and shouted back at slurs aimed to strip me of my humanity, this was the certainty behind my anger. When I sputtered in pain at well-meaning individuals who told me, "I just don't get what you are?" – this is what I meant. Today, *Transgender Warriors* is my answer. This is the core of my pride.

ACKNOWLEDGMENTS

I'VE BEEN FORCED TO PACK UP
and move quickly many times in the last twenty years – spurred by my inability to pay the rent or, all too often, by a serious threat to my life that couldn't be faced down. Yet no matter how much I was forced to leave behind, I always schlepped my cartons of transgender research with me. Thanks to my true friends who got up in the middle of the night, wiped the sleep from their eyes, and helped me move. You rescued my life, and my work.

Over the decades, my writings on trans oppression, resistance, and history have appeared as articles in *Workers World* newspaper, and *Liberation and Marxism* magazine. I have spoken about these topics at countless political meetings, street rallies, and activist conferences. So I thank the members of Workers World Party – of every nationality, sex, age, ability, gender, and sexuality – for liberating space for me, helping me develop, and defending a podium from which I could speak about trans liberation as a vital component of the struggle for economic and social justice.

Some special thanks. To Gregory Dunkel for waking me some twenty years ago to the need to archive the images I'd found, and then helping me every step of the way. To Sara Flounders, for proving to be such a good friend and ally to the trans communities – and to me. My gratitude and love for Dorothy Ballan is right here in my heart. I'm especially grateful for the unflagging support from my transsexual, transgender, drag, and intersexual comrades – especially Kristianna Tho'mas.

In 1992 I wrote the pamphlet *Transgender Liberation: A Movement Whose Time Has Come*, which became the basis for my slide show. I traveled the country showing slides in places as diverse as an auditorium at Brown University and a back room of a pizzeria/bar in Little Rock, Arkansas. Thousands of you asked questions during or after the program, which contributed to this finished work. Maybe you sent me a clipping, photo, or book reference. You've all offered me support. I am grateful for this kindness and solidarity.

My gratitude to each of the trans warriors included in this book. But many other transsexual, transgender, drag, intersexual, and bigender warriors gave me a heap of help and support, including: Holly Boswell, Cheryl Chase, Loren Cameron, Dallas Denny and the valuable resources of the National Transgender Library and Archive, Lissa Fried, Dana Friedman, Davina Anne Gabriel, James Green, David Harris, Mike Hernandez, Craig Hickman, Morgan Holmes, Nancy Nangeroni, Linda and Cynthia Phillips, Bet Power, Sky Renfro, Martine and Bina Rothblatt, Ruben, Gail Sondegaard, Susan Stryker, Virginia Prince, Lynn Walker, Riki Wilchins, and Jessy Xavier.

Chrystos, you really served as editor of Chapter 3; I loved working with you! Thanks to other friends and allies who also gently helped me to express my solidarity with people of other nationalities in the most sensitive possible way: Yamila Azize-Vargas, my beloved Nic Billey, Ben the Dancer, Spotted Eagle, Elias Farajaje-Jones, Curtis Harris, Larry Holmes, Leota Lone Dog, Aurora Levins Morales, Pauline Park, Geeta Patel, Doyle Robertson, Barbara Smith, Sabrina Sojourner, and Wesley Thomas.

Then there was the research. Leslie Kahn, you are my goddess of transgender library research. Miriam Hammer, I will always remember you coming to my home at the eleventh hour after I'd lost my manuscript and research to a computer virus. Thanks to Allan Berubé, Melanie Breen, Paddy Colligan, Randy P. Conner, Bill Dragoin, Anne Fausto-Sterling, Jonathan Ned Katz, and Julie Wheelwright.

My warmest thanks to Morgan Gwenwald and Mariette Pathy Allen – who worked on this project as photographic consultants and advisors. Amy Steiner, thanks! And I owe a debt of gratitude to the many brilliant documentary and art photographers, amateur shutterbugs, graphic artists, and a wildly popular cartoonist – who all contributed to this book. Special thanks to Marcus Alonso, Alison Bechdel, Loren Cameron, Stephanie Dumaine, Greg Dunkel, Robert Giard, Steve Gillis, Andrew Holbrooke, Jennie Livingston, Viviane Moos, John Nafpliotis, Lyn Neely, V. Jon Nivens, Cathy Opie, M. P. Schildmeyer, Bette Spero, Pierre Verger, and Gary Wilson. And my regards to the darkroom folks, particularly Ligia Boters and Brian Young at Phototechnica, and the guys at Hong Color.

As I saw how much archivists, librarians, and researchers all over the world cared about preserving our collective past and making it accessible, my respect for their work soared. Special thanks to archivist Janet Miller, and your Uncommon Vision, and the staffs of the Schomburg Collection, Museum of the American Indian, Smithsonian Institute (especially Vertis), Library of Congress, State Hermitage Museum of Russia, Mansell Collection, British Library, National Library of Wales, Royal Anthropological Institute, British Museum, Louvre, American Library Association, Bettmann Archive, New York Public Library, Musée de Beaux Arts de Rouen, Staatliche Museen, Clarke Historical Library, Verger Institute, Nationalmuseum Stockholm, Cleveland Museum of Art, Guildhall Library, and Art Resource.

For support that came in many forms, my gratitude to: John Catalinotto, Kate Clinton, Hillel Cohen, Annette Dragon, Bob Diaz, Ferron, Nanette Gartrell, Diane McPherson, Dee Mosbacher, Joy Schaefer, Adrienne Rich, Beth Zemsky, and Carlos Zúñiga.

To my agent, Charlotte Sheedy – it's an honor to work with a pioneer who marked the trail for so many of us. To Deb Chasman, my editor at Beacon – you've demonstrated that editing genius is sharp style, and a whole lot of sensitivity. My gratitude to Ken Wong for grammatically scrubbing this book. And I thank the whole staff at Beacon for their contributions – not the least of which was enthusiastic support.

Thanks to those whose astute reading of my drafts greatly developed this book – especially Elly Bulkin and Deirdre Sinnott. For teaching me how to be a journalist, over two decades, I credit you, Deirdre Griswold – longtime editor, longtime friend.

Now I go a bit deeper. Thanks to my sons – Ben and Ransom – for loving and supporting your Drag Dad. I love you each dearly. To my sister Catherine, and my "chosen family" – Star, Shelley, Robin, Brent and my mom Wyontmusqui – how else can I thank you for your love except to love you right back.

To my wife, my inspiration, and my dearest friend, poet-warrior Minnie Bruce Pratt – I couldn't have gotten through this without you. I've stoop-picked beans and stretch-picked apples, but this book was the hardest work I've ever done. Your brilliance, insight, and generous love got me through each day. How could I possibly thank you in the way you deserve? Tell you what – As we grow old happily – one day at a time – I'll try to find the ways.

The sum total of everyone's contributions to this book is a collective act of solidarity with trans liberation. Since the movement to bring a better world into birth developed me and my world view, I give this book – and every cent of the advance royalties, an author's wages – back to the struggle to end all oppression.

TRANS GENDER

Warriors

And when the enthusiastic
story of our time
is told,
for those
who are yet to be born
but announce themselves
with more generous face,
we will come out ahead
— those who have suffered most from it.

FROM *"Before the Scales, Tomorrow,"*
BY OTTO RENÉ CASTILLO,
Guatemalan Revolutionary,
EXECUTED IN 1967.

Part One

CHAPTER **1.**

WHEN I WAS BORN

in 1949, the doctor confidently declared, "It's a girl." That might have been the last time anyone was so sure. I grew up a very masculine girl. It's a simple statement to write, but it was a terrifying reality to live.

I was raised in the 1950s – an era marked by rigidly enforced social conformity and fear of difference. Our family lived in the Bell Aircraft factory housing projects. The roads were not paved; the coal truck, ice man's van, and knife-sharpener's cart crunched along narrow strips of gravel.

I tried to mesh two parallel worlds as a child – the one I saw with my own eyes and the one I was taught. For example, I witnessed powerful adult women in our working-class projects handling every challenge of life, while coping with too many kids and not enough money. Although I hated seeing them so beaten down by poverty, I loved their laughter and their strength. But, on television I saw women depicted as foolish and not very bright. Every cultural message taught me that women were only capable of being wives, mothers, housekeepers – seen, not heard. So, was it true that women were the "weak" sex?

In school I leafed through my geography textbooks and saw people of many different hues from countries far, far from my home. Before we moved to Buffalo, my family had lived in a desert town in Arizona. There, people who were darker skinned and shared different customs from mine were a sizeable segment of the population. Yet in the small world of the projects, most of the kids in my grade school, and my teachers, were white. The entire city was segregated right down the middle – east and west. In school I listened as some teachers paid lip service to "tolerance" but I frequently heard adults mouth racist slurs, driven by hate.

I saw a lot of love. Love of parents, flag, country, and deity were mandatory. But I also observed other loves – between girls and boys, and boys and boys, and girls and girls. There was the love of kids and dogs in my neighborhood, soldier buddies in foxholes in movies, students and teachers at school. Passionate, platonic, sensual, dutiful, devoted, reluctant, loyal, shy, reverent. Yet I was taught there was only one official meaning of the word *love* – the kind between men and women that leads to

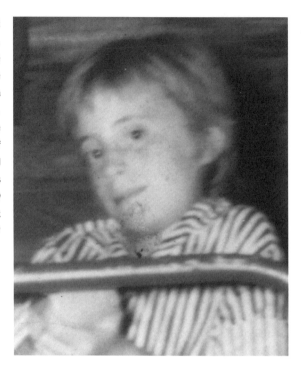

marriage. No adult ever mentioned men loving men or women loving women in my presence. I never heard it discussed anywhere. There was no word at that time in my English language to express the sheer joy of loving someone of the same sex.

And I learned very early on that boys were expected to wear "men's" clothes, and girls were not. When a man put on women's garb, it was considered a crude joke. By the time my family got a television, I cringed as my folks guffawed when "Uncle Miltie" Berle donned a dress. It hit too close to home. I longed to wear the boys' clothing I saw in the Sears catalog.

My own gender expression felt quite natural. I liked my hair short and I felt most relaxed in sneakers, jeans and a t-shirt. However, when I was most at home with how I looked, adults did a double-take or stopped short when they saw me. The question, "Is that a boy or a girl?" hounded me throughout my childhood. The answer didn't matter much. The very fact that strangers had to *ask* the question already marked me as a gender outlaw.

My choice of clothing was not the only alarm bell that rang my difference. If my more feminine younger sister had worn "boy's" clothes, she might have seemed stylish and cute. Dressing all little girls and all little boys in "sex-appropriate" clothing actually called attention to our gender differences. Those of us who didn't fit stuck out like sore thumbs.

Being different in the 1950s was no small matter. McCarthy's anti-communist witch hunts were in full frenzy. Like most children, I caught snippets of adult conversations. So I was terrified that communists were hiding under my bed and might grab my ankles at night. I heard that people who were labeled "reds" would discover their

names and addresses listed in local newspapers, be fired from their jobs, and be forced to pack up their families and move away. What was their crime? I couldn't make out the adults' whispers. But the lesson seeped down: keep your mouth shut; don't rock the boat. I overheard angry, hammering accusations on radio and television against grownups who had to answer to a committee of men. I heard the words: commie, pinko, Jew. I was Jewish.

We were the only Jews in the projects. Our family harbored memories of the horrors that relatives and friends had faced in Czarist Russia before the 1917 revolution and in Eastern Europe during World War II. My family lived in fear of fascism, and the McCarthy era stank like Nazism. Every time a stranger stopped us on the street and asked my parents, "Is that a boy or a girl?" they shuddered. No wonder. My parents worried that I was a lightning rod that would attract a dangerous storm. Feeling

ABOVE LEFT: This person is about to face a 1951 Chicago grand jury, charged with failure to report to the draft board for induction. ABOVE RIGHT: These two people are being led into Manhattan felony court in 1952. Their crime? They went to the movies together. The manager spotted them and called the police. FAR RIGHT: Police raid on a Manhattan Ball in 1962.

helpless to fight the powers that be, they blamed the family's problems on me and my difference. I learned that my survival was my own responsibility. From kindergarten to high school, I walked through a hail of catcalls and taunts in school corridors. I pushed my way past clusters of teenagers on street corners who refused to let me pass. I endured the stares and glares of adults. It was so hard to be a masculine girl in the 1950s that I thought I would certainly be killed before I could grow to adulthood. Every gender image – from my Dick and Jane textbooks in school to the sitcoms on television – convinced me that I must be a Martian.

In all the years of my childhood, I had only heard of one person who seemed similarly "different." I don't remember any adult telling me her name. I was too young to read the newspaper headlines. Adults clipped their vulgar jokes short when I, or any other child, entered the room. I wasn't allowed to stay up late enough to watch the television comedy hosts who tried to ridicule her out of humanity.

But I did know her name: Christine Jorgensen.

I was three years old when the news broke that Christine Jorgensen had traveled from the United States to Sweden for a sex change from male to female. A passport agent reportedly sold the story to the media. All hell broke loose. In the years that followed, just the mention of her name provoked vicious laughter. The cruelty must have filtered down to me, because I understood that the jokes rotated around whether Christine Jorgensen was a woman or a man. Everyone was supposed to easily fit into one category or another, and stay there. But I didn't fit, so Christine Jorgensen and I had a special bond. By the time I was eight or nine years old, I had asked a baby-sitter, "Is Christine Jorgensen a man or a woman?"

"She isn't anything," my baby-sitter giggled. "She's a freak." Then, I thought, I must be a freak too, because nobody seemed sure whether I was a boy or a girl. What was going to happen to me? Would I survive? Would Christine survive?

As it turned out, Christine Jorgensen didn't just endure, she triumphed. I knew she must be living with great internal turmoil, but she walked through the abuse with her head held high. Just as her dignity and courage set a proud example for the thousands of transsexual men and women who followed her path, she inspired me – and who knows how many other transgendered children.

Little did I know then that millions of children and adults across the United States and around the world also felt like the only person who was different. I had no other adult role model who crossed the boundaries of sex or gender. Christine Jorgensen's struggle beamed a message to me that I wasn't alone. She proved that even a period of right-wing reaction could not coerce each individual into conformity.

I survived growing up transgendered during the iron-fisted repression of the 1950s. But I came of age and consciousness during the revolutionary potential of the 1960s – from the Civil Rights movement to the Black Panther Party, from the Young Lords to the American Indian movement, from the anti-Vietnam War struggles to women's liberation. The lesbian and gay movement had not yet emerged. But as a teenager, I found the gay bars in Niagara Falls, Buffalo, and Toronto. Inside

those smoke-filled taverns I discovered a community of drag queens, butches, and femmes. This was a world in which I *fit;* I was no longer alone.

It meant the world to me to find other people who faced many of the same problems I did. Continual violence stalked me on the streets, leaving me weary, so of course I wanted to be with friends and loved ones in the bars. But the clubs were not a safe sanctuary. I soon discovered that the police and other enemies preyed on us there. Until we organized to fight back, we were just a bigger group of people to bash.

But we did organize. We battled for the right to be hired, walk down the street, be served in a restaurant, buy a carton of milk at a store, play softball or bowl. Defending our rights to live and love and work won us respect and affection from our straight co-workers and friends. Our battles helped fuel the later explosion of the lesbian and gay liberation movement.

I remember the Thaw Out Picnic held each spring during the sixties by the lesbian and gay community in Erie, Pennsylvania. Hundreds and hundreds of women and men would fill a huge park to enjoy food, dancing, softball, and making out in the woods. During the first picnic I attended, a group of men screeched up in a car near the edge of the woods. Suddenly the din of festivity hushed as we saw the gang, armed with baseball bats and tire irons, marching down the hill toward us.

"C'mon," one of the silver-haired butches shouted, beckoning us to follow. She picked up her softball bat and headed right for those men. We all grabbed bats and beer bottles and followed her, moving slowly up the hill toward the men. First they jeered us. Then they glanced fearfully at each other, leaped back into their car and peeled rubber. One of them was still trying to get his legs inside and shut the car door as they roared off. We all stood quietly for a moment, feeling our collective power. Then the old butch who led our army waved her hand and the celebration resumed.

My greatest terror was always when the police raided the bars, because they had the law on their side. They *were* the law. It wasn't just the tie I was wearing or the suit coat that made me vulnerable to arrest. I broke the law every time I dressed in fly-front pants, or wore jockey shorts or t-shirts. The law dictated that I had to wear at least three pieces of "women's" clothing. My drag queen sisters had to wear three pieces of "men's" clothing. For all I know, that law may still be on the books in Buffalo today.

Of course, the laws were not simply about clothing. We were masculine women and feminine men. Our *gender expression* made us targets. These laws were used to harass us. Frequently we were not even formally charged after our arrests. All too often, the sentences were executed in the back seat of a police cruiser or on the cold cement floor of a precinct cell.

But the old butches told me there was one night of the year that the cops never arrested us – Halloween. At the time, I wondered why I was exempt from penalties for cross-dressing on that one night. And I grappled with other questions. Why was I subject to legal harassment and arrest at all? Why was I being punished for the way I walked or dressed, or who I loved? Who wrote the laws used to harass us, and why? Who gave the green light to the cops to enforce them? Who decided what was normal in the first place?

These were life-and-death questions for me. Finding the answers sooner would have changed my life dramatically. But the journey to find those answers *is* my life. And I would not trade the insights and joys of my lifetime for anyone else's.

This was how my journey began. It was 1969 and I was twenty years old. As I sat in a gay bar in Buffalo, a friend told me that drag queens had fought back against a police bar raid in New York City. The fight had erupted into a four-night-long uprising in Greenwich Village – the Stonewall Rebellion! I pounded the bar with my fist and cursed my fate. For once we had rebelled and made history and I had missed it!

I stared at my beer bottle and wondered: Have we always existed? Have we always been so hated? Have we always fought back?

MY PATH TO CONSCIOUSNESS

Many lives of females who lived as men are reduced to headlines such as these. While we'll never know which of these individuals would today describe themselves as trans-sexual, transgender, drag king, butch, or some other contemporary identity, it is clear they could not live openly and proudly. Had I not spent twenty years in the movement for change and lived in a historical period in which a trans move-ment arose, my life could have also been diminished into a salacious headline.

CHAPTER 2

IT HAD NEVER OCCURRED

to me to search history for answers to my questions. I didn't do well in history classes in school. Actually, that's an understatement. I could never make sense out of history. I couldn't remember whether Greece or Rome came first. The Middle Ages were a monolithic boulder I couldn't chip. I always got confused about who were allies during which war.

I couldn't find *myself* in history. No one like me seemed to have ever existed.

But I *had* to know why I was so hated for being "different." What was the root cause of bigotry, and what was its driving force? Some people expect to find answers to questions like these in hallowed halls of learning. But I found what I was looking for on another path – by working in the factories and the political movement for justice.

Looking back, I can see that growing up blue-collar shaped my life and my consciousness in general, but it didn't automatically make me progressive. My parents instructed us not to be racist when we were kids because they thought it was wrong to teach children to hate. That was a good start, but it wasn't until I began working in the plants as a teenager that I really learned the function of institutionalized racism. I quickly understood the phrase "divide-and-conquer." Whenever a strike loomed, the foremen suddenly tried to cozy up to a few of the white workers, "advising" us not to trust the African-American, Latino, and Native workers. "Don't count on the women, either," they would whisper to the white men. "They've got their husband's paycheck, too. They won't stand with you." And the supervisors and their helpers hung out near the time clock as we all punched in, their voices rising on the epithets "bulldagger" and "faggot."

Sometimes other workers told me the foreman had informed them that all Jews were rich bankers and industrialists responsible for the suffering of the working class. But I'd remind my co-workers they labored alongside Jews like myself on the assembly line every day, and since when did the foreman care about *our* misery! It became clear to me that racism and anti-Semitism – like woman-hating and homophobia – were designed to keep us battling each other, instead of fighting together to win real change.

However, my understanding of class dynamics was limited to factory life. This was the 1960s. There were plenty of jobs. We had won livable wages. The system seemed to be working for me. It didn't occur to me that this economic prosperity was based on weapons production and government spending for the Pentagon's war against Vietnam. So I didn't make the connections as I sat, stalled in traffic on my motorcycle, as anti-war protestors marched down Main Street chanting "Big firms get rich, GI's die!"

My view of the world was limited to my factory, the gay bars, my friends, and my lover. Outside of my own small sphere, society was roiling. This struggle also raged in Buffalo. University students occupied the local campus. Tear gas wafted across Buffalo streets. The African-American community rebelled in righteous fury. I could even hear the impact of the women's movement in our conversations at work. Change was rocking the world outside my window. But it took one more event to radically change my consciousness – unemployment.

When factories were humming with production during the war years – and many young men were being shipped to Vietnam – everyone was considered employable. But as the boom economy receded during the early 1970s, we stood in block-long lines just to get a job application. If I forgot for a moment just how "different" I was, the recession reminded me. I was considered far too masculine a woman to get a job in a store, or a restaurant, or an office.

I couldn't survive without working. So one day I put on a femme friend's wig and earrings and tried to apply for a job as a salesperson at a downtown retail store. On the bus ride to the interview, people stood rather than sit next to me. They whispered and pointed and stared. "Is that a *man*?" one woman asked her friend, loud enough for us all to hear.

The experience taught me an important lesson. The more I tried to wear clothing or styles considered appropriate for women, the more people believed I was a man trying to pass as a woman. I began to understand that I couldn't conceal my gender expression.

So I tried another experiment. I called one of the older butches who I knew passed as a man on a construction gang. She lent me a pair of paste-on theatrical sideburns. After gluing them on, I drove to the Albright-Knox Art Gallery. As I walked around, nobody seemed to stare. That was an unusual experience and a relief. I allowed my voice to drop to a comfortably low register and chatted with one of the guards about the job situation. He told me there was an opening for a guard and suggested I apply. An hour later, the supervisor who interviewed me told me I seemed like a "good man" and hired me on the spot. I was suddenly acceptable as a human being. The same gender expression that made me hated as a woman, made me seem like a good man.

My life changed dramatically the moment I began working as a man. I was free of the day-in, day-out harassment that had pursued me. But I also lived in constant terror as a gender outlaw. What punishments would I face when I was discovered? The fear moved me to make a complex decision: I decided to begin taking male hormones, prescribed to me by a local sex-reassignment program. Through this program, I also located a surgeon who would do a breast reduction. Shaping my body was something I had long wanted to do and I've never had any regrets. But I started taking hormones in order to pass. A year after beginning hormone shots, I sprouted a full, colorful beard that provided me with a greater sense of safety – on the job and off. With these changes, I explored yet another facet of my trans identity.

The years I worked at the art gallery impacted my consciousness. I spent eight hours a day surrounded by centuries of artwork. Listening to the tour guides, I began to understand how developments in technology – like the camera – influenced art. I got a luxury education.

But I soon learned that the art gallery wasn't designed merely for the enlightenment of working-class people like myself. I discovered there was another class in Buffalo I'd never seen before, and the gallery was one of the elegant places where they entertained. They arrived in limousines. They wore tuxedos in mid-afternoon. They clinked champagne glasses served to them by waiters they didn't notice.

One morning as I punched in, the atmosphere at the gallery felt electrically charged. My supervisor ordered me to straighten my tie and polish my black shoes until they gleamed – Nelson Rockefeller would be paying a visit. I was assigned to be the guard at the entrance of the gallery when he arrived.

I paced around the front entrance, smoking one cigarette after another. "Is he here, yet?" the head guard asked again and again. I saw the glint off a line of sleek black limos as they turned into the parking circle in front of the gallery. Squinting to see through the dark glass, I noticed dozens of protesters waving placards that read "Attica's blood on Rockefeller's hands!" When the lead limo driver got out and opened the rear car door, I recognized Rockefeller from his pictures in the newspapers. He sneered at the demonstrators and flipped them the finger.

My boss shouted at me, "Open the door for him! Open the door!" As I reached forward and held the door open, Rockefeller stepped inside. "Thanks, boy," he muttered without looking at me.

That moment was an epiphany.

No matter how much passing as a man had changed my daily life, I understood then that the rock foundation of my class had not changed. Until that moment, I had directed all my rage against the foremen and the middle-class people – like small business owners – who were arrogant and rude to me. I had thought they held the reins of power. But suddenly I had an opportunity to watch Rockefeller and his wealthy associates stride down the hall, oblivious to a handful of middle-class art gallery volunteers hurrying to keep up with them. I snapped a new mental picture of middle-class people as literally caught in the middle – between Rockefeller and me.

I realized that the men in tuxedos who strolled through the gallery halls like they owned the world really did! Here was Rockefeller hobnobbing with the Knoxes and Schoellkopfs and other men who privately owned the very factories I had worked in and the banks where I cashed my checks. They represented just a few families, yet they claimed as their own industry, finance, and communications – all the massive tools that sustain human life.

I thought about the huge factories of Buffalo: Anaconda Copper, Chevrolet, Bethlehem Steel. People like me built them from the ground up. Our muscles set those tools of production into motion. So why did these families who didn't work there own it all? And why, after lifetimes of labor, did working-class people like myself own little else than the ability to toil for a paycheck?

I thought about the placards that demonstrators angrily waved at Rockefeller when he arrived. I knew the Attica prisoners were workers, too. Yet they were paid only pennies a day for their labor. When these prisoners – predominantly men of color – rose up and demanded to be treated as human beings, not beasts, Rockefeller ordered troopers to open fire and mow them down. I found several books on labor history at the library about miners who organized and demanded economic justice. They were cut down by bullets with another Rockefeller's name on them.[1]

Now I felt connected to this vortex of struggle.

Soon after the Rockefeller incident, I quit my job at the art gallery and found work as a third-shift dishwasher at a local diner. As I hauled heavy pans filled with dishes and silverware into the kitchen, I listened to the radio blaring from a shelf over the sink. The big news, night after night, was the bloody military coup in Chile. Newscasters reported tens of thousands of Chileans were being tortured or had fled in exile. The junta generals smashed the workers' organizations and boasted they would hang a Jew from every lamppost.

One morning after my shift, I told one of the short-order cooks who had been a merchant sailor how upset I was by a news report that the CIA was behind the coup in Chile. He explained to me that when the Chileans had elected a socialist as president, big U.S. companies like ITT and Anaconda Copper started plotting the coup with the CIA. He told me you can't just vote for socialism, you have to fight to win it.

I was angry and sickened at so much genocide by the U.S. military – from the massacre at Wounded Knee to the war against Vietnam. I wanted to travel to Latin America to join the resistance movement. But when I applied for merchant seaman papers and asked a clerk what was required to join, he said a physical exam. My idealistic dream hit a dead end.

Weeks later I asked one of the day-shift waitresses out on a date for Friday night. She said no, she attended meetings every Friday evening. Nobody I knew went to meetings about anything. "What are you?" I joked, "a communist?" All conversation stopped in the restaurant. She flushed. A co-worker dragged me into the kitchen. "What did you do that for?" she scolded me. "You could get us fired." She said they were both members of the Workers World Party.[2] I was working with two communist waitresses! I apologized profusely. I hadn't meant to hurt anyone. To me, "communist" had always been a meaningless slur, not a real person. I didn't even know what the word really meant.

I began to dawdle over breakfast during shift changes, asking both waitresses questions. After weeks of inquiries, they invited me to a demonstration, outside Kleinhan's Music Hall, protesting the Israeli war against Egypt and Syria. I was particularly interested in that protest. The state of Israel had been declared shortly before my birth. In Hebrew school I was taught "Palestine was a land without people, for a people without a land." That phrase haunted me as a child. I pictured cars with no one in them, and movies projected on screens in empty theaters. When I checked a map of that region of the Middle East in my school geography textbook, it was labeled Palestine, not Israel. Yet when I asked my grandmother who the Palestinians were, she told me there were no such people.

The puzzle had been solved for me in my adolescence. I developed a strong friendship with a Lebanese teenager, who explained to me that the Palestinian people had been driven off their land by Zionist settlers, like the Native peoples in the United States. I studied and thought a great deal about all she told me. From that point on I staunchly opposed Zionist ideology and the occupation of Palestine.

So I wanted to go to the protest. However, I feared the demonstration, no matter how justified, would be tainted by anti-Semitism. But I was so angered by the actions of the Israeli government and military, that I went to the event to check it out for myself.

That evening, I arrived at Kleinhan's before the protest began. Cops – in uniforms and plainclothes – surrounded the music hall. I waited impatiently for the protesters to arrive. Suddenly, all the media swarmed down the street. I ran after them. Coming over the hill was a long column of people moving toward Kleinhan's. The woman who led the march and spoke to reporters proudly told them she was Jewish! Others held signs and banners aloft that read: "Arab Land for Arab People!" and "Smash Anti-Semitism!" Now those were two slogans I could get behind! I wanted to know who these people were and where they had been all my life!

Hours later I followed the group back to their headquarters. Orange banners tacked up on the walls expressed solidarity with the Attica prisoners and the Vietnamese. One banner particularly haunted me. It read: Stop the War Against Black America, which made me realize that it wasn't just distant wars that needed opposing. Yet although I worked with two members of this organization, I felt nervous that night. These people were communists, Marxists! Yet I found it easy to get into discussions with them. I met waitresses, factory workers, secretaries, and truck drivers. And I decided they were some of the most principled people I had ever met. For example, I was impressed that many of the men I spoke with talked to me about the importance of fighting the oppression of gays and lesbians, and of all women. Yet I knew they thought they were talking to a straight man.

From then on, my Friday nights were also reserved for meetings of Workers World Party (WWP) and its youth group, Youth Against War and Fascism (YAWF). I saw that I didn't have to sail around the world to join the struggle for justice! But when I joined the organization, everyone thought of me as a man. I had a bushy beard, and I had been passing, full-time, for more than four years, so I didn't contradict their assumptions.

I divided my free time between educational meetings and protest demonstrations against racism and war, sexism and anti-gay bigotry, and in defense of Native sovereignty and prisoners' rights. The moment I joined a larger movement for social justice, I wasn't struggling alone anymore. It felt so good to win important battles. I felt connected to struggles around the world.

However, I lived in fear of what the police would do to me if I was arrested. And although my comrades fought alongside me, shoulder to shoulder, I felt they didn't really know me. I longed to live openly and proudly as a transgendered person – not as a man. But what if I told them about myself and they didn't accept me? Would I have to return to fighting back daily as an individual? The fear of loss began to tear me apart.

On March 8, 1973, I attended my first celebration of International Women's Day. Before the meeting began, all the Workers World Party women were reading over each other's speeches; all the men took organizational tasks, so I was on security. I watched the women together, and the men, and I couldn't find my place among either. Later that night I had a terrible dream: I was standing in a small, airless room; one of the walls was a dam with tremendous water pressure behind it; small cracks split the plaster. I woke up drenched in sweat.

I called Jeanette Merrill, who had helped found the Buffalo branch of Workers World Party. I remember asking her husband, Eddy, to leave the room. I can't recall how I explained my situation to Jeanette or what words I chose to explain that I was a "he-she" who had experienced such hatred and violence because of my gender expression that I couldn't live safely or find work. When I finished, Jeanette said she didn't completely understand, but she knew oppression when she heard it.

In the weeks that followed, the WWP's women's caucus meetings and women's self-defense classes were opened to me. The leading women sat down with each member to explain my situation and help them relate to me sensitively. One by one, the men and women of my organization visited me at home. Each brought a cake or pie or soup or an entire case of beer, and adjusted themselves to listen to me in a different way. I told them about my life; each one told me about their own.

Eddy Merrill, who I had asked to leave the room while I talked to Jeanette, waited patiently for an opportunity to talk to me. One night, he found me standing in the WWP literature room with tears in my eyes. The small storeroom was filled with pamphlets and books – slim and thick – about history, politics, and science. I had been an insatiable reader growing up, but I had stuck to fiction. Outside the classroom, I had made it a policy not to read non-fiction books, because I feared I wasn't smart enough to understand the facts inside.

But I had reached a point where I really wanted to educate myself about the past and present of the world I lived in. However, as I stood in the literature room leafing through book after book, I couldn't comprehend what I read. I told Eddy I felt stupid.

"Don't worry," he reassured me. "These are books you'll read later. First you need to understand the events and the people they're talking about. It's like a foundation. Pretend you're building a brick wall – one brick at a time."

"Eddy," I sighed, "I really want to learn. But I'm terrible at history. I don't even know how to approach the subject."

Eddy offered to help me study, so I took him up on it. But he didn't start me out on a diet of history. He dropped four quarters into the literature money box and handed me a pamphlet about an anti-racist struggle in a factory I knew very well. "Come over for dinner after you've read it," he offered, "and we'll talk." Eddy nodded toward the books. "Some of the answers you're looking for are in there. But whenever someone has the courage to talk about an oppression that hasn't been discussed before, they make a contribution. I have a feeling you will, too."

I spent many exciting hours talking to Eddy about politics. Before he lent me each book, he'd talk to me about it. After I'd read it, we would sit and discuss the ideas. I began studying political science ferociously. I had thought Marxists were all white men. Eddy introduced me to the important writings of Che Guevara, Nkrumah, Mao Zedong, Ho Chi Minh, and Rosa Luxemburg. I read insatiably and soon felt confident enough to attend weekly WWP classes, many of them led by women. I quickly learned that the real proof of understanding a complex idea was how clearly you could state it.

Like many among the generations of working-class Jews before me, I discovered that Marxism was a valuable science, not a religion. In fact, I began to view the anti-communism that had been drummed into me since childhood as an unexamined cult ideology.

Suddenly, history didn't seem boring at all. I began to see the seasons – or stages – of history. I learned that human society has undergone continuous development and has been transformed many times over the course of centuries.

One fact rocked my thinking: All of our earliest ancestors lived in communal societies based on cooperation and sharing. I knew that many Native peoples on this continent had still lived communally, even as colonialism stormed these shores. But I didn't know that was true all over the planet.

Group cooperation required respect for the contributions and insights of each individual. Communal societies were not severed into have and have-nots. No small group held power over others through private ownership of the tools necessary to sustain life. Therefore the earth, sky, and waters were not viewed as property that could be bought or sold. The word *communist* derives from communal.

All my life I had heard the cynical view that intolerance and greed were products of a flawed human nature. But "thou shalt not steal" would have been a bewildering command to people who lived in societies where everyone ate or everyone starved because their survival relied on teamwork. I realized that human nature has changed along with the organization of society.

While I didn't expect to find my own modern self-definitions or consciousness mirrored in the economic systems of our earliest ancestors, I wondered if some form of transgender had existed in early communalism. I began examining the roots of women's oppression. I studied Frederick Engels's classic work, *Origin of the Family, Private Property and the State.*[3] Then I turned to a pamphlet by Dorothy Ballan, one of the founding women of my organization, entitled *Feminism and Marxism.*[4] I read as much as I could find written by socialist feminists in the women's liberation movement who researched the material origin of sexual oppression.

I was surprised at what I discovered. In these ancient communal societies, blood descent – the basis for paternal inheritance today – was traced through mothers. Women enjoyed equality and respect for their vital roles in both collective production and reproduction. Women were the heads of *gens*, which were kinship groups that bore little resemblance to today's patriarchal nuclear family. Since blood descent was traced through the mothers, women headed these extended economic units.

A man lived with his mother's family. If he married a woman, he left his mother's economic unit and became a part of his wife's gens. There he was surrounded by all of her relatives in her household. And if the woman wanted a "divorce," she merely asked him to pack up his personal possessions and leave. He then had to move back to his own mother's household, with all of her relatives. How could a man beat or abuse a female partner in those societies? Where was the material power for male domination?

However, the material basis for women's oppression is precisely what today's ruling-class "fathers" do not want opened up to scrutiny. They seek to shape history in their own image. To hear the bible-thumpers, you'd think that the nuclear family, headed by men, has always existed. But I found that the existence of matrilineal societies on every continent has been abundantly documented. Up until the fifteenth century, a great majority of the world's population lived in communal, matrilineal societies. This was true throughout Africa, large parts of Asia, the Pacific islands, Australia, and the Americas. If all of human history were shrunk to the scale of one year, over 360 days of historical time belong to cooperative, matrilineal societies.

A deeper understanding of the roots of women's oppression had great meaning to me, particularly because of my experiences growing up as a girl in a woman-hating society. But my oppression was not just based on being "woman." Was there a material basis for transgender oppression? Surely transsexual women and men, or people like me who expressed their gender differently, were not merely products of a high-tech capitalist system in decline. I came full circle to one of my original questions as well: Have we always existed?

I felt further from an answer than ever before. Fortunately, feelings are not facts.

In the meantime, the economic crisis of 1973 was wreaking havoc on my life. I could not find work anywhere. Even the temp agencies had no job openings – at least not for a he-she like me. I made my decision to move to New York City. Since that's where the Workers World national headquarters was located, I knew I would get help in finding an apartment and a job, and I looked forward to becoming a journalist for Workers World newspaper.[5]

As I said tearful goodbyes to my friends in the Buffalo branch, I asked several of them, "Do you think I'll ever find the answers I'm looking for?" They each reassured me I would. As a parting gift, Jeanette and Eddy gave me one of their own old volumes of Lenin's writings. They had inscribed it: "To Les, with great expectations." That precious gift is next to me on my bookshelf as I write these words.

But at the time, I feared their expectations were unrealistic.

The author, circa 1973.

CHAPTER **3.**

that trans people have not always been hated in 1974. I had played hooky from work and spent the day at the Museum of the American Indian in New York City.

The exhibits were devoted to Native history in the Americas. I was drawn to a display of beautiful thumb-sized clay figures. The ones to my right had breasts and cradled bowls. Those on the left were flat chested, holding hunting tools. But when I looked closer, I did a double-take. I saw that several of the figures holding bowls were flat chested; several of the hunters had breasts. You can bet there was no legend next to the display to explain. I left the museum curious.

What I'd seen gnawed at me until I called a member of the curator's staff. He asked, "Why do you want to know?" I panicked. Was the information so classified that it could only be given out on a "need to know" basis? I lied and said I was a graduate student at Columbia University.

Sounding relieved, he immediately let me know that he understood exactly what I'd described. He said he came across references to these berdache* practically every day in his reading. I asked him what the word meant. He said he thought it meant transvestite or transsexual in modern English. He remarked that Native peoples didn't seem to abhor them the way "we" did. In fact, he added, it appeared that such individuals were held in high esteem by Native nations.

Then his voice dropped low. "It's really quite disturbing, isn't it?" he whispered. I hung up the phone and raced to the library. I had found the first key to a vault containing information I'd looked for all my life.

---

* "Berdache" was a derogatory term European colonizers used to label any Native person who did not fit their narrow notions of woman and man. The blanket use of the word disregarded distinctions of self-expression, social interaction, and complex economic and political realities. Native nations had many respectful words in their own languages to describe such people; Gay American Indians (GAI) has gathered a valuable list of these words. However, cultural genocide has destroyed and altered Native languages and traditions. So Native people ask that the term "Two-Spirit" be used to replace the offensive colonial word – a request I respect.

In a further attempt to avoid analyzing oppressed peoples' cultures, I do not make a distinction between sex and gender expression in this chapter. Instead, I use sex/gender.

"Strange country this," a white man wrote in 1850 about the Crow nation of North America, "where males assume the dress and perform the duties of females, while women turn men and mate with their own sex!"[1]

I found hundreds and hundreds of similar references, such as those in Jonathan Ned Katz's ground-breaking *Gay American History: Lesbians and Gay Men in the U.S.A.*, published in 1976, which provided me with additional valuable research. The quotes were anything but objective. Some were statements by murderously hostile colonial generals, others by the anthropologists and missionaries who followed in their bloody wake.

Some only referred to what today might be called male-to-female expression. "In nearly every part of the continent," Westermarck concluded in 1917, "there seem to have been, since ancient times, men dressing themselves in the clothes and per-forming the functions of women...."[2]

But I also found many references to female-to-male expression. Writing about his expedition into northeastern Brazil in 1576, Pedro de Magalhães noted females among the Tupinamba who lived as men and were accepted by other men, and who hunted and went to war. His team of explorers, recalling the Greek Amazons, renamed the river that flowed through that area the *River of the Amazons.*[3]

Female-to-male expression was also found in numerous North American nations. As late as 1930, ethnographer Leslie Spier observed of a nation in the Pacific Northwest: "Transvestites or berdaches ... are found among the Klamath, as in all probability among all other North American tribes. These are men and women who for reasons that remain obscure take on the dress and habits of the opposite sex."[4]

I found it painful to read these quotes because they were steeped in hatred. "I saw a devilish thing," Spanish colonialist Alvar Núñez Cabeza de Vaca wrote in the six-teenth century.[5] "Sinful, heinous, perverted, nefarious, abominable, unnatural, dis-gusting, lewd" – the language used by the colonizers to describe the acceptance of sex/gender diversity, and of same-sex love, most accurately described the viewer, not the viewed. And these sensational reports about Two-Spirit people were used to further "justify" genocide, the theft of Native land and resources, and destruction of their cultures and religions.

But occasionally these colonial quotes opened, even if inadvertently, a momentary window into the humanity of the peoples being observed. Describing his first trip down the Mississippi in the seventeenth century, Jesuit Jacques Marquette chronicled the attitudes of the Illinois and Nadouessi to the Two-Spirits. "They are summoned to the Councils, and nothing can be decided without their advice. Finally, through their profession of leading an Extraordinary life, they pass for Manitous, – That is to say, for Spirits, – or persons of Consequence."[6]

Although French missionary Joseph François Lafitau condemned Two-Spirit people he found among the nations of the western Great Lakes, Louisiana, and Florida, he revealed that those Native peoples did not share his prejudice. "They believe they are honored …" he wrote in 1724, "they participate in all religious ceremonies, and this profession of an extraordinary life causes them to be regarded as people of a higher order…."[7]

But the colonizers' reactions toward Two-Spirit people can be summed up by the words of Antonio de la Calancha, a Spanish official in Lima. Calancha wrote that during Vasco Núñez de Balboa's expedition across Panama, Balboa "saw men dressed like women; Balboa learnt that they were sodomites and threw the king and forty others to be eaten by his dogs, a fine action of an honorable and Catholic Spaniard."[8]

This was not an isolated attack. When the Spaniards invaded the Antilles and Louisiana, "they found men dressed as women who were respected by their societies. Thinking they were hermaphrodites, or homosexuals, they slew them."[9]

Finding these quotes shook me. I recalled the "cowboys and Indians" movies of my childhood. These racist films didn't succeed in teaching me hate; I had grown up around strong, proud Native adults and children. But I now realized more consciously how every portrayal of Native nations in these movies was aimed at diverting attention from the real-life colonial genocide. The same bloody history was ignored or glossed over in my schools. I only learned the truth about Native cultures later, by re-educating myself – a process I'm continuing.

Discovering the Two-Spirit tradition had deep meaning for me. It wasn't that

I thought the range of human expression among Native nations was identical to trans identities today. I knew that a Crow *badé*, Cocopa *warhameh*, Chumash *joya*, and Maricopa *kwiraxame'* would describe themselves in very different ways from an African-American *drag queen* fighting cops at Stonewall or a white *female-to-male transsexual* in the 1990s explaining his life to a college class on gender theory.

What stunned me was that such ancient and diverse cultures allowed people to choose more sex/gender paths, and this diversity of human expression was honored as sacred. I had to chart the complex geography of sex and gender with a compass needle that only pointed to north or south.

Barcheeampe, the Woman Chief, was an acclaimed hunter and warrior, praised in songs
composed by the Crow people. When all the chiefs and warriors assembled for council,
Barcheeampe sat as a chief, ranking third in a band of 160 lodges.

You'd think I'd have been elated to find this new information. But I raged that these facts had been kept from me, from all of us. And so many of the Native peoples who were arrogantly scrutinized by military men, missionaries, and anthropologists had been massacred. Had their oral history too been forever lost?

In my anger, I vowed to act more forcefully in defense of the treaty, sovereignty, and self-determination rights of Native nations. As I became more active in these struggles, I began to hear more clearly the voices of Native peoples who not only reclaimed their traditional heritage, but carried the resistance into the present: the takeover of Alcatraz, the occupation of Wounded Knee, the Longest Walk, the Day of Mourning at Plymouth Rock, and the fight to free political prisoners like Leonard Peltier and Norma Jean Croy.

Two historic developments helped me to hear the voices of modern Native warriors who lived the sacred Two-Spirit tradition: the founding of Gay American Indians in 1975 by Randy Burns (Northern Paiute) and Barbara Cameron (Lakota Sioux), and the publication in 1988 of *Living the Spirit: A Gay American Indian Anthology*. Randy Burns noted that the History Project of Gay American Indians "has documented these alternative gender roles in over 135 North American tribes."[10]

Will Roscoe, who edited *Living the Spirit*, explained that this more complex sex/gender system was found "in every region of the continent, among every type of native culture, from the small bands of hunters in Alaska to the populous, hierarchical city-states in Florida."[11]

Another important milestone was the 1986 publication of *The Spirit and the Flesh*[12] by Walter Williams, because this book included the voices of modern Two-Spirit people.

I knew that Native struggles against colonialization and genocide – both physical and cultural – were tenacious. But I learned that the colonizers' efforts to outlaw, punish, and slaughter the Two-Spirits within those nations had also met with fierce resistance. Conquistador Nuño de Guzmán recorded in 1530 that the last person taken prisoner after a battle, who had "fought most courageously, was a man in the habit of a woman. . . ."[13]

Just trying to maintain a traditional way of life was itself an act of resistance. Williams wrote, "Since in many tribes berdaches were often shamans, the government's attack on traditional healing practices disrupted their lives. Among the Klamaths, the government agent's prohibition of curing ceremonials in the 1870s and 1880s required shamans to operate underground. The berdache shaman White Cindy continued to do traditional healing, curing people for decades despite the danger of arrest."[14]

Native nations resisted the racist demands of U.S. government agents who tried to change Two-Spirit people. This defiance was especially courageous in light of the power these agents exercised over the economic survival of the Native people they tried to control. One such struggle focused on a Crow *badé* (*botê*) named *Osh-Tisch* (Finds Them and Kills Them). An oral history by Joe Medicine Crow in 1982 recalled the events: "One agent in the late 1890s . . . tried to interfere with Osh-Tisch, who was the most respected *badé*. The agent incarcerated the *badés*, cut off their hair, made them wear men's clothing. He forced them to do manual labor, planting these trees that you see here on the BIA grounds. The people were so upset with this that Chief Pretty Eagle came into Crow Agency, and told [the agent] to leave the reservation. It was a tragedy, trying to change them."[15]

How the *badés* were viewed within their own nation comes across in this report by S. C. Simms in 1903 in *American Anthropologist*: "During a visit last year to the Crow reservation, in the interest of the Field Columbian Museum, I was informed

We'Wha, a <u>lhamana</u>, wearing the ceremonial regalia of Zuni women. We'Wha was an accomplished weaver and potter and spent six months in Washington, D.C. in 1886, meeting President Grover Cleveland and others who never realized this six-foot Zuni was a <u>lhamana</u>. In 1896, We'Wha died and was buried in a woman's dress with a pair of men's pants underneath.

that there were three hermaphrodites in the Crow tribe, one living at Pryor, one in the Big Horn district, and one in Black Lodge district. These persons are usually spoken of as 'she,' and as having the largest and best appointed tipis; they are also generally considered to be experts with the needle and the most efficient cooks in the tribe, and they are highly regarded for their many charitable acts....

"A few years ago an Indian agent endeavored to compel these people, under threat of punishment, to wear men's clothing, but his efforts were unsuccessful."[16]

White-run boarding schools played a similar role in trying to force genera-

RIGHT: A <u>nadleeh</u> referred to as "Charlie" by photographer Adam Clark Vroman who took this photo at the Navajo hogans at Bitahoochee in 1895.
FAR RIGHT: Spotted Eagle holding grandson.

tions of kidnapped children to abandon their traditional ways. But many Two-Spirit children escaped rather than conform.

Lakota medicine man Lame Deer told an interviewer about the sacred place of the *winkte* ("male-to-female") in his nation's traditions, and how the *winkte* bestowed a special name on an individual. "The secret name a *winkte* gave to a child was believed to be especially powerful and effective," Lame Deer said. "Sitting Bull, Black Elk, even Crazy Horse had secret *winkte* names." Lakota chief Crazy Horse reportedly had one or two *winkte* wives.[17]

Williams quotes a Lakota medicine man who spoke of the pressures on the

winktes in the 1920s and 1930s. "The missionaries and the government agents said *winktes* were no good, and tried to get them to change their ways. Some did, and put on men's clothing. But others, rather than change, went out and hanged themselves."[18]

Up until 1989, the Two-Spirit voices I heard lived only in the pages of books. But that year I was honored to be invited to Minneapolis for the first gathering of Two-Spirit Native people, their loved ones, and supporters. The bonds of friendship I enjoyed at the first event were strengthened at the third gathering in Manitoba in 1991. There, I found myself sitting around a campfire at the base of tall pines under the rolling colors of the northern lights, drinking strong tea out of a metal cup. I laughed easily, relaxed with old friends and new ones. Some were feminine men or masculine women; all shared same-sex desire. Yet not all of these people were transgendered, and not all of the Two-Spirits I'd read about desired people of the same sex. Then what defined this group?

I turned to Native people for these answers. Even today, in 1995, I read research papers and articles about sex/gender systems in Native nations in which every source cited is a white social scientist. When I began to write this book, I asked Two-Spirit people to talk about their own cultures, in their own words.

Chrystos, a brilliant Two-Spirit poet and writer from the Menominee nation, offered me this understanding: "Life among First Nation people, before first contact, is hard to reconstruct. There's been so much abuse of traditional life by the Christian Church. But certain things have filtered down to us. Most of the nations that I know of traditionally had more than two genders. It varies from tribe to tribe. The concept of Two-Spiritedness is a rather rough translation into English of that idea. I think the English language is rigid, and the thought patterns that form it are rigid, so that gender also becomes rigid.

"The whole concept of gender is more fluid in traditional life. Those paths are not necessarily aligned with your sex, although they may be. People might choose their gender according to their dreams, for example. So even the idea that your gender is something you dream about is not even a concept in Western culture – which posits you are born a certain biological sex and therefore there's a role you must step into and follow pretty rigidly for the rest of your life. That's how we got the concept of queer. Anyone who doesn't follow their assigned gender role is queer; all kinds of people are lumped together under that word."[19]

Does being Two-Spirit determine your sexuality? I asked Chrystos. "In traditional life a Two-Spirit person can be heterosexual or what we would call homosexual," she replied. "You could also be a person who doesn't have sex with anyone and lives with the spirits. The gender fluidity is part of a larger concept, which I guess the most accurate English word for is 'tolerance.' It's a whole different way of conceiving how to be in the world with other people. We think about the world in terms of relationship, so each person is always in a matrix, rather than being seen only as an individual – which is a very different way of looking at things."[20]

Chrystos told me about her Navajo friend Wesley Thomas, who describes himself as *nadleeh*-like. A male nadleeh, she said, "would manifest in the world as a female and take a husband and participate in tribal life as a female person." I e-mailed Wesley, who lives in Seattle, for more information about the nadleeh tradition. He wrote back that "nadleeh was a category for women who were/are masculine and also feminine males."[21]

The concept of nadleeh, he explained, is incorporated into Navajo origin or creation stories. "So, it is a cultural construction," he wrote, "and was part of the normal Navajo culture, from the Navajo point of view, through the nineteenth century. It began changing during the first half of the twentieth century due to the introduction of western education and most of all, christianity. Nadleeh since then has moved underground."[22]

Wesley, who spent the first thirty years of life on the Eastern Navajo reservation, wrote that in his initial fieldwork research he identified four categories of sex: female/woman, male/man, female/man, and male /woman. "Where I began to identify gender on a continuum – meaning placing female at one end and male on the other end – I placed forty-nine different gender identifications in between. This was derived at one sitting, not from carrying out a full and comprehensive fieldwork research. This number derived from my own understanding of gender within the Navajo cosmology."[23]

I have faced so much persecution because of my gender expression that I also wanted to hear about the experiences of someone who grew up as a "masculine girl" in traditional Native life. I thought of Spotted Eagle, who I had met in Manitoba, and who lives in Georgia. Walking down an urban street, Spotted Eagle's gender expression, as well as her nationality, could make her the target of harassment and violence. But she is White Mountain Apache, and I knew she had grown up with her own traditions on the reservation. How was she treated?

"I was born in 1945," Spotted Eagle told me. "I grew up totally accepted. I knew from birth, and everyone around me knew I was Two-Spirited. I was honored. I was a special creation; I was given certain gifts because of that, teachings to share with my people and healings. But that changed – not in my generation, but in generations to follow."

There were no distinct pronouns in her ancient language, she said. "There were three variations: the way the women spoke, the way the men spoke, and the ceremonial language." Which way of speaking did she use? "I spoke all three. So did the two older Two-Spirit people on my reservation."[24]

Spotted Eagle explained that the White Mountain Apache nation was small and isolated, and so had been less affected early on by colonial culture. As a result, the U.S. government didn't set up the mission school system on the White Mountain reservation until the late 1930s or early 1940s. Spotted Eagle said she experienced her first taste of bigotry as a Two-Spirit in those schools. "I was taken out of the mission school with the help of my people and sent away to live with an aunt off reservation, so I didn't get totally abused by Christianity. I have some very horrible memories of the short time I was there."[25]

"But as far as my own people," Spotted Eagle continued, "we were a matriarchy, and have been through our history. Women are in a different position in a matriarchy than they are out here. It's not that we have more power or more privilege than anyone else, it's just a more balanced way to be. Being a woman was a plus and being Two-Spirit was even better. I didn't really have any negative thoughts about being Two-Spirit until I left the reservation."[26]

Spotted Eagle told me that as a young adult she married. "My husband was also Two-Spirit and we had children. We lived in a rather peculiar way according to standards out here. Of course it was very normal for us. We faced a lot of violence, but we learned to cope with it and go on."[27]

Spotted Eagle's husband died many years ago. Today her partner is a woman. Her three children are grown. "Two of them are Two-Spirit," she said proudly. "We're all very close."[28]

I asked her where she found her strength and pride. "It was given to me by the people around me to maintain," she explained. "If your whole life is connected spiritually, then you learn that self-pride – the image of self – is connected with everything else. That becomes part of who you are and you carry that wherever you are."[29]

What was responsible for the imposition of the present-day rigid sex/gender system in North America? It is not correct to simply blame patriarchy, Chrystos stressed to me. "The real word is 'colonization' and what it has done to the world. Patriarchy is a tool of colonization and exploitation of people and their lands for wealthy white people."[30]

"The Two-Spirit tradition was suppressed," she explained. "Like all Native spirituality, it underwent a tremendous time of suppression. So there's gaps. But we've continued on with our spiritual traditions. We are still attached to this land and the place of our ancestors and managed to protect our spiritual traditions and our languages. We have always been at war. Despite everything – incredible onslaughts that even continue now – we have continued and we have survived."[31]

Like a gift presented at a traditional give away, Native people have patiently given me a greater understanding of the diverse cultures that existed in the Western hemisphere before colonization.

But why did many Native cultures honor sex/gender diversity, while European colonialists were hell-bent on wiping it out? And how did the Europeans immediately recognize Two-Spiritedness? Were there similar expressions in European societies?

Thinking back to my sketchy high-school education, I could only remember one person in Europe whose gender expression had made history.

A 1594 Theodor de Bry engraving of Balboa using dogs to murder Two-Spirit Native people.

CHAPTER **4.**

wear men's clothes?" I asked a friend over coffee in 1975. She had a graduate degree in history; I had barely squeaked through high school. I waited for her answer with great anticipation, but she dismissed my question with a wave of her hand. "It was just armor." She seemed so sure, but I couldn't let my question go. Joan of Arc was the only person associated with cross-dressing in history I'd grown up hearing about.

I thought a great deal about my friend's answer. Was the story of Joan of Arc dressing in men's clothing merely legend? Was wearing armor significant? If a society strictly mandates only men can be warriors, isn't a woman military leader dressed in armor an example of cross-gendered expression?

All I knew about the feudal period in which Joan of Arc lived was that lords owned vast tracts of land and lived off the forced agricultural labor of peasants. But I made the decision to study Joan of Arc's life, and her story opened another important window on trans history for me.

In school, we'd quickly glossed over the facts of Joan of Arc's life. So I hadn't realized that in 1431, when she was nineteen years old, Joan of Arc was burned at the stake by the Inquisition of the Catholic Church because she refused to stop dressing in garb traditionally worn by men. And no one had ever taught me that her peasant followers considered Joan of Arc – and her clothing – sacred.

I discovered that more than ten thousand books have been written about Joan of Arc's extraordinary life. She was an illiterate daughter of the peasant class, who as a teenager demonstrated a brilliant military leadership that helped birth the nation-state of France. What impressed me the most, however, was her courage in defending her right to self-expression. Yet I was frustrated at how many texts analyzed Joan of Arc solely as an individual, removed from the dynamics of a tumultuous period and place. I was particularly interested in understanding the social soil in which this remarkable person was rooted.

Joan of Arc was born in Domremy, in the province of Lorraine, around 1412. Only half a century before her birth, the bubonic plague had torn the fabric of the feudal order. One-third of the population of Europe was wiped out, whole provinces were depopulated. Peasant rebellions were shaking the very foundations of European feudalism.

At the time, France was gripped by the Hundred Years War. French peasants suffered plunder and violence at the hands of the marauding English occupation armies. The immediate problem for the peasantry was how to oust the English army, a task the French nobility had been unable to accomplish.

Joan of Arc emerged as a leader during this period of powerful social earthquakes. In 1429, dressed in men's clothing, this confident seventeen year old presented herself and a group of her followers at the court of Prince Charles, heir to the French throne. In the context of feudal life, in which religion permeated everything, Joan asserted that her mission, motivation, and mode of dress were directed by God. She declared her goal: to forge an army of peasants to drive out the English. Prince Charles placed her at the head of a ten-thousand-strong peasant army.

The rest is history that has been replayed again and again in text and film. Unable to read or write, Joan of Arc dictated a letter to the King of England and the Duke of Bedford, leader of the English occupying army in Orleans, demanding they leave French soil, vowing, "[I]f you do not do so, you will remember it by reason of your great sufferings."[1]

On April 28, 1429, Joan led a march on Orleans. The next day, she entered the city at the head of her peasant army. By May 8, the English were routed. Over the next months, she further proved her genius as a military strategist and her ability to inspire the rank-and-file soldiers by liberating other French villages and towns and forcing the English to retreat.

Joan persuaded Charles to go to Rheims to receive the crown. It was an arduous trip – long and dangerous – through territory still occupied by English troops. Although her army was exhausted and famished along the way, they forced the English to yield still more turf. As Charles was crowned King of France, Joan stood

beside him, holding her combat banner. The French nation-state, soon to be fully liberated from occupation, was born.

On May 23, 1430, Joan was captured by the Burgundians, French allies of the English feudal lords. The Burgundians referred to her as *hommasse,* a slur meaning "man-woman," or masculine woman.[2] Had she been a knight or nobleman, King Charles would have offered a ransom for Joan's freedom, since ransom was the customary method of freeing knights and nobility captured in battle. Even the sums were fixed – one could ransom a royal prince for 10,000 livres of gold, or 61,125 francs.[3] Once ransom was offered, it *had* to be accepted. But Joan's position as military leader of a popular peasant movement threatened the very French ruling class she helped lift to power. The French nobility didn't offer a single franc for her release. What an arro-

BELOW FROM LEFT TO RIGHT:

1} Joan of Arc has been claimed as a symbol by everyone from Church fathers who canonized her to French right-wing nationalists. Frequently, Joan of Arc is portrayed in art as an extremely feminine woman. Given the charges of transgender that led to her murder, it's more likely Joan looked like this rendition in a seventeenth-century painting, attributed to Jean de Caumont.

2} A virgin (center figure) of the Klementi tribe in Albania, circa 1910. Daughters had no say about when and to whom they were married. But if a virgin swore before twelve witnesses that she would never marry, that person was then recognized and ranked as a man, wore men's clothing, carried weapons, ate with other men, and worked as herdsmen of sheep and goats.

3} Catalina de Erauso was a Basque who cross-dressed and traveled to South America in the early 1600s as a conquistador. S/he and fellow soldiers slaughtered many Native peoples. While the Church and French ruling class saw Joan of Arc and her transgender expression as a threat, de Erauso, who fought on the side of colonialism, won the Pope's blessing to continue cross-dressing.

4} Liberté (Angélique Brulon) was a decorated officer in Napoleon's infantry, serving in seven campaigns between 1792 and 1799 that liberated much of Europe from feudalism. Liberté joined her husband's regiment after he was killed in warfare. Liberté "came out" during the war and became a hero to French women who wanted to replace Joan of Arc for having been so loyal to the nobility.

TOP: While this portrait of Nzinga, King of Angola from 1624 to 1653, is quite idealized, she ruled as a king, cross-dressed, and defeated the Portuguese army in many battles. BOTTOM: Afro-Mexicana revolutionary from Michoacán, one of many cross-dressed female warriors and revolutionaries who have helped make history. Another example was Chui Chin, a Chinese revolutionary, cross-dressing feminist who was tortured and beheaded in 1907 for her efforts at organizing an uprising against the Manchu dynasty. She founded a militant newspaper in Shanghai called The Chinese Women's Journal, organized an army, and helped plan an insurrection.

gant betrayal. How anxious they must have been to be rid of her.

The English urged the Catholic Church to condemn Joan for cross-dressing. The king of England, Henry VI, wrote to the infamous Inquisitor Pierre Cauchon, the Bishop of Beauvais: "It is sufficiently notorious and well-known that for some time past a woman calling herself Jeanne the Pucelle (the Maid), leaving off the dress and clothing of the feminine sex, a thing contrary to divine law and abominable before God, and forbidden by all laws, wore clothing and armour such as is worn by men." Buried beneath this outrage against Joan's cross-dressing was a powerful class bias. It was an affront to nobility for a peasant to wear armor and ride a fine horse. This offense was later elaborated in one of the charges against Joan that claimed she dressed "in rich and sumptuous habits, precious stuffs and cloth of gold and furs."[4]

The Burgundians sold Joan of Arc to the English, who turned her over to the Inquisition in November 1430. Joan was held in a civil prison in Rouen, France, an English stronghold at that time. She was reportedly guarded by English male soldiers who slept in her cell, in violation of the Church's own rules. She was shackled in a small iron cage "in which she was kept standing, chained by her neck, her hands and her feet," according to the locksmith who built the cage.[5]

Joan's trial began in Rouen on January 9, 1431. The Grand Inquisitors condemned Joan for cross-dressing and accused her of being raised a pagan. Church leaders had long charged that the district of her birth, Lorraine, was a hotbed of paganism and witchcraft. One of the principal accusations against Joan was that she associated with "fairies,"[6] a charge leveled by the Church in their war against paganism. (Which, incidentally, derives from the Latin *paganus*, meaning rural dweller or peasant.) The Church was waging war against peasants who resisted patriarchal theology and still held onto some of the old pre-Christian religious beliefs and matrilineal traditions. This was true of peasants in the area of Lorraine, even in the period of Joan's lifetime. For instance, the custom of giving children the mother's surname, not the father's, still survived there.[7]

Scapegoating Joan of Arc and the area of her birth fueled the Church's reactionary campaign. And the more Joan of Arc was idolized by her followers, the more she posed a threat to the Church's religious rule. Article III of the Articles of Accusations stated this clearly: "Item, the said Joan by her inventions has seduced the Catholic people, many in her presence adored her as a saint…even more, they declared her the greatest of all the saints after the holy Virgin…."[8] No wonder the Church fathers feared her!

On April 2, 1431, the Inquisition dropped the charges of witchcraft against Joan, because they were too hard to prove. Instead, they denounced her for asserting that her cross-dressing was a religious duty compelled by voices she heard in visions, and for maintaining that these voices were a higher authority than the Church. Many historians and academicians view Joan of Arc's wearing men's clothing as inconsequential. Yet the core of the charges against Joan focused on her cross-dressing, the crime for which she ultimately was executed. However, the following quote from the verbatim court proceedings of her interrogation reveals it wasn't just Joan of Arc cross-*dressing* that enraged her judges, but her cross-*gendered* expression as a whole:

> You have said that, by God's command, you have continually worn man's dress, wearing the short robe, doublet, and hose attached by points; that you have also worn your hair short, cut *en rond* above your ears, with nothing left that could show you to be a woman; and that on many occasions you received the Body of our Lord dressed in this fashion, although you have been frequently admonished to leave it off, which you have refused to do, saying that you would rather die than leave it off, save by God's command. And you said further that if you were still so dressed and with the king and those of his party, it would be one of the greatest blessings for the kingdom of France; and you have said that not for anything would you take an oath not to wear this dress or carry arms; and concerning all these matters you have said that you did well, and obediently to God's command.
>
> As for these points, the clerks say that you blaspheme God in His sacraments; that you transgress divine law, the Holy Scriptures and the canon law; you hold the Faith doubtfully and wrongly; you boast vainly; you are suspect of idolatry; and you condemn yourself in being unwilling to wear the customary clothing of your sex, and following the custom of the Gentiles and the Heathen.[9]

Even though she knew her defiance meant she was considered damned, Joan's testimony in her own defense revealed how deeply her cross-dressing was rooted in her identity. "For nothing in the world," she declared, "will I swear not to arm myself and put on a man's dress."[10]

But by April 24, 1431, Joan's judges claimed she had recanted, after having been taken on a tour of the torture chamber, and brought to a cemetery where she was shown a scaffold that her tormentors said awaited her if she did not repent. Joan allegedly accused herself of wearing clothing that violated natural decency, and agreed to submit to the Church's authority and wear women's apparel. She was "mercifully" sentenced to life in prison on bread and water – in women's dress.

However, since Joan could neither read nor write, did she know the exact details of what she was signing? This is an important question, because cross-dressing was not a capital offense at that time. And the Inquisition did not have the power to turn a heretic over to the secular state for execution. But the church judges were empowered to condemn a *relapsed* heretic.[11]

Did Pierre Cauchon, the Inquisitor, trick Joan into making her mark on a document that signed away more than she'd realized? Perhaps Cauchon later revealed the exact contents of the phony confession in hopes she would renege. Or were parchments switched? Witnesses described Joan making her mark on a short declaration; the confession in the court records is very long.[12]

Whatever the case, Joan recanted the alleged abjuration within days and resumed wearing men's clothes. Her judges asked her why she had done so, when putting on male garb meant certain death. According to the court record she said she had done so "of her own will. And that nobody had forced her to do so. And that she preferred man's dress to woman's." Joan told the judges she "had never intended to take an oath not to take man's dress again."[13] The Inquisition sentenced her to death for resuming male dress, saying "time and again you have relapsed, as a dog that returns to its vomit. . . ."[14]

Joan of Arc was burned alive at the stake on May 30, 1431, in Rouen. She was nineteen years old. The depth of her enemies' hatred toward her transgender expression was demonstrated at her execution, when they extinguished the flames in order to prove she was a "real" woman. After her clothing was burned away and Joan was presumed dead, one observer wrote, "Then the fire was raked back and her naked body shown to all the people and all the secrets that could or should belong to a woman, to take away any doubts from people's minds."[15]

Joan of Arc suffered the excruciating pain of being burned alive rather than renounce her identity. I know the kind of seething hatred that resulted in her murder – I've faced it. But I wish I'd been taught the truth about her life and her courage when I was a frightened, confused trans youth. What an inspirational role model – a brilliant transgender peasant teenager leading an army of laborers into battle.

But one aspect of the information I'd gathered left me puzzled. Why did the feudal ruling class and the Church abhor her transgender so violently, while the peasants considered it so sacred? There's no question how much Joan of Arc was honored by the peasantry. Even the Church admitted that the peasants considered her the greatest of all the saints after the holy Virgin.

It's also clear that Joan of Arc's cross-dressing was central to that reverence. Gay historian Arthur Evans noted that before Joan was captured by the Burgundians: "[W]henever she appeared in public she was worshipped like a deity by the peasants. . . . The peasants believed that she had the power to heal, and many would flock around her to touch part of her body or her clothing (which was men's clothing). Subsequently her armor was kept on display at the Church of St. Denis, where it was worshipped."[16]

According to Professor Margaret A. Murray, "The enormous importance as to the wearing of the male costume is emphasized by the fact that as soon as it was known in Rouen that Joan was again dressed as a man the inhabitants crowded into the castle courtyard to see her, to the great indignation of the English soldiers who promptly drove them out with hard words and threats of hard blows."[17]

I could not answer, yet, why the peasants venerated Joan of Arc's cross-dressing. But I thought back to a clue buried in the condemnation of Joan by her judges. What did they mean when they charged that her cross-dressing was "following the custom of the Gentiles and the Heathen?" What custom? Were there other examples of cross-dressing among the peasantry? Did the peasants consider transgender itself to be sacred? If so, why?

I had no idea where to find the answers to these questions.

Franklin Thompson (Sarah Emma Edmonds) fought for the Union Army in the Civil War. Some 400 male Civil War soldiers were discovered to have been born female. Many of them fought for the pro-slavery Confederacy; just being transgendered doesn't automatically make each person progressive. Like the old trade union song asked, it's a question of "Which side are you on?"

*Concepts that have proved useful
in the constitution of an order of things
readily win such authority over us
that we forget their earthly origins
and take them to be changeless data.*

ALBERT EINSTEIN

Part Two

^{CHAPTER} **5.**∎

I REMEMBER RIDING A BUS

in the middle of the night during a bitter snowstorm in the early months of 1976. I was traveling, along with many other activists, to a political conference in Chicago. Unable to sleep, I read a xeroxed copy of a Workers World pamphlet so new the typeset copies weren't yet back from the printers.[1] That landmark pamphlet – a Marxist examination of the roots of lesbian and gay oppression – was authored by Bob McCubbin, a gay man I worked with in our New York City branch. I had known Bob was working on that history, but I'd had no concept of how his research and analysis would impact on my life.

I found *myself* in those pages. For the first time since I'd acknowledged my own sexual desire to myself, I felt released from a layer of unexamined shame. Bob presented an overview of human history so I could see that same-sex love had always been part of the spectrum of human sexuality. He provided examples of early communal societies that honored all forms of human love and affection. Bob analyzed how and why the division of society into classes led to increasingly hostile attitudes by rulers towards same-sex love. And to my surprise, he included examples of acceptance of transgender in cooperative societies.

As I shivered next to a bus window thick with ice, I cried with relief. I realized how important it was for me to know I had a place in history, that I was part of the human race.

As I read and reread that pamphlet in the years that followed, I saw that I could also approach trans history from a materialist point of view. So I went back and took another look at the charge by Joan's Inquisitors that she followed "the custom of the Gentiles and the Heathen." In my family, gentiles meant non-Jews. But I remembered Engels's use of the term *gens* – and it occurred to me that the French clerics were referring to free farming communities still organized into *gens*, the family unit of cooperative matrilineal societies.

I wanted to go back further, to dig around for prehistoric evidence of transgender in communal societies in Europe. But how could I? Although these early com-

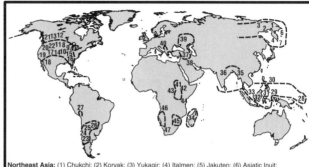

This map shows the many parts of the world where anthropologist Hermann Baumann documented male-to-female transsexual priestesses.

Northeast Asia: (1) Chukchi; (2) Koryak; (3) Yukagir; (4) Italmen; (5) Jakuten; (6) Asiatic Inuit;
North America: (7) Aleut; (8) Ojibwa; (9) Sauk-Fox; (10) Illinois; (11) Dakota; (12) Mandan-Minitari; (13) Crow; (14) Ponka, Omaha, Hansas, Oto, Osage; (15) Choctaw and other Muskogee; (16) Seminole; (17) Pueblo (Zuni, Acoma, Laguna, Navajo); (18) Yuma, Mohave; (19) Juaneño; (20) Yakut, Yuki, Yurok; (21) Shahaptin-Flathead; (22) Ute-Shoshone; (23) Puelche; (24) Araukaner; (25) earlier Guaycuru tribes of the Chaco; (26) Caduveo; (27) Titicaca villagers; **Southseas:** (28) Tahiti, Marquesas; (29) Palau; **Indonesia:** (30) Subanum (Mindanao); (31) Celebes (Bugis, Makas); (32) Borneo; (33) Malaysia; (34) Madagascar; **Burma:** (35) Lushai, the Arakan Coast; **India:** (36) Vallabhacharyas and area; **Near East:** (37) Ancient Babylonia; (38) Nogai; **Eurasia:** (39) Scythians; (40) Serbo-Croatians, Albanians; **Africa:** (41) Nuba, Kunama; (42) Konso, Galla; (43) Lango; (44) Rundi, Hunde; (45) Shona-Karanga, Lamba, Venda; (46) Humbe, Handa, Musho, Ovimbundu, Kimbundu; (47) Ambo-Kwanyama.

munities were cooperative up until about 4000 B.C.E.[*] – estimated to be the end of the Stone Age, or the Neolithic period – these ancient farmers and hunters left no written records.

So I combed through books, periodicals, and news clippings devoted to the history of Europe, Africa, Latin America, the Middle East, and Asia. I searched for the earliest written records of any forms of trans expression. Much to my surprise, I found a lot of information.

For example, I discovered abundant evidence of male-to-female transsexual women priestesses who played an important role in the worship of the Great Mother. Extensive research by scholars has revealed that this goddess, not male gods, was venerated throughout the Middle East, Northern Africa, Europe and western Asia.

The Great Mother was emblematic of pre-class communalism. Today, many scholars describe her as a female goddess. But perhaps those who revered her saw this divinity as more complex. While it's impossible today to interpret precisely how people who lived millennia ago viewed this goddess, Roman historian Plutarch described the Great Mother as an intersexual (hermaphroditic) deity in whom the sexes had not yet been split.[2]

The Great Mother's transsexual priestesses followed an ancient and sacred path of rituals that included castration. These transsexual priestesses continued to serve the Great Mother in societies in which class divisions were just developing. They are documented in Mesopotamian temple records from the middle of the third millennium B.C.E., and are also found in Assyrian, Akkadian, and Babylonian records.[3]

Many Mediterranean, Middle Eastern, and Near Eastern goddesses were served by transsexual priestesses, including the Syrian Astarte and Dea Syria at Hierapolis, Artemis, Atargatis, Ashtoreth or Ishtar, Hecate at Laguire, and Artemis (Diana) at Ephesus. Statues of Diana were often represented draped with a necklace made of the testicles of her priestesses.[4]

---

[*] *B.C.E. stands for "Before Common Era." It's an alternative to B.C., or "Before Christ." C.E. replaces A.D., or Anno Domini, which means "in the year of the Lord."*

Transsexual women priestesses known as *gallae* were found in such large numbers in Anatolia, an area which today is part of Turkey, that some classical texts report as many as five thousand in some cities.[5] The *gallae* served the Great Mother, known to the Phrygians as Cybele, whose worship is believed to date back to the Stone Age.[6]

Was the sacred service of transsexual priestesses a practice rooted in communal matrilineal societies? Or was it an example of men, living under patriarchy, castrating themselves in order to wrest this position from women? Not all researchers and historians agree.

For example, historian David F. Greenberg's findings seem to support the first position. He concludes that evidence of trans shamans, "among peoples whose later ways of life have been very diverse, suggests that the role does date back to the late Paleolithic (if not earlier)."[7]

Feminist researcher Merlin Stone is a prominent spokesperson for the latter argument. She wrote about the transition in Mediterranean and Middle Eastern cultures from communal to early class-divided societies. Stone argues: "It seems quite possible that as men began to gain power, even within the religion of the Goddess, they replaced priestesses. They may have initially gained this right by identifying with and imitating the castrated state of the son/lover; or in an attempt to imitate the female clergy, which originally held the power, they may have tried to rid themselves of their maleness by adopting the ritual of castration and the wearing of women's clothing."[8]

Stone's argument rests on a biological determinist definition of these transsexual priestesses as men. But how could priestesses who had "rid themselves of their maleness" expect to curry much favor with the new wealthy men who so valued males over females? Besides being bereft of "maleness," these priestesses continued the practice of matrilineal goddess worship that rivaled the patriarchal religions of new male-dominated ruling classes.

And what about the statement that the female clergy "originally held the power"? From where did women's "power" derive in cooperative societies? Was

TOP: The figure on the left is a trans <u>enaree</u> priestess. This image is from a gold plaque on a late fourth-century C.E. tiara from the Karagodeuaskh Tumulus on the Kuban River.

BOTTOM: A <u>galla</u> priestess of the goddess Cybele, from the mid-second century C.E.

it based on holding the spiritual reins?

Anthropologists have reconstructed patterns of life in Stone Age Europe, in much the same way as paleontologists have rebuilt models of dinosaurs. The Stone Age was a span of human development before the use of metals, when tools and hunting implements were fashioned from stone. Humans lived by hunting and food gathering; group labor was cooperative.

In these early societies, most men hunted while most women developed a division of labor in large centers of production and shared the responsibility of childcare. Women didn't rule *over* men, the way men dominate women in a patriarchal society. There were no signs of pharaohs and emperors, queens or presidents, who lived in luxury while others toiled in squalor. Leadership could not be coerced or bought, so it had to be earned through group respect.

The family structure of these societies was matrilineal and matrilocal – meaning women headed the family groupings and the collective homes. Blood descent and inheritance were traced through women. In these Stone Age societies, women were so respected that anthropologist Jacquetta Hawkes concluded, "Indeed, it is tempting

TOP: **Worshipping Heviosso, in Abomey, Africa. This is the region that is famous for Amazon warrior women.**
MIDDLE: **A Sakpota dancer in Dahomey, Africa.**
BOTTOM: **A Yoruba ritual in Brazil. Note the double-edged axe of Shangó, the deity who is represented as all sexes. The Amazons also reportedly carried double-edged axes.**
OPPOSITE: **A young male dressed as a Hindu deity at the Kumbh Mela festival in Allahabad, India in 1989.**

to be convinced that the earliest Neolithic societies throughout their range in time and space gave woman the highest status she has ever known."[9]

But did these cooperative societies only have room for two sexes, fixed at birth? It has become common for social scientists to conclude that the earliest human division of labor between women and men in communal societies formed the basis for modern sex and gender boundaries. But the more I studied, the more I believed that the assumption that every society, in every corner of the world, in every period of human history, recognized only men and women as two immutable social categories is a modern Western conclusion. It's time to take another look at what we've long believed was an ancient division of labor between only two sexes.

Our earliest ancestors do not appear to have been biological determinists. There are societies all over the world that allowed for more than two sexes, as well as respecting the right of individuals to reassign their sex. And transsexuality, transgender, intersexuality, and bigender appear as themes in creation stories, legends, parables, and oral history.

As I've already documented, many Native nations on the North American continent made room for more than two sexes, and there appeared to have been a fluidity between them. Reports by military expeditions, missionaries, ethnographers, anthropologists, explorers, and other harbingers of colonialism cited numerous forms of sex-change, transgender, and intersexuality in matrilineal societies – societies where men were not in a dominant position. In these accounts – no matter how racist or angrily distorted by the colonial narrative voice – it is clear that transsexual priestesses and other trans

ABOVE: A <u>nat</u> dancer in Myanmar (Burma). RIGHT: A Two-Spirit Tolowa medicine person.

spiritual leaders, or medicine people, have existed in many ancient cultures.

It's not possible in many of the following examples to make a distinction between transsexual, transgender, bigender, or mixed gender expression. However, trans spiritual leaders played a role in far-flung cultures all over the world.

For example, African spiritual beliefs in intersexual deities and sex/gender transformation among their followers have been documented among the Akan, Ambo-Kwanyama, Bobo, Chokwe, Dahomeans (of Benin), Dogon, Bambara, Etik, Handa, Humbe, Hunde, Ibo, Jukun, Kimbundu, Konso, Kunama, Lamba, Lango, Luba, Lulua, Musho, Nuba, Ovimbundu, Rundi, Shona-Karonga, Venda, Vili-Kongo, and Yoruba.[10]

Transgender in religious ceremony is still reported in the twentieth century in west Africa. And cross-dressing is a feature of modern Brazilian and Haitian ceremonies derived from west African religions.[11]

In addition, male-to-female shamans have been recorded among the Araucanians in southern Chile and parts of Argentina.[12] They are also reported among the Guajire, a cattle-herding people of northwest Venezuela and northern Colombia,[13] and the Tehuelche, who were hunter-gatherers in Argentina.[14]

Transgender historian Pauline Park, who is Korean American, wrote to me about trans spiritual expression in Asia:[15]

> Transgendered identities and practices have been documented in every traditional Asian society. In some Asian traditions, transgendered figures perform religious or quasi-religious functions. One such example is the *basaja* of the Indonesian island of Sulawesi (the

Celebes).[16] The *hijra* of India also can be understood in a religious context, in relation to the mother-goddess *Bahuchara Mata*, though some *hijras* also worship the Hindu god Shiva in his manifestation as the half-man, half-woman *Ardhanarisvara*.[17]

Finally, the *mudang* must be mentioned. The Korean *mudang* was a shaman or sorceress who frequently was a transgendered male, and like many other shamanic traditions, the idea that combining the characteristics of both sexes and both genders could connect one to a transcendent spiritual realm seemed to underlie the practice.[18]

In ancient China, the *shih-niang* wore a combination of female, male, and religious garb.[19] In Okinawa, some shamans took part in an ancient male-to-female ceremony known as *winagu nati*, which means, "becoming female."[20] And trans shamans were still reported practicing in the Vietnamese countryside in the mid-1970s.[21]

Female-to-male priests also exist – and most importantly, even co-exist with male-to-female shamans. Among the Lugbara in Africa, for example, male-to-females are called *okule* and female-to-males are named *agule*.[22] The Zulu initiated both male-to-female and female-to-male *isangoma*. While male-to-female shamans have been part of the traditional life of the Chukchee, Kamchadal, Koryak, and Inuit – all Native peoples of the Arctic Basin – Inuit female-to-males serve White Whale Woman, who was believed to have been transformed into a man or a woman-man.[23] And female-to-male expression is part of rituals and popular festivals with deep matrilineal roots in every corner of the world – including societies on the European continent.

Women and trans spiritual leaders continue to coexist in this century. Although South African Zulu diviners are usually women, some are male-to-female diviners.[24]

Among the Ambo people of southern Angola, even in this century, women – including trans women – serve the deity Kalunga.[25]

And in several areas of the world, the replacement of trans shamans with non-trans women spiritual leaders was a result of patriarchal pressure. For example, Walter Williams wrote that in South America, "Among the precontact Araucanians, the Mapuche, and probably other people, shaman religious leaders were all berdaches. When the Spanish suppressed this religious institution because of its association with male-male sex, the Indians switched to a totally new pattern. Women became the shamans."[26]

Although these brief examples of trans expression are limited to spiritual con-

texts, thousands of books, essays, and field research cite transgender, bigender, transsexuality, and intersexuality in societies on every continent, in every stage of development. I'm not arguing that all of these examples from diverse cultures are identical to modern Western trans identities. Nor am I trying to unravel the matrix of attitudes and beliefs around trans expression in these societies. The importance for me is the depth and breadth of evidence underscoring that gender and sex diversity are global in character, and that trans people were once revered, not reviled. How else could a trans person be a sacred shaman? In communal societies, where respect could not be bought or sold or stolen, being a shaman, or medicine person, was a position of honor.

So how and why, I wondered, did attitudes towards trans people plummet so drastically?

LEFT: **The African male youth on the left is representing a female.**

RIGHT: **A Haitian march through Brooklyn, New York, in 1993.**

CHAPTER **6.**

THE EARLIEST WRITTEN

edicts I could find against cross-dressing and sex-change were in Deuteronomy. Did that make Jews responsible for the rise of this bigotry? I hoped not, since I was sick to death of blame.

I grew up fighting anti-Semitism with balled-up fists. I was one of only four Jewish kids in my grade school. Our absence during religious holidays reminded the bullies who we were, so there was always a fight waiting for me around the school entrances. Jews were not allowed on the school playground. I thought the other kids made up the rule, but years later I discovered it was a parent who had given the instruction to his son and to others to enforce the edict, because, he said, "Jews killed our God!"

I can still remember the night in 1965 when my father, Irving, made an announcement to the whole family at the dinner table: "The pope says the Jews aren't responsible anymore for the crucifixion of Christ!" He added, "Tonight I'll get the first good sleep I've had in two thousand years!" Though it was funny, the so-called absolution didn't blunt the hatred I faced as a Jewish teenager.

But being Jewish presented me with my own questions. Why did the religious men I knew thank god every morning in their prayers that they weren't born women? And how could I reconcile myself to the fact that Deuteronomy and Leviticus – two of the five books of Mosaic law – condemned my cross-dressing and my sexual desire? My resolute insistence on cross-dressing had already cut short my religious education at our synagogue. So where, and to whom, could I go for understanding about how these laws came into being? I felt trapped between the anvil of religious laws I didn't want to defend and the hammer of anti-Semitism.

In my own life, Jews seemed to be a very small part of a larger, dominant culture steeped in bigotry and intolerance. I didn't see how Judaism could be responsible for that.

The more I researched the early Hebrews, the more I understood that blaming Judaism for the rise of biases against women, transsexuals, cross-dressers, intersexuals, lesbians, and gay men is not only anti-Semitic, it's a diversion from the real understanding of why oppression arose.

Where did the culpability really lie?

The Hebrews were one of many Semitic tribes that migrated from Arabia into the Fertile Crescent region over a long period, estimated by many scholars to be from about 1500–1250 B.C.E. These nomadic cattle breeders conquered one city after another from the inhabitants of Palestine, increasingly subjecting them to their rule. But what was won on the battlefield had to be defended by constant warfare. Other nomads were equally anxious for this fertile land. The territory conquered by the Hebrews stood at a crossroads of trade routes that allowed the Hebrews to develop extensive commerce.

The accumulation of wealth in the form of herds, agriculture, and trade led to deepening class divisions among the Hebrews, so no wonder the religious beliefs and laws began to reflect the interests of the small group who owned the wealth and their struggle to strengthen their control over the majority.

The communal religious beliefs of the Hebrews had not been fundamentally different from that of other polytheistic tribal-based religions of that region. They worshipped numerous deities, including *Yahweh*.

So where did trans-phobic and gender-phobic laws in Deuteronomy spring from? Deuteronomy flatly condemns cross-dressing: "The woman shall not wear that which pertaineth unto a man, neither shall a man put on a woman's garment: for all that do so are abomination unto the LORD thy God."[1] And male-to-female surgery was denounced: "He that is wounded in the stones, or hath his privy member cut off, shall not enter the congregation of the LORD."[2]

The patriarchal fathers wouldn't have felt the need to spell out these edicts if they weren't common practice. But why did they consider cross-dressing and sex-change such a threat? What was going on among the Hebrews at the time Deuteronomy was written?

Scholars hotly debate the date, as well as the authorship, of these laws. Estimates range from the eleventh to the seventh centuries B.C.E. But what is clear is that Deuteronomy reflects the deepening of patriarchal class divisions among the Hebrews, who lived in and around communal societies that still worshipped goddesses such as Astaroth, Ishtar, Isis, and Cybele. And remember, ritual sex-change was a sacred path for many priestesses of these matrilineal religious traditions.[3]

The condemnation against "cross-dressing," historians Bonnie and Vernon Bullough wrote, "formed part of a campaign against the Syrian goddess Atargatis, who was probably a Syrian version of the Assyrian goddess Ishtar. In some of the worship ceremonies, the followers of Atargatis dressed in the clothes and assumed the role of the opposite sex, just as their Greek counterparts did."[4]

In addition, the laws warned against Jews cross-dressing. These rules forbade Jewish men from using makeup, wearing brightly colored clothes, jewelry, or ornaments associated with women, or shaving their pubic hair. Women were told to keep their hair long, while men were to keep theirs clipped short.[5] On the one hand, these rules could be seen from the point of view that cross-dressing and cross-gendered expression as a whole retained an integral connection to the worship of the Mother Goddess.

But it's also important to remember that wealthy Hebrew males were trying to consolidate their patriarchal rule. That means they were very much concerned about making distinctions between women and men, and eliminating any blurring or bridging of those categories. That would also explain why the rules of ownership of property and the rights of intersexual people were extensively detailed in Jewish law.[6]

The Hebrews and Judaism were not to blame for the rise of patriarchy or oppression. Class divisions were responsible for the growth of laws that placed new boundaries and restrictions across bodies, self-expression, and desire – as well as fencing off property and wealth.

A statue of a bearded King Hatshepsut (1485 B.C.E.), from the Valley Temple of Hatshepsut at Deir-el-Bahri.

And the Hebrews weren't even the first society to split into classes, or to develop increasingly patriarchal laws. That transformation took place in societies all over the world.

More than a century ago, Frederick Engels explained the importance of these dramatic changes in human society. Engels compared the significance of research into early forms of kinship by Lewis H. Morgan[7] to Darwin's theory of evolution. Morgan, who studied the North American Haudenosaunee (Iroquois Confederacy) and numerous tribes in Asia, Africa, and Australia, documented that matrilineal kinship historically preceded patriarchal families. Engels and Karl Marx saw Morgan's studies as proof that the oppression of women began with the cleavage of society into male-dominated classes based on private ownership of property and the accumulation of wealth.

I believe the same historic overthrow of communalism was also responsible for trans oppression.

In every society in which human labor grew more productive with the use of improved tools and techniques, people stored up more than what they needed for immediate consumption. This surplus was the first accumulation of wealth. Generally, men, who had primarily been wild-game hunters, domesticated and herded large animals, which represented the first wealth. Men, therefore, were in charge of stockpiling this abundance: cattle, sheep, goats, horses, and the surplus of dried and smoked meats and hides, milk, cheese, and yogurt.

Prior to this surplus, tools, utensils, and other possessions were commonly owned within the matrilineal *gens*. As wealth accumulated in the male sphere of labor, the family structure began to change, and men began to pass on inheritance to their

The Assyrian King Ashurbanipal, in women's clothes, shown spinning with his wives.

male heirs. Those who had large families and other advantages gathered and stored more surplus. These inequalities, small at first, became the basis of the enrichment of some male tribal members over the women and the tribe as a whole.

This material imbalance led to the unplanned and unconscious transformation of human society. Communal societies, in which labor was voluntary and collective, gave way to unequal societies in which those who owned wealth forced others to work for them – an enforced social relationship of masters and slaves. This took place at different times in different places over a period of many centuries.

No matter where or when this occurred, everything that had once been considered natural was turned on its head in the service of the new owning classes. Creation of a slave class required the branding – either literally or figuratively – of some people as "different," and therefore unworthy of a free status. This stigma, whether race, nationality, religion, sex, or gender, was meant to dehumanize the individuals and justify their enslavement.

Shackling a vast laboring class meant creating armies, police, courts, and prisons to enforce the ownership of private property. However, whips and chains alone couldn't ensure the rule of the new wealthy elite. A tiny, parasitic class can't live in luxury off the wealth of a vast, laboring class without keeping the majority divided and pitted against each other. That is where the necessity for bigotry began.

I found the origin of trans oppression at this intersection between the overthrow of mother-right and the rise of patriarchal class-divided societies. It is at this very nexus that edicts like Deuteronomy arose. Law, including religious law, codified class relations.

The earliest overthrow of mother-right took place in the fertile river valleys of Eurasia and northeast Africa during the period of about 4500 to 1200 B.C.E. In this new social structure, riven by inequality, male ruling class attitudes toward women and trans people grew more and more hostile, even toward transgendered queens and kings.

For example, Hatshepsut, a woman who ruled Egypt in the fifteenth century B.C.E., "assumed masculine attire, was represented as god and king, and wore the symbolic false beard. In murals she was pictured with short hair, bare shoulders, and was usually devoid of breasts. S/he described herself by male names." Ruling with the support of the temple community, Hatshepsut built grand monuments in honor of the god Amun. Yet after her death, she and the god she honored faced a campaign of hostility, with her second husband attempting to erase all memory of her.[8]

Some eight hundred years later, in the seventh century B.C.E., King Ashurbanipal (Sardanapalus), the last of the Assyrian kings, was described by a physician in his court as spending a great deal of his time dressed in women's clothing. Key nobles used reports of Ashurbanipal's cross-dressing to justify overthrowing him. Ashurbanipal waged a defensive military campaign against these rivals but was twice defeated in battle. As a result, his rule was limited to his capital city. Finally facing defeat, Ashurbanipal set fire to his palace, killing everyone in it – including himself.[9]

Hostility to transgender, sex-change, intersexuality, women, and same-sex love became a pattern wherever class antagonisms deepened. As a Jewish, transgender, working-class revolutionary, I can't stress enough that Judaism was *not* the root of the oppression of women and the outlawing of trans expression and same-sex love. The rise of patriarchal class divisions were to blame.

And I found that wherever the ruling classes became stronger, the laws grew increasingly more fierce and more relentlessly enforced.

BUT THEY HAD SLAVES!

CHAPTER 7.

WHAT WAS I TAUGHT

in school about Greek antiquity? I recall only one moment. It was springtime, and I was gazing out the window, longing to be released from school. My teacher's voice droned, the harsh lights buzzed overhead, the giant clock ticked. At that very moment my teacher rapped on my desk and ordered me to pay attention. I sat bolt upright and tried to concentrate, which is the only reason I heard the following statement so clearly: "Greek democracy was the highest expression of ancient civilization."

I slumped back down in my chair and listened half-heartedly to a stream of facts and dates. Suddenly I heard the word "slaves." I urgently raised my hand and asked, "Were there slaves in Greece?" As the other kids giggled, I guessed I had missed that part of class. Later that day I wandered down to a stretch of woods tucked along the edges of my neighborhood. As I placed pennies on the train tracks and crouched waiting for the train to roar past, I thought about my teacher's earlier statement that "Greek democracy was the highest expression of civilization." If it was so civilized, how come they had slaves?

I've heard some gay men and lesbians exclaim that, out of all of human history, ancient Greek society was the most accepting of same-sex lovers. But I wonder, how happy were the gay slaves? The word democracy has a pleasant ring, but democracy for whom? The political reality is that Greek democracy was a form of state based on the authoritarian rule of the slave-owning patricians over the enslaved majority.

I found that, as with virtually every ancient people, the early tribes of Greece were communal and matrilineal. But the rise of the Greek city-states during the eighth to sixth centuries B.C.E. was based on slave labor, plunder, and trade. The longer the ruling patricians held power, the more women's status became degraded and expressions of human love became subject to legal dictate.

It's true I did find many, many trans references in Greek culture, religion, art, and mythology. But whatever homage trans expression still enjoyed was a holdover from the communal past. It was hard for the Greek patriarchs to diminish the honor

A terminal figure of
an intersexual feeding a
bird. Second century c.e.,
restored in the
eighteenth century.

that transgender and intersexuality still held among the laboring class. The patriarchal priests in Greece were hemmed in by the popularity of ancient religions – some dating from matriarchal times – and by schools of secular philosophers who played a vital role in politics and education.[1] Wherever ancient rituals still persisted in Greece, so did trans expression. There were numerous festivals, rituals, and customs in which men dressed in women's clothing, and women wore men's clothes and beards.[2]

Greek mythology was also filled with references to sex-change, intersexuality, and cross-dressing. Many mythological heroes and gods cross-dressed at one time or another, including Achilles, Heracles, Dionysus, and Athena. "Literal and metaphoric sex change," notes classical scholar P. M. C. Forbes Irving, "seems to have been a subject of considerable imaginative interest in the ancient world and had some importance in ancient religion."[3]

But changing attitudes toward trans people and the sharpening patriarchal class divisions are reflected in the Greek legends, in the same way that the mythological defeat of goddesses by male gods mirrored the overthrow of matrilineal societies. For example, Kaineus (Caeneus), a female-to-male figure in mythology, is viewed as a "scorner and rival of the gods."[4] He is driven into the earth by the Centaurs who considered Kaineus an outrage to their masculinity.

Dionysus, also known as Bacchus, was one of the gods who replaced the pre-class goddesses. But Dionysus was represented as a transgendered, cross-dressing god – a hybridization of the old beliefs and the new. During the rites of Dionysus, females – known as *ithyphalloi* – dressed in men's clothes and carried large phalluses, and men dressed in women's apparel.[5]

Dionysus held great popularity with the most downtrodden, notes Forbes Irving:

Perhaps the most striking feature of Dionysus, and one which seems particularly relevant
to his role as a shape-shifter, is that although he becomes
one of the greatest of all the gods he retains in his myths
and many of his cults a marginal character. He is above all
the god of the weak and oppressed, especially women, and
an opponent of the established order.[6]

The slave-owners were not easily able to impose their brutal system,
or their beliefs, on peoples who had once lived freely and worked
cooperatively. The patricians couldn't rule without fighting wars
and crushing rebellions.

To my surprise, I discovered that one particular group of warriors
who fought against this enslavement was considered transgendered,
at least by the Greeks – the Amazons. I knew a little about the Amazons
because they were such a symbol of freedom and resistance for modern
feminists. However, I had always thought of these warriors as
"woman-identified women." But were the Amazons also
an example of transgender resistance?

The ancient Amazons fought in the gateway
between freedom and slavery, between the overthrow of matrilineal communal societies and the
ascendancy of patriarchal class rule. Numerous
battles between Amazon warriors and the Greek
armies are documented in art and legends. The
double-edged axe the Amazons reportedly carried in battle has become a symbol of modern
feminist pride.

Yet while the Amazons are almost
always portrayed as feminine, there is
evidence the Greeks thought of them as
transgendered. Classical writer Pliny
the Younger referred to "the race of
the Androgynae, who combine the
two sexes.... Aristotle adds that in all
of them the right breast is that of a
man, the left breast that of a woman."[7]

The right breast of a man, the left
breast of a woman – this sounds very
much like a description of the Amazons. The only thing I had heard about
the legendary Amazons was that they surgically removed their right breast
because they were archers. But that had
always struck me as a rather simplistic
explanation.

THIS PAGE: A Greek intersexual statue.

LEFT: Athena as a male warrior.

To the Greeks, these Amazons were masculine women who bore themselves like men. And they weren't the only transgendered Scythians. The Greeks were well aware of the transsexual priestesses among the Scythians, who were trading partners and competitors in the Black Sea. And even in legends, the Amazon leaders were paired in battles with Greek male warriors such as Achilles, Theseus, and Heracles – all of whom were reported in mythology as having cross-dressed at one time. In addition, the Amazons were believed to have a spiritual connection with Dionysus, the transgendered god.[8]

And was the Amazon's weapon – the double-edged axe – a "man's" armament merely because it was a weapon of war, or did it symbolize intersexuality?

Greek historian Plutarch wrote that Heracles gave Queen Omphale the double axe he had taken from a defeated Amazon as a spoil of war; both Heracles and Omphale were reported to have cross-dressed. Eventually, the axe was given in homage to Zeus Labrandeus, who was represented in a bronze statue as a beardless deity holding the double axe, the upper body bearing four rows of breasts. So the axe passed, as Delcourt concluded, "from a warrior-woman to a hero and a queen who have exchanged clothing; afterwards it goes to a father-god represented as having breasts; indications of androgyny are particularly abundant here."[9]

Were the Amazons a shining example of transgender resistance? If so, Scythian Amazons are part of the overlapping history of women and trans people. And I knew that the Amazons were not the only female warriors associated with transgender.

I remembered the description of female-to-male warriors of the Tupinamba, in northeastern Brazil, described in 1576 by Pedro de Magalhães de Gandavo. He and other explorers renamed the river that flowed through that area the "River of the Amazons," after the Scythian warriors. And I recalled that both a double-edged axe and cross-gendered expression were central to worship by African and Brazilian followers of the Yoruba deity Shangó – a divinity believed to appear at times as a man and other times as a woman.

As I began to write this chapter, I thought about how the past has been interpreted

 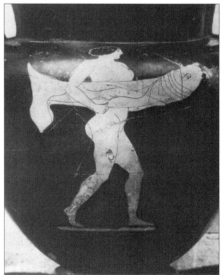

only from the standpoint of women and men, without taking transgender, bigender, transsexuality, or intersexuality into account. Later that afternoon I received an e-mail from Dr. Anne Fausto-Sterling, a respected bio-geneticist and feminist from Brown University. She called my attention to a short article that appeared in the *British Daily Telegraph* on February 13, 1995. The clipping, headlined "She-Men," announced the discovery of evidence of transgender, including women warriors, in Iron Age graves in southern Russia by British archeologist Timothy Taylor. "I think I have identified females who moved into a male sphere as well as men who cross-dressed," Taylor wrote.[10]

It's time for a fresh look at history. And this time, I don't intend to be left out!

OPPOSITE LEFT: **Heracles dressed in women's clothing.**

OPPOSITE RIGHT: **A woman carrying a phallus, an act attributed to female followers of Dionysus, who also cross-dressed.**

ABOVE: **A homosexual trans scene from a red-figure cup by Peithinos, fifth century B.C.E.**

CHAPTER 8.

a gender outlaw in modern society, it's not rhetoric. I have been dragged out of bars by police who claimed I broke the law when I dressed myself that evening. I've heard the rap of a cop's club on the stall door when I've used a public women's toilet. And then there's the question of my identity papers.

My driver's license reads *Male*. The application form only offered me two choices: *M* or *F*. In this society, where women are assumed to be feminine and men are assumed to be masculine, my sex and gender expression appear to be at odds. But the very fact that I could be issued a license as a male demonstrates that many strangers "read me" as a man, rather than a masculine woman.

In almost thirty years of driving I've heard the whine of police sirens behind my car on only three occasions. But each time, a trooper sauntered up to my car window and demanded, "Your license and registration – sir." Imagine the nightmare I'd face if I handed the trooper a license that says I am female. The alleged traffic infraction should be the issue, not my genitals. I shouldn't have to prove my sex to any police officer who has stopped me for a moving violation, and my body should not be the focus of investigation. But in order to avoid these dangers, I broke the law when I filled out my driver's license application. As a result, I could face a fine, a suspension of my license, and up to six months in jail merely for having put an *M* in the box marked sex.

And then there's the problem of my passport. I don't feel safe traveling with a passport that reads *Female*. However, if I apply for a passport as *Male*, I am subject to even more serious felony charges. Therefore, I don't have a passport, which restricts my freedom to travel. I could have my birth certificate changed to read *Male* in order to circumvent these problems, but I don't see why I should have to legally align my sex with my gender expression, especially when this policy needs to be fought.

Why am I forced to check off an *F* or an *M* on these documents in the first place? For identification? Both a driver's license and a passport include photographs! Most cops and passport agents would feel insulted to think they needed an *M* or an *F* to determine if a person is a man or a woman. It's only those of us who cross the boundaries of sex or gender, or live ambiguously between those borders, who are harassed by this legal requirement.

Many of my transsexual sisters and brothers are required legally to amend their birth certificates before they can change their other identification papers to conform to their lives. But states have different policies on changing birth certificates – some simple, some grueling. Why should transsexual men and women be harassed, or denied the right to travel, merely based on which state they were unlucky enough to have been born in?

I am told I must check off *M* or *F* because it is a legal necessity. But when I was a child, I was required to check off race on all legal records. It took mighty, militant battles against institutionalized racist discrimination to remove that mandatory question from documents. The women's liberation movement won some important legal victories against sex discrimination too, like ending the policy of listing jobs in "female" and "male" categories. So why do we still have to check off *male* or *female* on all records?

Why is the categorization of sex a legal question at all? And why are those categories policed? Why did these laws arise in the first place? I grew up thinking that law was wisdom that hovered above society. But I came away with another view after researching the ancient Roman edicts that segregated the sexes into separate and distinct legal categories.

As class divisions deepened in ancient Roman society, the sexes were assigned an increasingly unequal status. Once property-owning males ascended to a superior social position, those categories could not be bridged or blurred without threatening those who owned and controlled this new wealth. Ownership of property and its inheritance, paternity, legitimacy, and titles became vital legal questions for the new ruling elite. The heterosexual family, headed by the father, became a state dictate because it was the economic vehicle that ensured wealth would be passed on to sons.

Everyone who was not born a male heir to property bore the wrath of the new social system. Just as the status of women was degraded, so was everything that was "not male" – transgender, gender-bending, sex-change, and intersexuality. A woman could not become a man, any more than a slave could become a ruling patrician. Males who were viewed as "womanly" were an affront to the men in power.

Eventually, even a god like Dionysus couldn't get away with such feminine flamboyance. The rituals of Dionysus had endured in Rome even after Christianity became the state religion of the wealthy. But as the god became scorned by the Christian ruling classes, Dionysus's status was downgraded from a man-woman – a double-being, doubly powerful – to effeminate, an increasingly despised gender expression.[1]

Hatred and contempt for women partly accounts for the growing hostility of the ruling classes toward men they considered too feminine. The Romans also used the Greeks' acceptance of male same-sex relations as an ideological weapon against this imperial power they had supplanted. But the campaigns by Rome's rulers against the followers of Dionysus might also have been a militaristic appeal to create

Rambo-like soldiers. War was becoming a profitable business venture in Rome, and Dionysus was a "make love, not war" god who encouraged soldiers to desert their posts in battle.[2]

In 186 B.C.E., the Roman Senate banned the *bacchanalia* – the pleasure-centered festivals of the worshippers of Dionysus. Attitudes of the ruling elite toward women, same-sex love, and transgender are documented by Roman historian Livy's summary of a consul's argument in favor of the ban: "A great number of adherents are women, which is the origin of the whole trouble. But there are also men like women, who have joined in each other's defilement.... Do you think, citizens, that young men who have taken this oath can be made soldiers?"[3]

Of the some seven thousand people arrested under this ban, most were from the laboring class. That was no accident. "The class nature of this oppression is evident," notes gay historian Arthur Evans, "when we realize that the ancient worship of Bacchus was most popular with the lower classes."[4]

For a while, transgender expression, like same-sex love, was permissible for the wealthy Roman leisure class because it wasn't seen as a threat to the patricians. But when factional battles broke out among the rulers themselves, transgender sometimes became a convenient political charge. The most famous example is Elagabalus, emperor of Rome in 218 C.E., who often appeared in women's clothing and makeup, and publicly declared one of his male lovers to be his husband. The ruling class faction who opposed him ordered the Praetorian Guard to assassinate Elagabalus in 222 C.E. His mutilated body was dragged through the streets of Rome, and thrown into the Tiber River.[5]

In 342 C.E., Emperor Constantine elevated Christianity to the status of a state religion. The fusion of religion with state power set the stage for strengthening antitrans laws during slavery, as well as sweeping feudal witch hunts that later targeted trans people.

The laws continued to tighten like a noose. Less than four decades after Constantine's act, on August 6, 390 C.E., the rulers Valentinian, Arcadius, and Theodosius addressed an edict to the vicar of the city of Rome:

> We cannot tolerate the city of Rome, mother of all virtues, being stained any longer by the contamination of male effeminacy.... Your laudable experience will therefore punish among revenging flames, in the presence of the people, as required by the grossness of the crime, all those who have given themselves up to the infamy of condemning the manly body, transformed into a feminine one, to bear practices reserved for the other sex, which have nothing different from women, carried forth – we are ashamed to say – from male brothels, so that all may know that the house of the manly soul must be sacrosanct to all, and that he who basely abandons his own sex cannot aspire to that of another without undergoing the supreme punishment [death by fire].[6]

But shortly after the law passed, at least one dramatic act of resistance to this murderous anti-trans legislation was recorded. The head of the militia in Thessalonica in northern Greece, a Goth named Butheric, arrested a famous circus performer who was well-known for his femininity. But the performer was loved by the masses. When news spread of his arrest, the people rose up in rebellion and killed Butheric. The outraged Gothic authorities reportedly rounded up the nearby population and butchered three thousand people as collective punishment.[7]

The very fact that these rulers were still trying to ban any form of trans expression demonstrates deep beliefs still persisted from communalism. But the repressive laws aimed at further oppressing trans people, gay and lesbian love, and women formed part of the *Corpus juris civilis* – the Roman body of law that was later used as the foundation for religious and secular law in Europe, England, and the United States.[8]

However, in its decline, the hierarchy of the Roman empire was too weak to wage an all-out war against transgender and same-sex love. Slavery contained the kernel of its own destruction – people who were chained, starved, and beaten didn't work at peak efficiency, and the economic system required constant warfare to replenish slaves. These huge military expenditures bankrupted Rome. That's why the Roman empire and its slave-based system of production disintegrated – not because of moral degeneration.

I wondered why the Roman edicts and terror hadn't been enough to reshape all trans people into the strictly defined categories of what was legally appropriate behavior and dress for women and men. Then I realized that I am part of a vast movement of people who have been shamed and threatened and beaten and arrested because of the way we define our sex or express our gender. And many of us have emerged stronger and prouder.

God/dess of love known as Cupid by the Romans and Eros by
the Greeks. The legend of Cupid/Eros, child of Hermes and
Aphrodite, was the root of the term "hermaphrodite".

"HOLY WAR" AGAINST TRANS PEOPLE

You may write me down in history
With your bitter, twisted lies,
You may trod me in the very dirt
But still, like dust, I'll rise.

MAYA ANGELOU
from Still I Rise

Part Three

CHAPTER 9.

ALTHOUGH I MAY HAVE
daydreamed my way through the Middle Ages, I do remember leaving high school with a certain feeling about feudalism. I had the impression that it was an epoch in which the Catholic Church rounded up Jews, Muslims, women of all sexualities, gay men, herbalists, scientists – anyone they could get their hands on – for torture and execution, and the serfs did nothing but subserviently till the land.

As a Jewish, transgendered lesbian, I wasn't wild about returning to study this period of Western European history, but I really wanted to understand more about the cryptic charge that Joan of Arc's cross-gendered expression was "following the custom of the Gentiles and the Heathen." I'm glad I did take another look at this period, however, because I realized why transgender was such a threat to both the Church and the feudal ruling class as a whole.

The feudal landlords waged war against communalism from the mid-eighth century well into the twelfth century. Feudal warlords and their powerful armies tried to privatize communally-held land. But both communal and enslaved peasants fiercely resisted feudal bondage. Peasant rebellions erupted throughout these centuries.

The Catholic Church, a powerful ally of the ruling class, played a pivotal role in suppressing this resistance. The Church was the one powerful institution that could bring all of Western Europe under one political system, because it provided the learning, organization, and structural framework. As a result, the Church became the defining institution of feudal life.

But the interests of the Church were decidedly economic, since it claimed ownership of one-third of the soil of the Catholic world – by far the biggest landowner.[1] And forcing peasants to bow to the belief that private ownership of the land and gross inequality was divinely inspired very much served the interests of the entire feudal ruling class.

But turning free peasants into enslaved serfs necessitated breaking communal bonds and beliefs. That's why, I believe, ritual and festival trans expression were targeted.

The association of transgender with communal religious worship and beliefs so enraged the Christian hierarchy that in 691 C.E. the Council of Constantinople decreed: "We forbid dances and initiation rites of the 'gods,' as they are falsely called among the Greeks, since, whether by men or women, they are done according to an ancient custom contrary to the Christian way of life, and we decree that no man shall put on a woman's dress nor a woman, clothes that belong to men."[2]

The Church tried to demonize transgender by linking it with witchcraft, and by banning and suppressing it from all peasant rituals and celebrations. As early as the sixth century C.E., the Christian writer Caesarius of Arles (now in southern France) denounced the pagan practices of ritual transgender. Sixth- and seventh-century synods repeatedly condemned cross-dressing during the popular New Year's holiday. In the ninth century, a Christian guidebook dictated penance for men who practiced ritual cross-dressing and cross-gender behavior. And a thirteenth-century Inquisitor in southern France denounced trans religious expression.[3]

In about 1250, a group of males dressed as women danced their way into the house of a wealthy landowner, singing: "We take one and give back a hundred." That verse referred to a popular belief that the "good people" – *bonae* in Latin – exercised the power to bestow prosperity upon any house in which they were given gifts. According to one account:

> The suspicious wife of the farmer did not accept the claim of the female impersonators to be *bonae* and tried to end their revel, but in spite of her protestations they carried out all the goods from her house. Perhaps for this as well as similar reasons bishops were requested to look out for throngs of demons transformed into women, which seems like a prohibition against male cross-dressing.[4]

Yet while the early Church fathers denounced all cross-gender behavior, they demonstrated their hypocrisy by canonizing some twenty to twenty-five female saints who cross-dressed, lived as men, or wore full beards. According to medieval legends, these cross-dressed female-to-male saints lived and worshipped as men for their entire adult lives. Their birth sex was only discovered after their deaths. These saints included Pelagia, Margarita, Marinus (Marina), Athanasia (Alexandria), Eugenia, Appollinaria, Euphrosyne, Matrona, Theodora, Anastasia, Papula, and Joseph (Hildegund). In addition, the Church canonized women with full beards: Galla, Paula, and Wilgefortis (Uncumber).[5] The legendary Pope Joan, who was chronicled during the thirteenth century, allegedly ruled as John Anglicus. His statue stood with those of other popes in the Cathedral of Siena in the fourteenth century, but by the sixteenth century, historians considered the account of his reign to be merely legend.[6]

Had the Church fathers forgotten the edicts of Deuteronomy? That's hard to believe, since they continued to invoke the injunctions throughout the Middle Ages. I believe that since a fusion of matrilineal beliefs with patriarchal culture was prevalent during the early development of class society, these cross-gendered saints could be attributed to the persistence of ancient worship and beliefs about transgender.

More than a century ago, German scholar Herman Usener argued that the similarity of the legends about female-to-male saints represented survival of the beliefs surrounding the goddess Aphrodite of Cyprus. Usener noted that Aphrodite was also named Pelagia and Marina – the same names as two of the cross-dressed Catholic saints. Aphrodite's female followers reportedly dressed in men's garb to sacrifice to her, and male-to-female transsexual priestesses served this goddess.[7]

Historians Vern and Bonnie Bullough, who have made enormous contributions to the study of cross-dressing during feudal times, attribute the Church's acceptance of female-to-male saints to the fact that they were admired for aspiring to the higher social status of men. It's true that men were considered superior, but female-to-male expression was specifically censured, even for the pious. Saint Jerome denounced it in the fourth century, and a canon of the Synod of Ver in the ninth century demonstrates that the Church had encountered and condemned transgendered females centuries before Joan of Arc was born.

The canon stated, "If women who choose chastity in the cause of religion either take on the clothes of a man or cut their hair, in order to appear false to others, we resolve that they should be admonished and criticized, because we consider that they err through a great ignorance rather than zeal."[8]

The charges of cross-dressing lodged against Joan of Arc certainly were political – as were all the accusations she faced. But she didn't just challenge men on their own playing field. Nor was she merely a pawn in the bloody war between England and France. Joan of Arc was also a prisoner of the class war waged by the French feudal nobility against their own peasantry. Of course she made the French rulers tremble; this transgendered female saint led a peasant army.

As I argued earlier, I believe the French nobility and the Church feared both Joan of Arc's assertion that her

While Pope John Anglicus (Pope Joan) is believed to be merely a legend, it's true that the Church canonized scores of female-to-male saints.

transgender expression was a religious duty, and the fact that her transgender was held in such reverence by the peasants, because both recalled beliefs in an ancient rival religion from a competing economic system. Scapegoating Joan of Arc and the "radical" region of her birth fed the counter-revolutionary terror against the communal farmers and the peasantry as a whole.

I think the Church fathers may have canonized a constellation of female-to-male trans saints because they were forced to compete with the old religion still popularly embraced by the peasants. The Church hierarchy must have had a tough time trying to convert peasants from their joyous, pro-sexual, cross-gendered religious rites to the gloom and doom of medieval Catholicism. I believe the clerics tried to co-opt popular images of transgender, but with a twist – these female-to-male saints were remarkably pious. Trans images that drew the devotion of peasants to the religion of the owning class would have been valuable in recruitment.

Several of these saints paid dearly for their renunciation of their birth sex, and all of them had to keep their change of sex secret. In cooperative societies, transgender, transsexual, and intersexual people lived openly, with honor. But in a class-divided society like medieval Western Europe, the Church's legends of the female-to-male saints introduced the concept of "passing" – being forced to hide a trans identity.

There are no known Christian male-to-female saints. Throughout the Middle Ages, this expression was only officially permitted during carnivals and festivals, when the laws of the land were temporarily lifted. Otherwise, male-to-female transgender and cross-dressing were stigmatized by the Church as witchcraft.[9]

Yet cross-gendered expression, whether male or female, was part of virtually all peasant festivals – including Halloween, a holiday with roots in Celtic, matrilineal society. After Celtic society transformed from matrilineal to patriarchal, the ruling classes bowed to patriarchal gods, while the laboring class maintained its beliefs in the ancient nature-based goddess religion.[10] The Celt feast days included *Samhain*, a festival celebrated on November 1, that Christians later called All Hallow's Eve – Halloween. The Celt Winter Solstice persisted under Christianity as the Feast of Fools. Transgender played a prominent role in both holidays. Maybe this had something to do with why I was exempt from arrest for cross-dressing on Halloween!

While the Church denounced male-to-female trans expression as witchcraft, they co-opted it for their theatrical productions. Trans theatrical performance in many parts of the world was rooted in communal rituals in which trans expression was considered sacred. For example, trans actors are famous in Japanese Noh drama, which stems from *dengaku*, a folk dance performed during rice planting and harvesting, and Chinese opera derives from the songs and dances of ancient religious festivities. In early Greek Athenian drama, male actors played the female roles; these dramas were originally performed during the festivals honoring Dionysus, a time when women and men engaged in cross-gendered worship.[11]

In Western Europe, theater had become such a popular ideological vehicle throughout the periods of slavery and early feudalism that by the tenth century the Catholic Church appropriated the transgender it had not been able to uproot from peasant festivals and rituals into its own dramatic rituals. In Church pageants and liturgical dramas, male actors were allowed to flaunt Deuteronomy by wearing women's clothing.[12] While priests denounced male femininity and cross-dressing, they didn't mind exploiting for their own interests the popularity of transgender in Church dramas.

And what about the flamboyant style of the Church fathers themselves? To this day, priests dress in floor-length gowns, bright colors, jeweled rings, and other adornments that many men wouldn't be caught dead in. In fact, sending a boy into the priesthood used to be referred to as putting a boy "into skirts."[13] Did this trans fashion in the Church evolve from the transsexual priestesses of the goddess religions?

The Church fathers may have hoped to co-opt the transgender expression that the peasants still revered, but it became the undoing of liturgical drama. "Indeed, festive and anarchic components steadily infiltrated liturgical drama," concluded historian Peter Ackroyd, "taking their final shape when Latin was replaced by vernacular in the thirteenth century. Just as the Church authorities were mocked by cross-dressers during the Feast of Fools, so the comic uses of transvestism slowly despiritualized religious drama."[14]

Although the Church encouraged peasants to kneel before bearded or female-to-male saints and enjoy transgender in liturgical drama, it opposed any trans customs that were connected to pre-class matrilineal beliefs. By the late fifteenth century, the Catholic Church fathers were slowly banishing the Feast of Fools from cathedrals.[15] Transgender was one of many targets of the landowner's war, waged under a religious banner.

The "Holy" Inquisition, begun in 1233, and the witch trials were weapons of terror and mass murder that took a staggering toll in human life from Ireland to Poland. Twenty years after Joan of Arc's execution, in 1451 the Inquisition was officially authorized to battle witchcraft as a major crime. Many peasant women, accused of being witches, were tortured and killed. These included women who followed the older rural-based religions, lived independently, held small amounts of land, or passed down folk medicinal knowledge, such as midwives who shared their knowledge of methods of birth control and abortion. Significantly, witches were accused of having the power to change sex.[16]

Because of the feudal landlords' economic interest in strengthening patriarchal inheritance and rule, they increasingly partitioned the sexes in the name of god. This drive to differentiate man from woman fueled a frenzied campaign against intersexuality. In the fifteenth century, for example, the Church put a rooster on trial at Basel. The cock was charged with having laid an egg. The rooster's lawyer argued that the act was involuntary, and that animals were not capable of making pacts with the devil. The court found the cock innocent, but attributed the act of laying the egg to a sorcerer masquerading as a cock. As a result, the rooster and the egg in question were burned at the stake.[17]

Although the Church engaged in rivalries with landowners and monarchs, it knew where its overall class interests lay. Trans people, women charged with lesbianism, gay men, Muslims, Jews, herbalists, healers – anyone who challenged feudal rule was considered a threat and faced extermination. Even scientists were targeted because their research negated religious dogma. The Inquisitors came armed with the Bible, as well as with swords and instruments of torture to put down

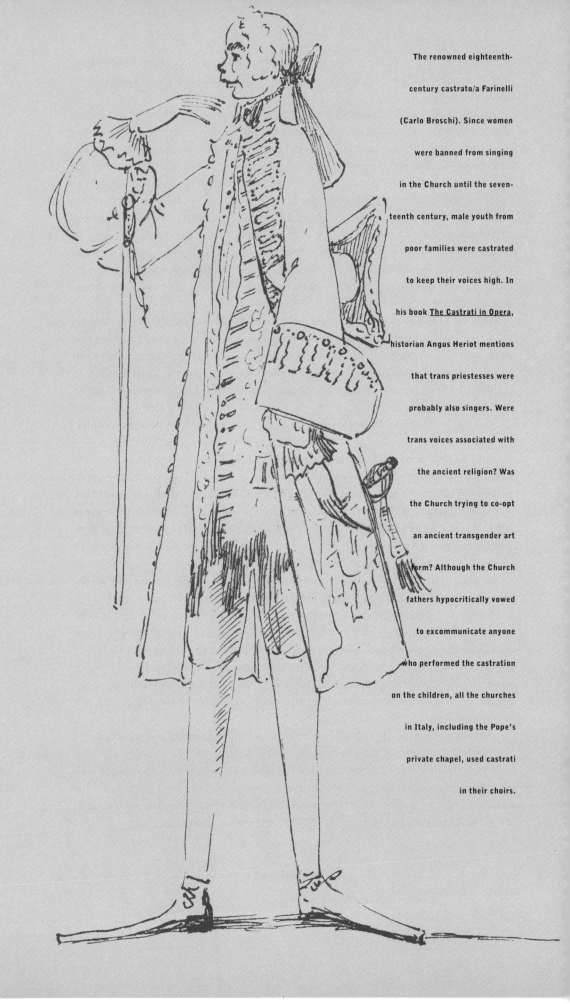

The renowned eighteenth-century castrato/a Farinelli (Carlo Broschi). Since women were banned from singing in the Church until the seventeenth century, male youth from poor families were castrated to keep their voices high. In his book The Castrati in Opera, historian Angus Heriot mentions that trans priestesses were probably also singers. Were trans voices associated with the ancient religion? Was the Church trying to co-opt an ancient transgender art form? Although the Church fathers hypocritically vowed to excommunicate anyone who performed the castration on the children, all the churches in Italy, including the Pope's private chapel, used castrati in their choirs.

peasant uprisings. But all the might of the feudal landowners didn't crush the resistance of the peasants once and for all – they continually rose up against the rule of powerful landlords and their feudal theology.

Frequently the feudal period is explained simply from the point of view of the growth of the Church, but as I have shown, religion itself became a propaganda weapon of the ruling rich. For example, under feudalism, which was based on private ownership of the land, the Lord's Prayer urged, "Forgive us our trespasses." Trespassing was a crime that could only have arisen in a society where individuals claimed vast expanses of soil as their own. But as a money-based capitalist system overthrew feudalism, the prayer changed to, "Forgive us our debts."

As agricultural feudalism grew more efficient, requiring fewer serfs, peasants struck off to the cities, dreaming of making their fortunes there. Some cities were administrative centers, most were commercial, grown up from market towns. An economy based on money, not land, was beginning to emerge. By the fifteenth century, towns in Western Europe were more vital to society than the feudal kingdoms. In the cities and the rural areas, the ranks of propertyless workers who were dependent on daily wages swelled. Hardly better off were the many small farmers who tilled their plots of land as leaseholders, renters, and sharecroppers.

Yet whether the spark was the privatization of commonly-held forests or urban bread shortages, impoverished farmers and laborers rose up in righteous rebellions.

One night, as I stayed up late reading a popularly written book about "drag" history, I was startled to read a paragraph about an uprising of farmers in which the leaders cross-dressed. To my great frustration, there was no source cited for this information. However, that brief paragraph proved to be all I needed.

CHAPTER 10.

AT DUSK ON MAY 13, 1839,

a call of horns, drums, and gunfire could be heard across the western Welsh countryside. The turnpike gatekeeper, accustomed to insults from farmers who had to
pay tolls to use the roads, may have thought little of the sounds. But if the gatekeeper assumed it was simply revelers, he was wrong. Armed male peasants, dressed
as women, thundered up on horseback, waving pitchforks, axes, scythes, and guns.
As they stormed the gate their leader roared: "Hurrah for free laws! Toll gates free
to coal pits and lime kilns!" These demands were punctuated by a cacophony of
music, shouts, and shotgun blasts. The rebel troops smashed the toll barriers and
rode away victorious.

They called themselves "Rebecca and her daughters."[1]

During the next four years many Rebeccas, leading thousands of their cross-
dressed daughters from diverse parts of Wales, led local constables and British
troops on a merry chase as they destroyed the turnpike toll barriers that were bleed-
ing the poor even poorer. Farmers frequently could not afford to travel to get sup-
plies or sell at the markets because the labyrinth of roads was privately owned by
individuals who charged steep tolls at every interval. "Rebecca and her daughters"
received widespread popular support, which reflected the "growing solidarity,
resolve, and openness of the disaffected population."[2]

Imagine turning on the news channel and seeing male-to-female cross-dressers
leading an angry demonstration against the Ku Klux Klan. Or watching a movie in
which powerful and dignified striking male workers wore dresses and wigs and
called each other sister. That was not the image of cross-dressers I grew up seeing
portrayed in popular culture. At best, transgender has been treated as comedic. At
worst, this form of self-expression has been characterized as anti-social behavior.

That's why I think it's important for everyone, particularly trans people, to
know that cross-gendered warriors led important battles that helped shape history.
I say cross-gendered because these activists didn't just cross-*dress*, they also adopted
the names, identities, and familial relationships of another sex. The male-to-female
leaders went to the trouble to curl the coifed horsehair wigs on their heads. That's
cross-*gendered* behavior.

And many of these leaders didn't just cross-dress in their lifetime in order to lead a rebellion, but rather they were part of ongoing trans groups that organized festivals, which mocked authorities and sometimes erupted into uprisings. "In fact, the donning of female clothes by men and the adopting of female titles for riots were surprisingly frequent, in the early modern period," wrote historian Natalie Zemon Davis, who made a ground-breaking study of these rebellions.[3]

Throughout Europe in the later Middle Ages into the sixteenth century, masking and cross-dressing as another sex were still an integral part of urban carnivals with ancient roots.[4] These festivals were organized by male societies – begun in rural times as organizations of young, single men. In France and northern Italy, they were called the Abbeys of Misrule; in England and Scotland, the Lords of Misrule and the Abbots of Unreason. In French cities, the male leaders of these groups took titles using words like Princess, Dame, and especially Mother: Mère Folle and her Children in Dijon, Langres, and Chalon-sur-Saône, Mère Sotte and her Children in Paris and Compiègne, and Mère d'Enfance in Bordeaux.[5]

The Abbeys acted as courts, with mock jurisdiction over marriages. The courts punished transgressions among their own members, elders, and neighbors. The

LEFT: **A male-to-female trans expression by a carnival participant. This is a detail from the painting "Dulle Griet" (Mad Margot), by Pieter Breugel.** ABOVE: **Welsh guerrilla Rebecca leading her daughters into battle.**

Abbots issued coins, which were tossed to spectators lining the festival routes. Between carnival days, these organizations defended popular concepts of morality through noisy masked demonstrations known as *charivaris, scampanate, katzenmusik,* and *cencerrada.* In Wales this tradition was known as the *ceffyl pren.*[6]

Trans leaders were in the front ranks when the licensed days of festival "misrule" exploded into real rebellion. City fathers in Rouen in 1541 ordered their sergeants to pull an Abbot right off a festival float because the pointed anti-clerical political satire attacked them too sharply. At Dijon in 1576, Mère Folle and her children humiliated the King's Grand Master of Streams and Forests in Burgundy – both for beating his wife and for destroying for his own profits the forests he was supposed to protect. In Lyon in the 1580s, the Lord of Misprint and his followers took advantage of festival license to protest war, the high cost of bread, and empty market stalls. In 1630, Mère Folle and her Infanterie led an uprising against royal tax officers in Dijon. As a result, a furious royal edict abolished the Abbey.[7]

For the most part, historians report male-to-female trans leadership in these urban uprisings and earlier rural rebellions. But does that mean there were no cross-gendered female leaders? As a social science, history, like anthropology, is subject to all the prejudices of the society in which it is based, so historians' sexism may well have skewed their observations, resulting in under-documenting the role of female-to-male leadership.

Some historical accounts, however, do note rebellions led by cross-dressed women described as masculine. One account from England mentions an unruly crowd of cross-dressed women and men in 1531. Another report from England in 1629 noted: "'Captain' Alice Clark, a real female, headed a crowd of women and male weavers dressed as women in a grain riot near Maldon in Essex." In still another instance, "The tax revolt at Montpellier in 1645 was started by women and led down the streets by a virago [masculine woman] named La Branlaire, who shouted for death for the tax collectors that were taking the bread from their children's mouths."[8]

The depictions of

"Rebecca and Her Daugh-

ters" in the British news-

papers made these popular

insurrectionists look

grotesque. However, some

cartoons depict them

smashing unfair taxation

by the Church, anti-poor

laws and prisons, and

other hated institutions

of domination.

And whether or not masculine women were in the lead, women took to the streets. "Women turn up rebuking priests and pastors, being central actors in grain and bread riots in town and country, and participating in tax revolts and other rural disturbances." Davis notes that "In England in the early seventeenth century . . . a significant percentage of the rioters against enclosures and for common rights were female, while David Jones has found them an important element in enclosure riots in Wales into the nineteenth century."[9]

As demonstrated by the "Rebeccas," cross-gendered leadership of uprisings was not just an urban tradition. In 1631, bands of rebels in the dairy and grazing areas of Wiltshire, England, rioted against the king's enclosure of their forests, led by cross-dressed males who referred to themselves as Lady Skimmington. In 1829, the War of the Demoiselles in the Pyrénées erupted after passage of a harsh new forest code. The peasants dressed in long white shirt-dresses and wore women's hats, as they fought to defend their rights to wood and pasturage in the forests.[10]

Many historians dismiss the female attire the male peasants wore as simply a convenient disguise. It's frustrating to me that historical examples of cross-dressing are so casually dismissed. When women military leaders like Joan of Arc cross-dressed, some historians claim men's clothes were most suited for warfare. Then why would male peasants choose women's clothes for battle? And since when is a dress an effective disguise? Cross-dressing is a pattern in rebellions in far-flung countries. And most importantly, this tradition appears to have ancient roots.

For instance, references to fairies crop up in a number of accounts of peasant rebellions continents apart. The Catholic Church had waged systematic war against belief in fairies, which it linked to paganism – a holdover from matrilineal communal beliefs. And remember Joan of Arc had been accused by her Church judges of consorting with fairies.

Belief in fairies continued to be linked to struggles against large landowners. In England, for example, the "servants of the Queen of the Fairies" led Cade's Rebellion in 1450–51 in Kent and Essex. These peasants broke into the Duke of Buckingham's land and took his bucks and does.[11] Of the White Boys of Ireland, known by their feminine white overshirts, a 1762 Tipperary informant wrote "... above 500 men frequently assemble with shirts over their clothes doing whatever mischief they please by night, under the sanction of being fairies, as they call themselves.... The fairies are composed of all the able young fellows from Clonmel to Mitchelstown." These resisters announced that their goal was "to do justice to the poor.... if any farmer dismissed a servant or a shepherd no one dared to take his place unless 'he had more interest with the fairies.'"[12] In Beaujolais in the 1770s, French male peasants dressed as women attacked surveyors assessing their lands for a new landlord. "In the morning, when the police agents came, their wives knew nothing, and said they were 'fairies' who came from the mountains from time to time."[13]

The economic interests of the eighteenth-century British ruling classes were challenged at home and abroad by urban and rural workers, many of whom were cross-dressed. In England: "To cite but four examples, toll gates were demolished by bands of armed men dressed in women's clothing and wigs in Somerset in 1731 and 1749, in Gloucester in 1728 and in Herefordshire in 1735."[14]

Just as the European ruling class faced fierce resistance when it tried to impose cultural and physical genocide on Native nations of the Americas, the British elite ran into intense insurgency when it tried to impose its cultural values and colonial aims on its "empire." In 1736 in Edinburgh, Scotland, "the Porteous Riots, which were sparked by a hated English officer and oppressive custom laws and expressed resistance to the union of Scotland with England, were carried out by men disguised as women and with a leader known as Madge Wildfire."[15]

Some of the most extensive examples of trans leadership are documented in the rural and anti-colonial struggles in Ireland. From 1760 to 1770, the White Boys created peasant troops in Ireland for "restoring the ancient commons and redressing other grievances" and they "leveled great numbers of enclosures, sent many threatening letters, rescued property which had been seized by landlords for non-payment of rent, compelled cloth weavers to lower the price of their goods" and forced masters to release unwilling apprentices.[16] Although ultimately the White Boy movement was suppressed by sheer force of arms, their legacy inspired the rise of the nineteenth-century Molly Maguires and Ribbon Societies.[17]

Still other guerrilla bands formed in Ireland. "By the 1820s the 'Lady Rocks' were frequent; their robing was complete with bonnet and veil. In the early 1830s a whole new society calling themselves the 'Lady Clares' was to mushroom in Clare and adjoining counties; in this case the 'official' costume was women's clothing."[18] The Ribbonmen and the Molly Maguires were part of this militant peasant tradition. The Molly Maguires, who dispensed popular justice around 1843 in Ireland, "were generally stout active young men, dressed up in women's clothes," according to historian Trench.[19]

I was excited to find these detailed accounts of nineteenth-century guerilla warfare by cross-dressed farmers and agricultural workers in Ireland and Wales. Once I feared examining history, terrified that I might find that trans people have always been hated. Instead I've discovered that bigotry is a relatively recent historical development that had to be forced on human beings for several thousand years before it took hold. Buried in the history of the Middle Ages and right up to the dawn of the industrial revolution, the ancient respect for transgender had not been rooted out, even after centuries of illegality and violent punishment under slavery and feudalism.

And despite numerous local and royal edicts banning masking and mumming, festival days continued to be marked by women dressing and masking as men, and men as women. Trans expression emerged in culture throughout Europe in holiday celebrations, rituals, carnival days, masquerade parties, theater, literature, and opera. That's why cross-dressing is still part of holiday festivals today in the United States, like the Mummer's parades, Mardi Gras, and Halloween.

Halloween! Finally I'd found the answer to why I did not face arrest for "cross-dressing" that one day of the year. I could never have guessed as a young butch in the bars that I was safe from police arrest on October 31 because peasants held onto a transgender tradition throughout centuries of repression. It seemed incredible to me that centuries of draconian laws and sheer terror couldn't suppress these trans customs.

Yet although trans expression continued to exist among all classes in society, what a difference social privilege made! For the ruling elite, transgender expression could still be out in the open with far less threat of punishment than a peasant could expect. For example, when Queen Christina of Sweden abdicated in 1654, she donned men's clothes and renamed herself "Count Dohna."[20] Henry III of France was reported to have dressed as an Amazon and encouraged his courtiers to do likewise.[21] But for the most oppressed, trans expression was not only a part of their belief systems and their festivals, it was incorporated into their battles against the ruling classes.

And this tradition continued right up to the start of the industrial era. In the early nineteenth century, cross-dressed workers led some early labor struggles against the growth of capitalism. Even after many peasants were driven from the countryside into urban production, a number of accounts show that the tradition of transgender leadership of militant rebellion persisted. The peasants packed their traditions, along with their few belongings, and brought them to the cities. In the early 1830s, for example, striking miners in southern Wales terrified scabs who were stealing their jobs by paying midnight visits dressed in cattle skins or women's clothes.[22]

A significant chapter from labor history is the early Luddite Rebellions in which weavers, angered at how their bosses exploited them, smashed the looms they operated. One revolt occurred in Stockton, England, in 1812, where "General Ludd's wives" – two male workers dressed as women – led an angry crowd of hundreds to destroy the looms and burn down the factory. An account of the rebellion states:

> [O]n Sunday, April 14, crowds milled about the town, broke windows, and threatened vengeance on the owners of the steam looms. Led by two men disguised as women, who were hailed by their followers as 'General Ludd's wives,' they stoned the house of Joseph Goodair, an owner of steam looms, at Edgeley and later returned with reinforcements to fire his house and cut up the work in the looms before destroying the looms themselves. When, four days later, rioting was stopped by the military at Stockport, it broke out at Oldham.[23]

For laborers, the rise of the Industrial Revolution in Europe, signalled greater anonymity and its flip-side, alienation. When the capitalists were the underdog, fight-

ing feudalism and all its ideological baggage, they prided themselves on their enlightened and scientific view of the world and society. But once in power, they became afraid of the very laborers they had called into the streets to overthrow feudalism. So the capitalists increasingly made use of many of the old prejudices, particularly those that suited their own divide-and-rule policies.

I don't imagine that the peasants and workers who cross-dressed for battle thought about themselves in the same way as modern-day drag queens or transsexuals or heterosexual cross-dressers do. I grew up as a factory worker, so I can't compare my consciousness to that of a serf under feudalism, either.

But "Rebecca" was, and I am, part of huge, exploited laboring classes. This is an important connection between a cross-dressed peasant and me. Transgender has been outlawed by the ruling classes of both our systems – feudal nobility and modern industrialists alike. The Stonewall Rebellion in Greenwich Village led by Black and Latina drag queens and the insurgency of Rebecca and her daughters in Wales are both uprisings against oppression, led by cross-dressed individuals.

These examples of transgendered leadership have great meaning for me. I grew up unable to find myself anywhere in history. Now I have examples of transgender in the leadership of social change. Here were peasants who cheered their cross-gendered leaders. Here were moments in history when transgender was a call to arms, when cross-dressed people fought for justice in the front ranks.

This is part of our history as trans people. And every single child today – no matter how their sex or gender is developing – needs to know about these militant battles and the names of those who led them: Joan of Arc, Rebecca, Mère Folle, Captain Alice Clark, Madge Wildfire, Molly Maguire, General Ludd's wives.

If I had known about these heroic struggles, I might have imagined as a child that cross-dressed workers could lead their trade union sisters and brothers on picket lines or that trans housing activists could inspire tenants to keep the rent strike strong. I might have pictured myself in those ranks!

Luisa Capetillo, a cross-dressed Puerto Rican socialist, trade union leader, author, and feminist, circa 1914, in Havana, Cuba. She never married, and had three children. Capetillo was arrested in Cuba on cross-dressing charges. On her island home, she is remembered in a popular song that says: "Doña Luisa Capetillo, intentionally or not, has created a tremendous uproar because of her culottes."

11.

CHAPTER

SOME OF THE MALES

who regularly cross-dressed during festivals, and were part of transgender festival organizations, may have been much like heterosexual *bigendered* males today who can only cross-dress in the safety of their own homes, support groups, or during certain holidays. But how did people who were *transgendered* survive?

I'm not the first person to live as another sex. Throughout the seventeenth and eighteenth centuries there were many accounts of people criminally charged with living as another sex. Passing from female-to-male was so widespread throughout Europe during those centuries, particularly in Holland, England, and Germany, that it was the theme of novels, fictionalized biographies and memoirs, plays, operas, and popular songs.

But those who passed became gender outlaws. Courtroom and police records cite punishments carried out against transgendered people – from flogging to death. As a result, we'll never know the depth and breadth of the passing population, because it was an underground phenomenon.

Most accounts passed down to us today are of those who were caught and exposed. The reasons that these individuals offered for their life decisions were made under duress in front of police and magistrates. I can glean little from their words, except how frightened they must have been. Today, although the authentic stories of their lives have been lost to us, many people speculate about those individuals, and why they chose to pass. My life is subject to the same conjecture.

"No wonder you've passed as a man! This is such an anti-woman society," a lesbian friend told me. To her, females passing as males are simply trying to escape women's oppression – period. She believes that once true equality is achieved in society, humankind will be genderless. I don't have a crystal ball, so I can't predict human behavior in a distant future. But I know what she's thinking – if we can build a more just society, people like me will cease to exist. She assumes that I am simply a product of oppression. Gee, thanks so much.

I've heard this same argument applied to the life and death of jazz musician Billy Tipton, who in 1989 painfully bled to death from an ulcer rather than go to a doctor. The coroner lost no time in announcing to the world that Billy Tipton had been born female. Since Billy Tipton left no personal records, all we really know is that he lived his life as a man. That was his almost lifelong identity, and it should be respected.

But a great debate has raged about why Tipton chose to live as a man. One group argued that he and others passed solely because of women's oppression – specifically economic inequality – at a time when women couldn't easily become successful jazz musicians in this country. Another group argues that Billy Tipton passed in order to escape lesbian oppression. Do either of these arguments fully explain the lives of thousands of females who have lived as men?

First, let's talk about who *can* pass as another sex. My same friend reminds me periodically that she too might have passed as a man a century ago to escape women's oppression. She stares right past my gender expression as she speaks. I study her as she's talking: she is about 5'3", has narrow shoulders and broad hips, tiny hands and feet, and delicate features, and her gender expression is definitely *not* masculine. How could she pass?

I don't want to burst her bubble. Everyone deserves untrammeled dreams. But I want to tell her that perhaps I could believe that, in the dead of winter, if she was bundled up against the cold, with a hood or hat covering her head, some man

TOP: Charley Wilson, born Catherine Coombes in 1834 in England, lived as a man for over forty years. After being imprisoned in the poorhouse at age sixty-three, the authorities forced him to wear a blue print dress and red shawl. "If I had money," Charley reportedly told a visitor, "I would get out of here in men's clothes and no one would detect me."

MIDDLE: Hannah Snell reportedly dressed as a man in order to search for her/his missing husband. But after not finding him, Snell became a sailor. After being exposed as female, Snell wrote a biography, appeared on stage as "Bill Bobstay the Sailor," and later opened a pub in London's dock district.

BOTTOM: Jack Bee Garland, also known as "Babe Bean," was born Elvira Mugarietta in 1869. His father was San Francisco's first Mexican consul. Garland—who lived as a man for forty years—was a popular writer and journalist. Two days before he collapsed and died, Garland came home exhausted because he had given his last dollar—his only car fare—to a frightened, runaway boy. After his death, the <u>San Francisco Chronicle</u> ran a front page story announcing that Garland was born female.

A female-to-male trans person with husband. Are they a heterosexual couple? Two gay men?

in a deli *might* call her "sir." But could she pass as male on board ship, sleeping with and sharing common facilities with her fellow sailors for decades and not be discovered?

Of course, hundreds of thousands of women have dreamed of escaping the economic and social inequities of their lives, but how many could live as a man for a decade or a lifetime? While a woman could throw on men's clothing and pass as a man for safety on dark roadways, could she pass as a man at an inn where men slept together in the same beds? Could she maintain her identity in daylight? Pass the scrutiny of co-workers? Would she really feel safer and more free?

How could females have lived and been accepted as men without hormones or surgery? They must have been masculine; they must have been trans*gendered.* If they were not, how could they pass? We don't know how each of the thousands who passed from female to male over the centuries would define themselves today – whether as transgender or transsexual or drag or any other modern definition. The point is that their gender expression allowed them to transition.

I just don't believe that the debate about why "women pass as men" can be understood only in the light of women's, or of lesbian and gay, oppression. It has to be viewed in the context of trans history in order to make sense.

I'm no stranger to women's oppression. I know that it operates like destructive machinery that grinds up even those who are born female but grow up identifying as another sex. But if passing from female to male is just an attempt to escape economic inequality, then why do we find transgendered individuals – both female-to-male and male-to-female – among the ruling elite and the privileged leisure classes? What about King

TOP: Violette Morris lived openly as a cross-dresser. In the 1920s, Morris sued the French Federation of Feminine Sports for 100,000 francs for withdrawing her license to wear trousers. ABOVE RIGHT: The writing on the back of this photograph of such a strong, proud trans person reads: Florence Alice Compson Brown. Born Sept. 26, 1897. Died Oct. 20, 1918. One son, Thomas Compson Brown.

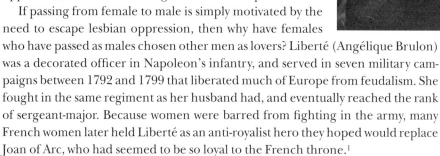

Ashurbanipal of Assyria or Queen Christina of Sweden? And what about the artists' circles in Paris of transgendered authors and painters from wealthy families like John (Radcliffe) Hall and Gertrude Stein?

Look at George Sand, the nineteenth-century novelist. It's true that she could not have published without a male *nom de plume* at that time. But if that's all there was to her identity, why did she wear men's clothing? Why was she attacked for masculine behavior? And if it was just a question of lesbian oppression, what was she doing in bed with Chopin?

If passing from female to male is simply motivated by the need to escape lesbian oppression, then why have females who have passed as males chosen other men as lovers? Liberté (Angélique Brulon) was a decorated officer in Napoleon's infantry, and served in seven military campaigns between 1792 and 1799 that liberated much of Europe from feudalism. She fought in the same regiment as her husband had, and eventually reached the rank of sergeant-major. Because women were barred from fighting in the army, many French women later held Liberté as an anti-royalist hero they hoped would replace Joan of Arc, who had seemed to be so loyal to the French throne.[1]

And many females knew when they made their life decision to live as men that they might never be able to risk the danger of revealing their secret by taking any lover.

Finally, if so many females have passed as men only to escape women's oppression, then why have so many males passed as women? While it is biologically easier for a female to pass as a young boy than for a male to pass as a woman, there are many, many examples in the modern era of those who passed from male to female.

Mlle. Jenny Savalette de Lange, for example, was only discovered to have been born male after her death in 1858. She had managed to get hold of a birth certificate that designated her female, was reportedly engaged to men six times, and had been given a pension and a free apartment by the king of France. Newspaper and magazine accounts include many other cases of women who were discovered to have been born male, including a woman who had been married for more than six years before she was exposed in 1937, Josephine Montgomery who was in a San Quentin women's prison in 1950 when authorities made the discovery, and Mrs. Adele Best who had lived as a woman for fifty-four years and had been married to men three times.[2]

At the close of the seventeenth century, the punishment for cross-dressing in England was to be dragged in an open cart through streets filled with a hostile mob to be publicly hanged.[3] Yet even in the face of such terrifying penalties, transgender males, known then as "mollies," continued to gather in underground societies. Between 1707 and 1730, when Societies for the Reformation of Manners launched attacks against "effeminate sodomites among the London poor," more than twenty "molly houses" were raided in London, and a number of those patrons were hanged or pilloried as a result.[4] But, in a striking parallel to the Stonewall Rebellion over three hundred years later, when a Covent Garden molly house was raided in 1725, the crowd, "many of them in drag, met the raid with determined and violent resistance."[5]

TOP: Chevalier D'Eon, born Charles D'Eon in France in 1728, was a famous male-to-female trans person whose birth sex was a hotly debated question in eighteenth-century France. ABOVE: Charles Edward Stuart, dubbed "Bonnie Prince Charlie," in women's clothing. BOTTOM L & R: "Mollies," or male-to-female trans people, were officially hanged in the early 1700s after raids on the "molly houses" where they gathered in large numbers. Others were said to have committed suicide after their arrests, knowing that was to be their fate. But in at least one raid on a molly house – more than 300 years before the Stonewall Rebellion – trans people fought back!

In the 1770s, German historian Johann Wilhelm von Archeholz described a London pub called the Bunch of Grapes: "On entering the room the guard found two fellows in women's attire, with muffs and wide shawls and most fashionable turban-like bonnets ... it turned out that each member of the club had a woman's name...."[6]

Transgender gatherings were seemingly widespread throughout seventeenth- and eighteenth-century Europe. Drag balls were reported in seventeenth-century Lisbon. In early eighteenth-century France, there were societies of male cross-dressers who wore ribbons and powder and called each other by women's names. And in the eighteenth-century Dutch Republic, some transgender males referred to each other by female nicknames.[7]

An 1813 account of a police raid in Victorian England described the patrons of a pub: "Many of the habitués took on female appellations as well as female dress..." Police who raided one of their meetings were reportedly so fooled by at least one of the patrons that they didn't arrest the person.[8] At a trans ball in Paris in 1864, "there were at least 150 men, and some of them so well disguised that the landlord of the house was unable to detect their sex."[9]

A famous case of transgender persecution in nineteenth-century England was the arrest of male-to-female theater performers Stella (Ernest) Boulton and Fanny (Frederick) Park outside the Strand Theater on April 28, 1890. They were tried on charges of "conspiracy to commit a felony." Boulton's mother testified in defense of Stella and explained that her child had dressed as a girl since age six. Stella and Fanny were both acquitted.[10]

The lives of people who have transitioned from female to male can't be understood without taking into account those who have passed as male to female. In order to understand the lives of people who have passed as another sex in any direction, it must be remembered that trans people have always existed, but were once viewed with respect as vital, contributing members of our societies.

We have not always been forced to pass, to go underground, in order to work and live. We have a right to live openly and proudly. When we are denied those rights, we are the ones who suffer that oppression. But when our lives are suppressed, *everyone* is denied an understanding of the rich diversity of sex and gender expression and experience that exist in human society.

I have lived as a man because I could not survive openly as a transgendered person. Yes, I am oppressed in this society, but I am not merely a *product* of oppression. That is a phrase that renders all our trans identities meaningless. Passing means having to hide your identity in fear, in order to live. Being forced to pass is a recent historical development.

It is *passing* that is a product of oppression.

BELOW: Actors Stella Boulton (born Ernest) and Fanny Park (born Frederick) being arrested in 1870 as a result of having worn women's clothing in public. After Boulton's mother testified that her child had cross-dressed since age six, both Stella and Fanny were acquitted. But the charges against Boulton and Park were a harbinger of the witch hunt against feminine men – assumed to be gay – that led to the trial of Oscar Wilde.

By the nineteenth century, drag – male and female – took centerstage in English-speaking theater, yet most European cities in the nineteenth century enforced laws against public cross-dressing. Female-to-male cross-dressers were regularly arrested in Berlin and St. Petersburg.

The philosophers have only interpreted *the world in various ways; the point, however, is to* change *it.*

KARL MARX, 1845

Part Four

WHEN I WAS A TEENAGER, during moments when I was under siege, I wondered if anyone would ever fight alongside me as if my battle were their own. What would motivate someone who didn't face the same hatred and abuse to join me as an ally?

I owe an enormous debt to Frederick Douglass – the great orator, writer, and abolitionist – for helping me answer that question. As a young adult, I was gripped by the power of Douglass's thinking and his use of language. As I read I came across this set of questions he had posed: "Why am I a slave? Why are some people slaves, and others masters? Was there ever a time when this was not so? How did the relations commence?"[1]

I shivered with recognition. It wasn't that the racism, brutality, and bondage this former slave had endured mirrored my own experiences. Yet his oppression made him burn with questions that sounded so similar to mine. What connects us, Douglass was explaining to me, is that we're up against a common enemy.

As I read further, I discovered that Frederick Douglass had steadfastly defended the right of women to vote. Douglass was one of thirty-one men who attended the first Women's Rights convention at Seneca Falls, New York. All the men, including Douglass, risked being labeled "Hermaphrodites" and "Aunt Nancy Men" by enemies of women's suffrage.[2]

Douglass was the only man to address that convention. He declared that women's suffrage was a right, and "Our doctrine is that 'right is of no sex.'"[3] Those wise words could apply to the trans communities today.

But we as trans people can't liberate ourselves alone. No oppressed peoples can. So how and why will others come to our defense? And whom shall we, as trans people, fight to defend? A few years before he died, Douglass told the International Council of Women, "When I ran away from slavery, it was for myself; when I advocated emancipation, it was for my people; but when I stood up for the rights of women, self was out of the question, and I found a little nobility in the act."[4]

I believe this is the only nobility to which we should aspire – that is, to be the best fighters against each other's oppression, and in doing so, build links of solidarity

and trust that will forge an invincible movement against all forms of injustice and inequality.

If you are not transsexual, transgender, or intersexual, if you're not a cross-dresser, bigender, or drag queen or king, then perhaps you already understand that defending our right to be who we are is inextricably tied to your own right to explore and define who you are. Each individual has a stake in trans liberation.

But what relationship does trans liberation have to already existing movements for change? For example, what is the basis for the coalitions that have already been cemented between lesbian, gay, bisexual, and trans people in many parts of the United States? What does trans liberation mean for the women's movement? And ultimately, what kind of larger movement will it take to win lasting social and economic justice?

As to the question of what connects lesbian, gay, bi, and trans people, I think the answer can only be found by examining the relationship between body, desire, and gender expression. Since I was a teenager I have pondered the connection between my sexuality and my gender expression. Every aspect of my spirit and style as I walk down the street, straighten my tie, or touch a child's hair is a demonstration of my individual gender expression in motion; the white-capped river of my desire for the woman I am married to is my sexuality. Since these are tightly braided aspects of my identity, I fight for my right to be whole.

However, perhaps the biggest societal misunderstanding about the trans population continues to be the assumption that all transgender or transsexual people are gay. That's not true. The majority of lesbian women, gay men, and bisexuals are not transgendered or transsexual, and the majority of trans people are not lesbian, gay, or bisexual. Nor can the sexuality of some trans people be easily categorized.

Although it's important to mark the broad boundaries of "lesbian, gay, and bi" in order to fight the oppression and build community, what happens to the borders of these categories for the trans community when the dunes of sex and gender shift? When a masculine female-to-male cross-dresser is married to a bisexual drag queen, is this a heterosexual relationship? The trans population is a reminder that not everyone who is heterosexual is straight!

Some people refer to my love relationship as lesbian, because they consider the fact that my wife and I are female to be a biological determinant of our sexuality. Others, who label me as "looking like a man," assume we live in a safe heterosexual space. Neither exactly corresponds to my life.

People stare at me wherever I go. Some who gawk at me shift between seeing me as a very feminine man and an extremely masculine woman. I unnerve them because they can't determine my sex. So are my love and I lesbian women, mother and son, lesbian woman with gay male friend, or some other combination? Our relationship is Teflon to which no classification of sexuality sticks.

But to those fueled by hatred of diversity, anyone who cross-dresses or changes their sex is "queer." As a result of the fact that masculine women and feminine men are assumed by bigots to be lesbian and gay, the oppressions have overlapped. And this has been true for many centuries.

TOP LEFT: Queen Allyson Ann Allante with King Farrell Armstrong. Allyson was fourteen the night she fought the police at the Stonewall rebellion, during which she was injured and arrested. Today she is president of the Imperial QUEENS & KINGS of New York City, Long Island, and New Jersey. When asked if the Stonewall Rebellion was a lesbian and gay rebellion or a trans rebellion, she replied, "It was both, because it was the first time that both came together to fight off the oppressor and it set a good precedent to do it many times since. It was a big milestone for both communities because they were both in unity to fight the common oppressor, which at that time was the police and the mafia, who controlled many of the gay clubs— whether for males or females."

THIS PAGE: On October 5, 1982, some thirty uniformed police entered a predominantly African-American drag bar called "Blues," which used to operate across the street from the New York Times building. The cops reportedly locked the doors and beat people senseless with clubs and pistol butts while shouting epithets. All of the patrons were reportedly injured, many seriously. On October 15, more than one thousand people of many nationalities, sexes, genders, and sexualities took to the streets of Times Square to protest.

For example, today's bible-thumpers condemn gay and lesbian love by quoting 1 Corinthians 6:9, which lumps together homosexuality with all forms of "immorality." But from the Geneva Bible (1560) to the American Standard Bible (1901), the word used was "effeminate." Even the Phillips Translation as late as 1958 still uses the word "effeminate." The Revised Standard Bible in 1946 was the first text to revise "effeminate" to "sexual perverts," which later became "homosexual perversion" in the New English Bible in 1961.[5]

And brutal laws that decreed death for the crime of male femininity – like the Code of Theodosius in 390 C.E. – have been recorded by historians as anti-gay laws. But those laws were also murderously anti-trans. Theodosius the Great condemned "All of those who are accustomed to condemn their own manly body, transformed into a womanly one, to undergo sexual practices reserved for the other sex, and who have nothing different from women, will pay for this crime among the avenging flames, in front of the people."[6] *Feminine* homosexuals were targeted under these

TOP: Assotto Saint (Yves Lubin) – a Black, gay, trans author whose death, as a result of AIDS, is grieved by many. Assotto was born in Haiti in 1957 and died in New York City in 1994.

MIDDLE: From left to right: Terry White, Cross Dressers International; Coco LaChine, Celestial Dragon Empress, Imperial Court of New York; Monica Pedone, president of the Greater New York Gender Alliance; and Lynn Walker, vice-president of the Greater New York Gender Alliance.

BOTTOM: Bearded Puerto Rican lesbian and trans activist Laurie Auffault holds a poster of John (Radcliffe) Hall – the lesbian trans author of The Well of Loneliness – in the Lesbian Herstory Archives contingent at a Pride March in Manhattan in 1993.

RIGHT: Rollerarena, who says she was born a coal miner's daughter in the hills of Kentucky, is famous for skating around the mean streets of Manhattan in this persona. She is a staunch anti-racist activist whose consciousness was shaped by the Civil Rights movement.

broad gender laws, while some masculine homosexuals were considered exempt.

Even as recently as the last century, feminine cross-dressing males caught up in sweeping arrests have been assumed by prosecutors to be gay. In the nineteenth century, most European cities enforced civil statutes against public cross-dressing, and female-to-male cross-dressers were regularly arrested in Berlin and St. Petersburg.[7] While drag performance – male and female – took center stage in nineteenth-century English speaking theater, well-known drag actors who wore women's clothing in public faced arrest. Transgendered performers Boulton and Park were arrested on felony charges for just that reason, and their trial was a harbinger of the witch hunt against male femininity that later led to the trial of Oscar Wilde in 1895.[8]

So were these trials focused on the sexuality of those arrested, or their gender expression? The two "crimes" were entwined in prosecutors' minds. Yet of fourteen drag actors studied by a German physician at the turn of the century – eight of whom wore women's clothes at home – only six were gay.[9]

But there are lesbian and gay trans people – transsexual, transgender, and drag – and we have played a leadership role in the birth of two major movements for lesbian and gay liberation in the last century.

Many of us have come to think of the 1969 Stonewall Rebellion as the birth of the lesbian and gay liberation movement. But in fact, the first historic wave of gay liberation, from 1869 to 1935, began in Germany. It was a dynamic and widening movement that grew to be international in scope, and left its mark on other social and political movements, as well as on literature and the arts.

In this movement, which rose on the ground swell of a struggle by German workers to win the most basic democratic rights, transgender activists were in the lead. In 1897, the first gay liberation organization was born in Germany – the Scientific Humanitarian Committee. Its founder and notable leader throughout much of the organization's thirty-five years was Dr. Magnus Hirschfeld – who was gay, Jewish, socialist, and reportedly a cross-dresser.[10] Hirschfeld coined the word *transvestite* in 1910 and wrote the germinal works on the subject.[11] One of Hirschfeld's contributions was his conclusion, based on his research, that sex and gender expression were not automatically linked, meaning that not all lesbian women and gay men are transgendered and not all transgendered people are lesbian or gay.

The Committee published a yearbook that reported on movement activities, as well as on literary, historical, anthropological, and scientific studies on same-sex love, and transgender. The stated goals of the Committee were to win the abolition of the anti-gay German law Paragraph 175, to enlighten public opinion, and to encourage sexually oppressed people to fight for their rights. In order to carry out its objectives, the Committee held regular public forums, organized speaking tours nationally and internationally, and sent literature to other governments about the need for the decriminalization of same-sex love.[12]

One of the debates that took place in the context of this movement is still being hotly argued: Are we born with our sexuality already coded for life, do we develop sexuality as we mature and interact with the world, or is there an as yet undetermined connection between the two? Karl Heinrich Ulrichs – the grandfather of gay liberation – and Hirschfeld were part of this debate. They believed that homosexuals were members of a third sex. For example, a gay man was thought to be a female mind in a male body. As a result, some German lesbians and gays fought against their persecution on the basis that they could not change their sexual orientation because it was inborn. Others argued that this was a weak, defensive argument, and that human rights should be fought for on the basis of justice, not pathology.[13]

But there was a big difference between the internal debate over nature versus nurture within the movement, and the rise of the Nazi eugenics movement that used the argument of "birth defects" to carry out mass genocide. The German lesbian and gay movement won significant support from the working class and the socialist movements, but the rise of fascism smashed all the workers' organizations. The Nazis also crushed the German Homosexual Emancipation Movement – which was largely middle-class in character. As a result, much of the valuable history that had been gathered has been lost to us forever. Hirschfeld was forced to flee the country and, while in exile, watched a film of his Institute being burned to the ground. More than ten thousand volumes from the Institute's special library were destroyed in those flames.[14]

The Homosexual Emancipation Movement, which had begun to spread to other countries, is an important example of one of the historic moments when lesbian, gay, and transgendered struggles have been entwined.

> "Like I've always said, 'You're born naked and the rest is drag.'
>
> "But when I give out my job description, people always attach 'Sex Fetish' to my career choice. No one ever thinks twice about the priest in his robe or the Supreme Court justice in his gown. And if you ever went up to a motorcycle cop and asked if he was into leather and domination, you would probably be arrested.
>
> " ...it's easy for people to label and categorize other people; in this way they make them small, trite, and ultimately inhuman.
>
> "But I will not be ignored. I am here to stay.
>
> "And I am here to say that we are all gods and goddesses, each and every one of us."
>
> *From* Lettin It All Hang Out: An Autobiography by RuPaul. *Hyperion: New York, 1995.*

I was lucky enough to be part of the second wave of lesbian and gay liberation in the 1960s and 1970s. When I came out as a young butch, I found those pre-Stonewall bars filled on weekends with other transgender outlaws. On weekdays, in the factories, butches like myself were referred to as "he-shes" much as our drag queen sisters were labeled "she-males." Some bigots referred to me as "it," which was meant to strip me of my humanity. The hyphenated pronouns illuminated a limitation of pronouns in the English language. "She" and "he" are customarily used to describe *both* the birth sex *and* the gender expression of an individual. But "he-she" and "she-male" describe the person's gender expression with the first pronoun and the birth sex with the second. The hyphenation signals a crisis of language and an apparent social contradiction, since sex and gender expression are "supposed" to match. That was our crime: our gender expression didn't match the one we were socially assigned at birth. That's what made us gender outlaws.

Some people used to say we "looked gay," but unless we were holding hands with our lovers or walking out of a gay bar, it was not our sexual desire that made us visible – it was our gender expression. As drag kings and drag queens, we were the visible tip of a huge iceberg. We were gay gender-benders. (Language is an imprecise tool. You can only be considered gender-bent in a society that is gender-rigid.) Since no one had ever seen the diversity of the lesbian, gay, and bi populations, most people assumed that being gay meant being transgendered. We thought so, too.

Our daily life was so hard for us that we couldn't help but struggle. That's why we were on the front lines of battles that helped birth the early gay liberation movement. And that's why it was no accident that gender outlaws led the Stonewall Rebellion. That historic uprising against police violence began shortly after 1 A.M. on June 28, 1969, when the cops raided the Stonewall, a gay bar in New York's Greenwich Village.[15]

The patrons of the bar, particularly the African-American and Latina drag queens, kings, and transsexuals, were expected to endure humiliation, slurs, and brutality in silence. But on that muggy summer night, gay trans anger exploded. The patrons of the bar, and the crowd that gathered, fought back against the police so valiantly that the cops were forced to retreat. The uprising continued for four nights running, and has come to be known as the Stonewall Rebellion.

In the years that followed, lesbian and gay liberation was born. As thousands of lesbians and gay men took to the streets in cities all over the country, our diversity was visible – race, nationality, class, abilities, region, and many other differences.

The spectrum of gender expression within this huge population also became apparent. The erroneous belief that being lesbian or gay meant you were automatically transgendered was visibly challenged.

Today, a quarter century after the Stonewall Rebellion rocked the world, a new rising movement is demanding trans liberation. The coalescing of this young movement, organizing and fighting back against sex and gender oppression, is enabling the world to see the diversity in trans communities. We are now able to challenge the assumption that transgender is an expression of sexuality, because for the first time in history the wide range of sexuality in the trans community is clear: we are heterosexual, bisexual, lesbian, gay, and asexual.

So I view the trans population as a broad circle and the lesbian, gay, and bisexual communities as another large circle. These two circles partially overlap. I am one of the people who has a foot in each of these communities, and, like a person with a foot in one of each of two rowboats, I have a deep personal hope that they don't move in opposite directions.

I hope those of us who do overlap can serve as bridges, because I think our communities are natural allies and all our strengths are magnified by solidarity. However, there are obstacles placed in our path to keep us from uniting.

The lesbian, gay, and bi communities in the United States have been subject to a steady stream of gender-baiting attacks. For instance, during the campaign in New York City for a lesbian and gay civil rights law (this was before bi inclusion), our movement was baited by newspaper editorials which asked: "What do these people want, men in high heels to be firefighters?" The only correct answer is: "Any cross-dresser would know to wear sensible shoes on a job like that! This is gender-phobia and job discrimination as well. We won't stand for it!" That's how to defeat gender-baiting.

A timid denial that "We're not all like that" only serves to weaken the entire fight-back movement. We can never throw enough people overboard to win approval from our enemies. Should we try to argue that we're as "normal" as those who organize against our civil rights? Forget it! I am *queer* and proud of it.

As a longtime butch lesbian activist, I urge my lesbian, gay, and bi sisters and brothers to take the initiative to form a lasting coalition to struggle against trans oppression. And as a transgendered fighter, I call on transsexuals, transgender, bigender, and intersexual activists to fight the oppression faced by lesbians, gay men, and bisexuals. Like trans-phobia and gender-baiting, homophobia has been used in an attempt to drive a dangerous wedge between potential allies.

I understand that many heterosexual transsexual and transgender people have been justly angered by a lifetime of accusations that their sex-change or gender expression is merely a result of being ashamed to admit they are gay. No one wants the identity they are willing to live for – or to die for – to be invalidated or misunderstood. But while not all lesbian, gay, and bi people face trans oppression, all trans people experience anti-gay bigotry. To the bigots and bashers, all trans expression is "queer." Distancing ourselves from the lesbian, gay, and bi movement will not make us safer. But fighting lesbian and gay oppression head-on will.

While the lesbian, gay, and bi and trans populations do not experience identical oppressions, or voice the same grievances and demands, in the current-day United

Part of the national trans contingent in the Stonewall 25 march. The drag queens were placed first in the march – which was the right thing to do, but the trans contingent was much further back. The sign this person holds makes clear that it was only the placement in the line of march that separated our communities.

States, our communities have been strengthened by forming coalitions on campuses, in workplaces, and in political protests.

At the same time, the trans communities – made up of a majority of heterosexuals with decades of their own organizational history – are also an independent, autonomous movement. Like lesbians who are also active in both the L/G/B/T coalition and the women's movement, or like lesbians and gays of color who are also vital leaders in their national liberation movements – many lesbian, gay, and bi trans people play an integral role in an autonomous trans movement as well.

Those who are truly committed to building coalitions know that listening and demonstrating sensitivity to each others' oppressions and demands will create greater mutual understanding and unity. While there are centuries-old misconceptions about trans people, the most powerful way for peoples who face different oppressions to understand each other is by fighting back shoulder to shoulder.

Frederick Douglass, and the diverse combatants at Stonewall, helped me realize that people who don't experience a common oppression *can* make history when they unite to fight a common enemy.

CHAPTER 13.

female, right?" The reporter asked me for the third time. I nodded patiently. "So do you identify as female now, or male?"

She rolled her eyes as I repeated my answer. "I am transgendered. I was born female, but my masculine gender expression is seen as male. It's not my sex that defines me, and it's not my gender expression. It's the fact that my gender expression appears to be at odds with my sex. Do you understand? It's the social contradiction between the two that defines me."

The reporter's eyes glazed over as I spoke. When I finished she said, "So you're a *third* sex?" Clearly, I realized, we had very little language with which to understand each other.

When I try to discuss sex and gender, people can only imagine woman or man, feminine or masculine. We've been taught that nothing else exists in nature. Yet, as I've shown, this has not been true in all cultures or in all historical periods. In fact, Western law took centuries to neatly partition the sexes into only two categories and mandate two corresponding gender expressions.

"The paradigm that there are two genders founded on two biological sexes began to predominate in western culture only in the early eighteenth century," historian Randolph Trumbach notes in his essay, "London's Sapphists: From Three Sexes to Four Genders in the Making of Modern Culture."[1] Trumbach explains that as late as the eighteenth century, in northwestern Europe, feminine men and masculine women – known as mollies and tommies respectively – were thought of as third and fourth genders.

But how many sexes and genders *do* exist? All too frequently, this question is presented as an abstract one, like how many angels can dance on the head of a pin? But the search for the answer to this question has to be understood within the context of oppression.

Those of us who cross the "man-made" boundaries of sex and gender run afoul of the law, are subject to extreme harassment and brutality, and are denied employment, housing, and medical care. We have grown up mostly unable to find ourselves represented in the dominant culture.

So how can we have a discussion of how much sex and gender diversity actually exists in society, when all the mechanisms of legal and extralegal repression render our lives invisible? Gender theorists can't just function as census takers who count how much sex and gender diversity exists; they must be part of the struggle to defend our right to exist, or most of us will be forced to remain underground.

The more inclusive the trans liberation movement becomes, and the more visible our movement is in society, the more clearly sex and gender variation will be seen. However, as the trans movement grows and develops, part of its impact has been to pose questions: What is the relationship between birth sex, gender expression, and desire? Does the body you are born with determine your sex for life? How many variations of sex and gender exist today?

The gradations of sex and gender self-definition are limitless. When I first opened an America Online account, I tried to establish the *nom de net* "stone butch" or "drag king." I discovered these names were already taken. As I later prowled through AOL and UNIX bulletin boards, I found a world of infinite sex and gender identities, which cyberspace has given people the freedom to explore with a degree of anonymity.

But although this fluidity and variation exists, there still aren't many more words to express sex and gender than there were when I was growing up. All of the complexity of my gender expression is reduced to looking "like a man." Since I'm not a man, what does it mean when people tell me I look like one? When I was growing up, other kids told me I pitched baseballs and shot marbles "like a boy." As a young adult, I suffered a torrent of criticism from adults who admonished me for standing, walking, and sitting "like a boy." Strangers felt free to stop me on the street to confront me with this observation. Something about me was inappropriate, but what?

The "gender theory" I learned in school, at home, in books, and at the movies was very simple. There are men and women. Men are masculine and women are feminine. End of subject. But clearly the subject didn't end there for me.

I had no words to discuss this with anyone. The way I expressed myself was wrong. There was no language to dispute this because the right way was assumed to be natural. Thank goodness, by the time I was sixteen years old the women's liberation movement was beginning to vocally denounce the outrageously separate and unequal indoctrination of girls and boys. For the first time, I was able to separate my birth sex from the gender education I received as a girl. Since sex and gender had always been seen as synonymous when I was growing up, disconnecting the two was a very important advance in my own thinking.

In addition, one of the gifts the women's movement gave me was a closer look at the values that have been attached to masculinity and femininity. In my social education, masculinity had been inaccurately contrasted as stronger, more analytical, more stable, and more rational than femininity.

But it was not until the rise of the movement for transgender liberation that I began to see the important distinction between the negative gender *values* attached to being masculine or feminine and my right to my own gender *expression*. I am subjugated by the values attached to gender expression. But I am not oppressing other people by the way I express my gender when I wear a tie. Nor are other people's clothing or makeup crushing my freedom.

Both women's and trans liberation have presented me with two important tasks. One is to join the fight to strip away the discriminatory and oppressive values attached to masculinity and femininity. The other is to defend gender freedom – the right of each individual to express their gender in any way they choose, whether feminine, androgynous, masculine, or any point on the spectrum between. And that includes the right to gender ambiguity and gender contradiction.

It's equally important that each person have the right to define, determine, or change their sex in any way they choose – whether female, male, or any point on the spectrum between. And that includes the right to physical ambiguity and contradiction.

This struggle affects millions of people, because, as it turns out, sex and gender are a lot more complicated than woman and man, pink and blue. As the brochure of the Intersex Society of North America explains: "Our culture conceives sex anatomy as a dichotomy: humans come in two sexes, conceived of as so different as to be nearly different species. However, developmental embryology, as well as the existence of intersexuals, proves this to be a cultural construction. Anatomic sex differentiation occurs on a male/female continuum, and there are several dimensions."[2] (*See Appendix B.*)

In an article entitled, "The Five Sexes: Why Male and Female Are Not Enough," geneticist Dr. Anne Fausto-Sterling stresses that "Western culture is deeply committed to the idea that there are only two sexes." But, she adds, "If the state and the legal system have an interest in maintaining a two-party sexual system, they are in defiance of nature. For biologically speaking, there are many gradations running from female to male; and depending on how one calls the shots, one can argue that along that spectrum lie at least five sexes – and perhaps even more."[3]

The right to physical ambiguity and contradiction are surgically and hormonally denied to newborn intersexual infants who fall between the "poles" of female and male. If doctors refrained from immediately "fixing" infants who don't fit the clear-cut categories of male and female, we would be spared the most commonly asked question: "What a beautiful baby! Is it a boy or a girl?"

And imagine what a difference it would make if parents replied, "We don't know, our child hasn't told us yet."

Why are infants being shoehorned into male or female? As Fausto-Sterling points out, "For questions of inheritance, legitimacy, paternity, succession to title, and eligibility for certain professions to be determined, modern Anglo-Saxon legal systems require that newborns be registered as either male or female." As a result, infants are surgically and hormonally

Ardhanariswara, from Rajasthan, India.

manipulated into one sex or the other after birth, sometimes without even the parents' knowledge. Fausto-Sterling concludes that society, therefore, "mandates the control of intersexed bodies because they blur and bridge the great divide."[4]

Intersexuality is not news; it's been recorded since antiquity. Creation legends on every continent incorporate a sacred view of intersexuality. But with the rise of patriarchal, sex-segregated societies in Greece and Rome, for example, intersexual babies were burned alive, or otherwise murdered. In recent centuries, intersexuals were ordered to pick one sex in which to live, and were killed if they changed their minds.[5]

What's news is hearing courageous intersexual people voice their own demands. Day-old infants can't give informed consent to genital surgery. Intersexed babies have a right to grow up and make their own decisions about the body they will live in for the rest of their lives. Parents need counseling; intersexual youth need intersexual advisors. These are basic human rights, yet they are being violated every day. Cheryl Chase, founder of the Intersex Society of North America describes this nightmare:

> When an intersexual infant is born, the parents are confronted with a shocking fact that violates their understanding of the world. Physicians treat the birth of such an infant as a medical emergency. A medical team, generally including a surgeon and an endocrinologist, is roused from bed, if need be, and assembled to manage the situation. Intersexual bodies are rarely sick ones; the emergency here is culturally constructed. The team analyzes the genetic makeup, anatomy, and endocrine status of the infant, "assigns" it male or female, and informs the parents of their child's "true" sex. They then proceed to enforce this sex with surgical and hormonal intervention.
>
> The parents are so traumatized and shamed that they will not reveal their ordeal to anyone, including the child as he/she comes of age. The child is left genitally and emotionally mutilated, isolated, and without access to information about what has happened to them. The burden of pain and shame is so great that virtually all intersexuals stay deep in the closet throughout their adult lives.[6]

Even reactionaries might agree with the struggle against the surgical alteration of infants, but with a twist: Let no man put asunder what God has brought together. However, this argument must not be used as a weapon against the rights of transsexual adults who choose sex-reassignment surgery. Not all transsexuals want or can afford that elective. But for those who do, there's no contradiction between the rights of transsexuals and those of intersexuals. The heart of the struggle of both communities is the right of each individual to control their own body.

I can remember standing in front of an abortion clinic in Buffalo, my arms linked with others in the dim glint of dawn, with cold rain dripping off my face. We were defending the women's health clinic against a right-wing assault on the right of women to choose abortion. I certainly knew politically what I was supporting. But that morning, perhaps because I was so miserably cold and wet, I felt the intersection of the demands of the trans movement and the women's movement in my own body. The heart of both is the right of each individual to make decisions about our own bodies and to define ourselves.

That is a right of each woman, each inter-sexed person, each transsexual man or woman – each human being. I believe that people who don't identify as transsexual also have a right to hormones and surgery. There are many of us who have wanted to shape our bodies without changing our sex. Since sex-reassignment pro-grams won't prescribe hormones or arrange surgery for a person who does not identify as a transsexual, we have to lie, buy hormones on the street, or go to quacks who sell prescriptions for a hefty fee.

Legions of people in this society do all sorts of things to make themselves more comfortable in their own bodies: myriad types of cosmetic surgery, nose jobs, piercing, tattooing, augmen-tation, liposuction, dieting, bodybuilding, cir-cumcision, bleaching, coloring, and electrolysis. But many of the people who add, subtract, reshape, or adorn their bodies criticize those transsexuals who elect surgery for *their* life deci-

<u>Uli</u> figure used in a chief's funeral, New Ireland Lelet Plateau, Papua New Guinea.

sions. I believe that the centuries-old fears and taboos about genitalia, buried deep in the dominant Western cultures, make the subject of surgical sex-change highly sensational. Today some opponents of sex-reassignment argue that sex-change is merely a high-tech phenomenon, a consequence of people being squeezed into narrow cultural definitions of what it means to be a woman or a man because sur-gical and hormonal options are now available. It's true that the development of anesthesia, and the commercial synthesis of hormones, opened up new opportu-nities for sex-reassignment. However, the argument that transsexuals are merely escaping rigid sex roles doesn't take into account ancient surgical techniques of sex-change developed in communal societies that offered more flexible sex and gender choices.

It all comes down to this: Each person has the right to control their own body. If each individual doesn't have that right, then who gets to judge and make decisions? Should we hand over that power to the church or the state? Should we make these rights subject to a poll?

And equally important to me is the right of each person to express their gender in any way they choose. But currently, strangers don't have to ask a parent if their infant is a boy or a girl if the child is dressed in pink or blue. Even gender color-coded diapers are now marketed in the United States.

ABOVE: An intersexual deity in Nepal. RIGHT: From the fifteenth-century painting, <u>The Land of the Hermaphrodites</u>.

As I researched this book, I was surprised to discover that this pink-for-girls, blue-for-boys gender assignment is a relatively recent development in the United States.[7] In the last century in this country, babies of all sexes wore little white dresses, which didn't seem to skew the gender expressions of these generations of children. Furthermore, the pink-blue gender values used to be just the opposite.

"Gender-based color schemes were adopted only at the onset of the twentieth century, as plumbing, cloth diapers, and color-fast fabrics became more available," wrote historians Vern and Bonnie Bullough. "However, different countries adopted different color schemes. In fact, there were heated arguments in the American popular press that pink was a more masculine color than light blue."[8]

How did the current pink and blue finally get assigned? Pink became a "girl's" color and blue a "boy's" in the United States in the early twentieth century after a media circus surrounding the acquisition of Thomas Gainsborough's painting *Blue Boy* and Sir Thomas Lawrence's *Pinkie* by wealthy art aficionado Henry Edwards Huntington.[9]

But the problem with the binary categories of pink and blue is that I'm not so easily color-coded, and neither are a lot of people I know. I've been taught that feminine and masculine are two polar opposites, but when I ride the subways or walk the streets of New York City, I see women who range from feminine to androgynous to masculine and men who range from masculine to androgynous to feminine. That forms a circle – a much more liberating concept than two poles with a raging void in between. A circle has room on it for each person to explore, and it offers the freedom for people to move on that circle throughout their lives if they choose.

Even today, when sex and gender choices have been so narrowed, when there are such degrading and murderous social penalties for crossing the boundaries of sex and gender, many of us can't – and don't want to – fit. We have to fight for the right of each person to express their gender in any way they choose. Who says our self-expression has to match our genitals? Who has the right to tell anyone else how to define their identities? And who has the right to decide what happens to each of our bodies? We cannot let these fundamental freedoms be taken away from us.

But those rights can't be won and protected without a fight. Strong bonds between the women's and trans liberation movements would put even more muscle into that struggle.

CHAPTER 14

I FEEL THE COMBINED

weight of women's and trans oppression in my own life. I am forced to battle both, simultaneously. As a result, I personally experience the relationship between women's and trans liberation, because these demands overlap in my own life.

Everywhere I've traveled across the United States talking about fighting trans oppression – from a crowded potluck supper in Tuscaloosa, Alabama, to an overflow audience in a cavernous university auditorium near Northampton, Massachusetts – women of all ages turn out, enthusiastically ready to discuss how the trans movement impacts on women's liberation.

We need to expand that dialogue, because women don't just need to understand the links between what they and trans people suffer in society, they need to realize that the women's and trans liberation movements need each other. Sex and gender oppression of all forms needs to be fought in tandem with the combined strength of these two movements and all our allies in society.

The development of the trans movement has raised a vital question that's being discussed in women's communities all over the country. The discussion revolves around one pivotal question: How is *woman* to be defined? The answer we give may determine the course of women's liberation for decades to come.

The question can't be considered without understanding that women face such constant dangers and harassment, day-in and day-out, that the attempt to define woman is generated by the need for safe space and clear-cut allies. That's a completely valid need. But how can we create safe space for women?

I think that if we define "woman" as a fixed entity, we will draw borders that would need to be policed. No matter what definition is used, many women who should be inside will be excluded.

Let's look first at the question of how woman can or cannot be defined. Some women hold an "essential," or biological definition, that one is born woman. Others, who define themselves as social constructionists, argue that women share a common experience. I don't think we can build women's communities or a liberation movement based on either.

A biological definition of woman is a dangerous direction for the women's movement to take. To accept that biological boundary would mark a definite break with the key principle of the second wave of women's liberation in the United States: that biology is not destiny. Simone de Beauvoir wrote, "One is not born but one becomes a woman."[1] The heart of that wisdom is that one should not be limited in life or oppressed because of birth biology. This is a truth that has meaning to all trans people and all women.

Of course, as a result of the oppression women face growing up in such a violently anti-woman environment, some women draw a line between women as allies and men as enemies. While it's understandable that an individual might do so out of fear, this approach fails as theory. It lumps John Brown and John D. Rockefeller together as enemies and Sojourner Truth and Margaret Thatcher together as allies. This view of who to trust and who to dread will not keep women safe or keep the movement on course.

One of the gifts of the women's liberation movement in the seventies was the understanding that our oppression as women is institutionalized – or built into the economic system. But this same system also tyrannizes entire nationalities, subjugates people because of who they love, denies people their abilities, works people near to death, and leaves many homeless and hungry. And last but not least, this system grinds up those who don't fit a narrow definition of woman and man.

A view that the primary division of society is between women and men leads some

TOP: Fifteenth-century engraving of North American Timicuan women and Two-Spirits, working together gathering food.
ABOVE: An Acoma mojaro, flanked by sister and niece (1900).

women to fear that transsexual women are men in sheep's clothing coming across their border, or that female-to-male transsexuals are going over to the enemy, or that I look like that same enemy. Where is the border for intersexual people – right down the middle of their bodies? Trans people of all sexes and genders are not oppressors; they, like women, rank among the oppressed.

After years of television and Hollywood movies and schooling full of prejudice, all of us have absorbed a biological definition of what is "normal" and what is not. But in a society rife with internal struggle, even a hard science like biology can be misused in an attempt to justify inequality and oppression. While we were dissecting frogs, biological determinism crept into our classrooms.

Biological determinism isn't just a recognition that some people have vaginas and others have penises. It is a theoretical weapon used in a pseudo-scientific way to rationalize racism and sexism, the partitioning of the sexes, and behavior modification to make gender expression fit bodies.

As I argued earlier, historical accounts suggest that although our ancestors knew who was born with a vagina, who was born with a penis, and whose genitals were more multi-faceted, they were not biological determinists. And although women's reproductive abilities contributed to a general division of labor, it was not a hard-and-fast boundary and it was not the only boundary.

It's true that women's ability to bear children and breast-feed in many cases helped to determine an *overall* division of labor. Human babies go through a long period of infancy during which they need to be nursed and nurtured. But by all accounts, childcare in communal cultures was a *collective* task, not the responsibility of each mother, nor of every woman, since not every woman bore children.[2]

I would suggest that we haven't had all the information with which to challenge the cultural construction of the modern view of childcare. For instance, in some pre-class societies, both parents went through the ritual pain of bearing a child and both were responsible for infant care.[3]

Any look at the early division of labor in cooperative societies has to take into account the reports by hundreds of social scientists of "women" in early cooperative societies who hunted and were accepted as *men* and "men" who worked among the women and were accepted as *women*. Then why do anthropologists continue to refer to them as *women* hunters and *men* gatherers, particularly when this insistence on their "immutable" biology flies in the face of the way these people were accepted by their own societies?

So although reproduction delineated a rough boundary of human labor, it was not decisive in determining sex/gender. Many communal societies accepted more than two sex/genders and allowed individuals to find their own place within that spectrum.

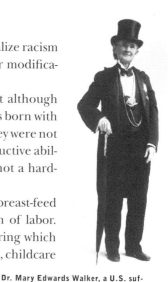

Dr. Mary Edwards Walker, a U.S. suffragist, wearing her Congressional Medal of Honor. Walker began cross-dressing in the early 1850s, inspired by the feminist dress-reform movement. She was suspended from Bowen Collegiate Institute after refusing to resign from the all-male debating society. Despite opposition, in 1863 she was appointed an assistant surgeon in the Union army and adopted the same uniform as her fellow soldiers. After the war, she was elected president of the National Dress Reform Association.

The people we would call male-to-female transsexuals in these early societies ritually menstruated and wore "the leaves prescribed for women in their courses."[4] That means that *all* the women had a relationship to fertility and birth – including those born with penises. A 1937 account of the North American Mohave by Alfred L. Kroeber describes a male-to-female initiation ritual for youths of ten to eleven years old, which, though provided by a white anthropologist, contrasts with the dominant Western view that sex/gender is fixed at birth.

In the morning the two women lift the youth and take him outdoors. One of the singers puts on the skirt and dances to the river in four stops, the youth following and imitating. Then all bathe. Thereupon the two women give the youth the front and back pieces of his new dress and paint his face white. After four days he is painted again and then is an *alyha*. Such persons speak, laugh, smile, sit, and act like women.[5]

A further account of the youths after the ceremony shows that they assumed female names. In addition:

> They insisted that their genitals be referred to by female terminology. After finding a husband, they would simulate menstruation by scratching between their legs with a stick until blood was drawn. When they were "pregnant," "menstruations" would cease. Before "delivery" a bean preparation would be ingested that would induce violent stomach pains dubbed "labor pains." Following this would be a defecation, designated a "stillbirth," which was later ceremoniously buried. There would then ensue a period of mourning by both husband and "wife."[6]

At the other end of the spectrum are accounts that some of the men hunters in communal societies who had been born female were believed not to menstruate.[7] So all the men – even those born with vaginas – were seen as outside the women's reproductive circle.

We need to combat the idea that a simple division of labor between women and men in communal societies has left us with today's narrow sex and gender system. Much evidence exists that many pre-class societies respected many more paths of self-expression. It was the overthrow of communalism and the subsequent division of society into classes that mandated the partitioning of the sexes and outlawed any blurring of those "man-made" boundaries. And we are left with those arbitrary and anti-human restrictions today.

Our histories as trans people and women are inextricably entwined. In the past, wherever women and trans people were honored, you can find cooperative, communal production. And societies that degrade women and trans people are already cleaved into classes, because those patriarchal divisions mandate a rigid categorization of sex and gender.

But how does this understanding help us today? If we reject a fixed biological boundary to define women as a group, what about the view that women share a common oppression? I believe this is also a perilous approach that can particularly lead to glossing over racism and class oppression.

Two broad currents emerged within the second wave of women's liberation in the United States. One was represented by feminists who analyzed women's oppression from a socialist-materialist viewpoint, the other by those who examined the psychological construction of woman. Both branches identified women as a group defined by oppression. Both currents recognized that arguments of biological determinism have been used by the patriarchal ruling classes for centuries as a weapon to justify women's oppression.[8]

However, since the rise of feminism, the definition of "woman" has been increasingly linked to a number of shared bodily experiences, like rape, incest, forced pregnancy, and battering. The underlying assumption is often that this physical oppression, experienced as a result of having a biologically female body, is the defining element of "womanhood." But women are not the only ones who experience the horrors of rape, incest, sexual humiliation, and brutality. And common bodily experiences that the majority of women on this planet share are hauling water and carrying firewood or working on an assembly-line – those are *class* experiences.

Do all women share the same experiences in society? What about the male-to-female transsexual women who have helped build the women's movement over the years? They experience women's oppression on a daily, even hourly basis. So if facing women's oppression defines being a woman, how long do you have to live it before you're "in"? Many lesbians went through a long period of heterosexuality before coming out. Would anyone argue that they should be excluded from lesbian gatherings because they were heterosexual during their formative years?

Do white women share the exact same experience as women of color? Do poor women and rich women share an identical experience? What about the experiences of disabled women, single mothers, lesbians, Deaf women? Women endure many different hardships and experiences. The sum total of our experiences and our resulting strengths and insights are just a small part of how many ways there are to be "woman" in this society.

Recently I had coffee with someone I've known since she was a teenager. "I don't think of you as a woman," she explained to me quite cheerily, "but as a very, very sensitive man – the kind that is so sensitive they don't really exist." I asked her how she arrived at this categorization.

"Well," she said, "I grew up without any real power as a girl. So I learned how to use being a woman to get around men's power, and that's not something I see you doing."

What she really meant was she learned to use being "feminine" to get around

Sex workers line up for free condom distribution as part of a safer-sex campaign in Recife, Brazil.

This cartoon, created especially for <u>Transgender Warriors</u>, is by Alison Bechdel, who draws the wildly popular lesbian cartoon series "Dykes to Watch Out For."

men's power. But I grew up very masculine, so the complex and powerful set of skills that feminine girls developed to walk safely through the world were useless to me. I had to learn a very different set of skills, many of them martial. While we both grew up as girls, our experiences were dissimilar because our gender expressions were very different. Masculine girls and women face terrible condemnation and brutality – including sexual violence – for crossing the boundary of what is "acceptable" female expression. But masculine women are not assumed to have a very high consciousness about fighting women's oppression, since we are thought to be imitating men.

As the women's movement of the seventies examined the negative values attached to masculinity and femininity in this society, some thought that liberation might lie in creating a genderless form of self-expression and dress. But of course androgyny was itself just another point on the spectrum of gender expression.

And remember the adage that you can't tell a book by its cover? Well, you can't read a person's overall consciousness by their gender expression.

In addition, gender doesn't just come in two brands, like perfume and cologne. Take masculinity, for example, particularly since there's an underlying assumption that the brutal and insensitive behavior of some men is linked to masculinity. Yet not all men dress, move, or behave in the same way. The masculinity of oppressed African-American men is not the masculinity of Ku Klux Klan members. Gender is expressed differently in diverse nationalities, cultures, regions, and classes.

And not all men in any given group express their masculinity in the same way. At a recent speaking event, I couldn't help but notice a man in the audience who was very masculine, but there was something in his gender expression that held my attention. At a later reception, he told me that he learned his masculinity from women – butches had mentored him as a young gay male. He learned one variation of an oppressed masculinity.

Those who are feminine – male and female – don't fare any better when it comes to assumptions about their gender expression. Feminine girls and women endure an extremely high level of sexual harassment and violence simply because of their gender expression. A great deal of woman-hating resides in attitudes towards femininity. And a great many bigoted generalizations are made about femme expression like: "The higher the heels, the lower the IQ; the higher the skirt the lower the morals." So femme women are also not assumed to have a very high consciousness about fighting women's oppression.

And what about males who are considered "effeminate"? Feminists have justifiably pointed out that the label is inherently anti-woman. But it is also anti-trans, gender-phobic, and anti-*feminine*.

The oppression of feminine men is an important one to me, since I consider drag queens to be my sisters. I've heard women criticize drag queens for "mocking women's oppression" by imitating femininity to an extreme, just as I've been told that I am imitating men. Feminists are justifiably angry at women's oppression – so am I! I believe, however, that those who denounce drag queens aim their criticism at the wrong people.

This misunderstanding doesn't take gender oppression into account. For instance, to criticize male-to-female drag performers, but leave out a discussion of gender oppression, lumps drag queen RuPaul together with men like actor John Wayne! RuPaul is a victim of gender oppression, as well as of racism.

There is a difference between the drag population and masculine men doing cruel female impersonations. The Bohemian Grove, for example, is an elite United States club for wealthy, powerful men that features comedy cross-dressing performances. But that's not drag performance. Many times the burlesque comedy of cross-dressed masculine men is as *anti-drag* as it is *anti-woman*.

In fact, it's really only drag performance when it's transgender people who are facing the footlights. Many times drag performance calls for skilled impersonations of a famous individual, like Diana Ross or Judy Garland, but the essence of drag performance is not impersonation of the opposite sex. It is the cultural presentation of an oppressed gender expression.

Our oppression and our identities – as drag queens and kings – are not simply based on our clothing. The term "drag" only means "cross-dressing" to most people. By that definition, we are people who put on garb intended for the opposite sex as a kind of masquerade. It's true that the word *drag* is believed to have originated as a stage term, derived from the drag of the long train of dresses male actors wore. But in fact, it is our gender expression, not our clothes, that shapes who we are.

Hopefully, the trans liberation movement will create a deeper understanding of sex and gender oppression. Everyone has a stake in the struggle to uncover how much cultural baggage is attached to the social categories of man and woman.

In addition, the women's movement has an opportunity to make a tremendous contribution by reaching out to all who suffer from sex and gender oppression. Drag queens and kings, and many women who have not been a part of the women's liberation movement, do not necessarily reflect the same consciousness as those who have been part of a collective movement for change for twenty years. But that doesn't mean that they don't feel their oppression or don't want to fight for their liberation.

The women's liberation movement that shaped my consciousness exposed the institutionalized oppression of women. The movement revealed that inequality begins at a very early age. But simply looking at the differences between what boys and girls are taught only reveals a broad analysis of sexual oppression. Just as girls experience different messages based on whether they are feminine, masculine, or androgynous, boys do too. It's absurd to think that messages of woman-hating and male privilege will produce the same consciousness in a male youth who grows up believing he will be part of the "good-ole boys club" and one who grows up fearing humiliation and violence at the hands of men. If the consciousness of male-to-female transsexuals was shaped early on by "male privilege," then why would they give it up?

What is the consciousness of a child who is assigned one sex at birth, but grows up identifying strongly with another sex? We need to examine how many ways there are to be a woman or a man, and how gender oppression makes sex-role conditioning more complex.

Everyone who is living as a woman in this woman-hating society is dealing with oppression every day and deserves both the refuge of being with other women and the collective power of the women's movement.

All women need to be on the frontlines against *all* forms of sex and gender oppression in society, as well as in fighting all expressions of gender-phobia and trans-phobia. In the simplest of terms, these twin evils are prejudices we have been taught since an early age. Gender-phobia targets women who are not feminine and men who are not masculine. Trans-phobia creates fear of changing sex. Both need to be fought by all women, as well as by all others in society.

As a rape survivor, I understand the need for safe space together – free from sexist harassment and potential violence. But fear of gender variance also can't be allowed to deceptively cloak itself as a women's safety issue. I can't think of a better example than my own, and my butch friends', first-hand experiences in public women's toilets. Of course women need to feel safe in a public restroom; that's a

Tala Candra Brandeis:
"Biology is not destiny."
From "Our Vision, Our
Voices: Transsexual
Portraits and Nudes,"
a photo exhibit by
Loren Cameron.

serious issue. So when a man walks in, women immediately examine the situation to see if the man looks flustered and embarrassed, or if he seems threatening; they draw on the skills they learned as young girls in this society to read body language for safety or danger.

Now, what happens when butches walk into the women's bathroom? Women nudge each other with elbows, or roll their eyes, and say mockingly, "Do you know which bathroom you're in?" That's not how women behave when they really believe there's a man in the bathroom. This scenario is not about women's safety – it's an example of gender-phobia.

And ask yourself, if you were in the women's bathroom, and there were two teenage drag queens putting on lipstick in front of the mirror, would you be in danger? If you called security or the cops, or forced those drag queens to use the men's room, would they be safe?

If the segregation of bathrooms is really about more than just genitals, then maybe the signs ought to read "Men" and "Sexually and Gender Oppressed," because we all need a safe place to go to the bathroom. Or even better, let's fight for clean individual bathrooms with signs on the doors that read "Restroom."

And defending the inclusion of transsexual sisters in women's space does not threaten the safety of any woman. The AIDS movement, for example, battled against the right-wing characterization of gay men as a "high-risk group." We won an understanding that there is no high-risk group – there are high-risk behaviors. Therefore, creating safety in women's space means we have to define unsafe behavior – like racist behavior by white women towards women of color, or dangerous insensitivity to disabilities.

Transsexual women are not a Trojan horse trying to infiltrate women's space. There have always been transsexual women helping to build the women's movement – they are part of virtually every large gathering of women. They want to be welcomed into women's space for the same reason every woman does – to feel safe.

And our female-to-male transsexual brothers have a right to feel welcome at women's movement events or lesbian bars. However, that shouldn't feed into the misconception that all female-to-male transsexuals were butches who just couldn't deal with their oppression as lesbians. If that were true, then why does a large percentage of post-transition transsexual men identify as gay and bisexual, which may have placed them in a heterosexual or bisexual status before their transition? There are transsexual men who did help build the women's and lesbian communities, and still have a large base of friends there. They should enjoy the support of women on their journey. Doesn't everyone want their friends around them at a time of great change? And women could learn a great deal about what it means to be a man or a woman from sharing the lessons of transition.

If the boundaries around "woman" become trenches, what happens to intersexual people? Can we really fix a policy that's so clear about who was born "woman"? And there are many people, like myself, who were born female but get hassled for not being woman enough. We've been accused of exuding "male energy." Now that's a frighteningly subjective border to patrol. Do all women – or *should* all women – have to share the same "energy"?

If we were going to decide who is a "real" woman, who would we empower to decide, and how could the check-points be established? Would we all strip? How could you tell if a vagina was not newly constructed? Would we show our birth certificates? How could you determine that they hadn't been updated after sex-reassignment? DNA tests? The Olympics tried it, but they had so many false results they went back to relying on watching somebody pee in a cup for the drug test as the "sex" test.

I understand that it took the tremendous social upheavals of the sixties and seventies to even begin to draw the borders of women's oppression. When I was growing up, no one even acknowledged that the system was stacked against women. But the women's liberation movement laid bare the built-in machinery of oppression in this society that's keeping us down. It's not your lipstick that's oppressing me, or your tie, or whether you change your sex, or how you express yourself. An economic system oppresses us in this society, and keeps us fighting each other, instead of looking at the real source of this subjugation.

The modern trans movement is not eroding the boundaries of women's oppression. Throughout history, whenever new lands and new oceans have been discovered, maps have always been re-charted to show their relationship to each other. The modern trans liberation movement is redrawing the boundaries to show the depth and breadth of sex and gender oppression in this society. It is this common enemy that makes the women's and trans communities sister movements for social justice.

What does it mean to be a woman in this society? How many different paths lead to woman? How varied are our experiences, and what do we share in common? Isn't this the discussion we need to have in order to continue to build a dynamic women's movement? And yet, we can't even begin the examination until all those who identify as women are in the movement. It's not a definition that's going to create safe space. Definitions have created some pretty unsafe space for many of us who were born female.

Let's open the door to everyone who is self-identified as woman, and who wants to be in women's space. (Not every woman wants that experience.) Let's keep the door unlocked. Together we can plot tactics and strategy for movement-building. And we can set some good-sense ground rules for what constitutes unsafe behavior.

What should the sign on the door of the women's movement read? I think the key to victory are these three simple words: "All women welcome."

But in addition to fighting women's oppression, we need to recognize and defend other sites of sex and gender oppression and organize an even larger struggle. The women's and trans liberation movements are comprised of overlapping populations and goals. Perhaps the unity of our two huge movements for justice will birth a new movement that incorporates the struggles against all forms of sex and gender oppression.

The combined power of women, trans people, and all of our allies could give rise to a powerful Sex and Gender Liberation movement!

RESOLUTION

WHEREAS, gender discrimination is at the heart of Feminist politics;

WHEREAS, the Transgendered and Transsexual Communities confront the same gender system that oppresses women and therefore are the target of marginalization, loss of medical care and economic and civil rights;

WHEREAS, there is a lack of understanding and information on the issue;

THEREFORE LET IT BE RESOLVED that NOW-NJ adopt a policy that supports the lives and identities of Transgendered and Transsexual people;

LET IT FURTHER BE RECOMMENDED that NOW-NJ chapters examine current policies and practices that discriminate against the Transgendered and Transsexual Communities and engage in dialogue with organizations and groups fighting for the rights of Transgendered and Transsexual people.

LET IT ALSO BE RECOMMENDED that this resolution be submitted to the National NOW Conference in 1995.

A resolution in support of trans lives and identities, passed on October 29, 1994 at the state conference of the New Jersey National Organization for Women (NOW-NJ).

*If there is not struggle, there is no
progress. Those who profess to favor
freedom, and yet depreciate
agitation . . . want crops without
plowing up the ground. They want rain
without thunder and lightning. They
want the ocean without the
awful roar of its many waters. . . .
Power concedes nothing without a
demand. It never did, and it never will.*

FREDERICK DOUGLASS

CHAPTER 15

WHENEVER PEOPLE WHO

have been silenced and persecuted for millennia begin to organize and voice their demands, others who are wounded by oppression lift their heads and sniff the air, sensing instinctively that a fresh wind of change is blowing. The trans liberation movement is ushering in just such change.

Change is the thing that most of us hope for, especially when we are suffering, but it's not something we necessarily have come to expect. We've all heard the cynical recitations, "You can't fight City Hall," or "The more things change, the more they stay the same." And we've been taught that the way things are today is pretty much the way they've always been – dog eat dog.

But that's a damn lie! Change and development are characteristics of everyone and everything that exists – including human society.

The history I've presented in this book is the granite basis for my belief that oppression is not the future of humanity. If world history had really been accessible to all of us, we would have been taught early on in life that our ancestors lived in societies that enjoyed much more humane social relations than we do. That fact, in and of itself, would have given many of us confidence about our ability to change the society we live in.

Similarly, I am heartened by the realization that hatred of sex and gender variation is not rooted in human nature. The more I dig, the more I find that although what we think of as gender today has been expressed differently in diverse historical periods, cultures, regions, nationalities, and classes, there appears to have always been gender diversity in the human population. And there is just as much evidence that sexes have not always been arbitrarily squeezed into hard-and-fast categories of woman and man, and that fluidity between sexes is an ancient path.

I have presented all this information, gleaned from thousands of books, essays, oral accounts, articles, and other sources about societies in which trans people were honored. And I've offered an overview about the oppression of trans people under slavery, feudalism, and capitalism. In the face of all this information, our trans liberation movement needs to examine the economic structures of the societies in which trans people were honored and those in which we were condemned. It is time to talk about class divisions, because a society of haves and have-nots is based on just that – divisions.

The fact that on a scale of one year, more than 360 days of human history belongs to cooperative, communal life gives me concrete hope about what could be achieved, with the powerful tools and technology that exist today, if we plan all production to meet the needs of everyone, without having to take the question of profitability into account. Eliminating the race for profits from manufacture and exchange removes the *motive* for pitting people against each other.

Tolerance and respect for human variation, including sex and gender diversity, resulted from the fact that people worked cooperatively with collectively owned tools and other materials. But everything around us today that supports life – factories, agricultural machinery and land, hospitals, scientific laboratories – was all built through collective human labor, yet most of it is privately owned by individuals.

Just recently, a front page article in the *New York Times* reported that one percent of the families in the United States own forty percent of the wealth that we all produce week-in and week-out. In fact, the *Times* noted that the polarization of wealth and poverty in the United States was greater than in any other industrialized country.[1] What the *Times* didn't see fit to print was that the rich get richer *because* the poor get poorer. That's an important cause-and-effect to omit!

As a messenger on Wall Street years ago, I remember seeing an old man, dressed in dirty rags, eating out of a garbage can next to a sleek double-stretch limousine. Some good-hearted person might think the solution to such glaring economic disparity would be to redistribute the wealth from rich people to poor people.

Anyone who has ever played Monopoly knows that when you've run out of little pieces of paper money at the end of the game, you lose. But even if the banker were to give you some more money, you'd still lose. That's because the one who owns Boardwalk and Park Place and all those utilities is just going to take your money *again* when you land on their property.

Real-life monopoly is not a game for people who can't find a job, or who have run out of money altogether. Recently a young woman at a party asked me, "What do you do for a living?" I replied, "I don't know," and my own answer made me anxious. I don't own property, a business, or a factory, so I don't live off other people's labor. I have to work for wages or I'd starve. But since I am gender-ambiguous, it's almost impossible for me to get a job. Every month it's a scramble for my half of the rent, and it's even harder to deal with working full-time at survival, when at the same time I have to cope with threats on the street, or harassment on the subway. This system I live under doesn't work for me!

Capitalism is one of the most irrational economic systems imaginable: those who do the most, get the least, and those who do the least, get the most. How can such a system continue? It couldn't if the vast, laboring majority got together to fight for a new, more equitable economy.

Keeping people divided – that's the purpose of making people fearful of those who dress differently, or who change their sex, or whose sex is not either-or. That's

Some of those arrested in a sweeping raid on the National Variety Artists Exotic
Carnival and Ball held at the Manhattan Center in October, 1962.

the function of pitting lighter-skinned people against those with darker skin, nationality against nationality, men against women, straight against lesbian, gay, or bi, abilities against disabilities, young against old. Divide-and-conquer is a crude weapon, but it has proven historically effective – that is, right up to the point where people wake up and realize that they have a material need for unity.

So what is the solution? Are sex and gender oppression so ingrained in people after centuries of campaigns to justify trans persecution that this bigotry can no longer be eradicated? Should we even try? Where would we begin?

When I was growing up in the stifling repression of the 1950s, I couldn't have imagined that the wave after wave of revolutionary struggles throughout the 1960s and 1970s would follow. The Stonewall Rebellion was part of those battles for change. I can remember seeing the banners of the young gay liberation movement flying at rallies in defense of the Black Panther Party, and against the Vietnam War.

But many of us who were working in the sixties enjoyed a higher standard of living, partly because the powers that be decided a liberal guns-and-butter approach would be most effective to dampen any domestic struggle against the Vietnam War. That's why the Johnson administration beefed up spending for social services – the

Venus Xtravaganza, one of the stars of the popular documentary, "Paris is Burning," was murdered before the film was released.

same vital services that are being slashed today. It was an attempt to keep the youth who were opposing the war and the Black, Latino, and Native liberation movements isolated from the mainstream of the working class.

But today, the system *isn't* working for the majority of people. Many millions are holding down two or three part-time jobs, lack health care, or are one paycheck away from homelessness. Those in the ruling summits of power in the United States are emboldened by the setbacks for workers in the former Soviet Union and Eastern Europe, and are trying to crush the trade unions, as well as the gains, like Social Security, unemployment, and welfare, won by militant struggles over the last seven decades.

At a time when there is no real economic safety net for most working people and our standard of living is under attack, is it any wonder that we are witnessing well-coordinated state-by-state ballot campaigns to strip lesbians, gays, bisexuals, and trans people of any recourse against discrimination by characterizing our progressive civil rights legislation as "special rights"?

And is it any surprise that the same well-funded movers-and-shakers of these "family values" hate crusades are frequently in the same ranks as those who are violently attacking women's right to reproductive freedom, and are trying to scapegoat immigrants?

This is divide-and-rule. But that doesn't mean we shouldn't fight for reforms! All trans people need basic civil rights, and we need them right now. In the United States at the present time, for instance, we have very little recourse against discrimination and are struggling to even be included in the broad human rights laid out in the Constitution.

As our contemporary trans movement gathers more and more oppressed sex and gender communities into its vortex, we will formulate extensive demands in the course of our struggle. We must demand the decriminalization of all forms of outlawed sex and gender expression, and gear education to winning social acceptance of sex and gender variance. We have a right to something as basic as clean toilets that are not marked "women" or "men."

Transsexual women and men, and other trans people, have a right to affordable surgery and hormones. And all trans people need access to basic health care, without fear of being turned away because of bigotry or lack of money. The trans community is also ravaged by AIDS; we need AIDS education and services that are offered in trans-friendly space.

We need to fight discrimination against us in housing and employment, in the military, and in child custody and visitation cases. We need to fight violations of the rights of trans prisoners, and trans victims of police brutality.

High schools, colleges, and universities need to include trans individuals and struggles in their curricula. In addition, the very concept that our current narrow sex and gender system is eternal needs to be challenged by exploring the diversity that has existed throughout human history. We need a fresh reexamination of history, anthropology, and medical science in order to weed out any concepts that sex and gender variation are "abnormal."

Sex categories should be removed from all basic identification papers – from driver's licenses to passports – and since the right of each person to define their own sex is so basic, it should be eliminated from birth certificates as well. And affirmative action – first won to redress some of the historic discrimination based on race and sex – needs to be defended and expanded to include more victims of sex and gender oppression.

Each person should have the right to determine and change their sex – and express their gender in any way they choose.

But those rights won't just fall from the sky. People have a right to food and shelter, and to be free from the threat of sexual or racist violence, too, but all of this takes a struggle.

When I grew up, Jim Crow segregation ordinances were the law of the land. It took the mighty upheavals of the Civil Rights and the Black Liberation movements to remove some of the most reactionary laws and win progressive anti-discrimination and affirmative action legislation. For the first time since the Reconstruction period following the Civil War, the movement won Black elected officials – mayors, governors, congressional representatives. But the crisis of capitalism still remained, and conditions for African Americans in the inner cities are worse now due to years of deep and protracted economic depression.

The development of high tech rendered many of the occupational divisions between men and women obsolete. But it took the women's movement to scrap the categories of "women's" jobs, to make discrimination on the basis of sex illegal, and to demand equal pay for comparable work. Yet, as women as a whole are sinking deeper into poverty, these reforms are not enough!

Law codifies the economic inequality built into a class-divided society. Whether a law has been cloaked as the word of a deity or as springing from precepts of human morality, it is presented as fixed and unchangeable, but it is *not*. However, advances in production or changes in human consciousness don't automatically change laws. Progressive legislation reflects the gains won through militant marches, rallies, picket lines, and grass-roots organizing; action is what makes laws change.

But it's like a union contract – first you fight to get it, then you still have to fight to defend what you've won from being snatched back.

For trans people, winning progressive legislation and repealing bigoted laws are

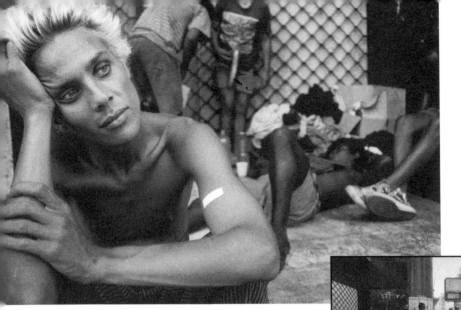

ABOVE: Sharon (Bruno),
who lives with other youths
in a street gang in Brazil,
has just been diagnosed
HIV-antibody positive.
RIGHT: Businessmen don't
even notice Sharon and
her street gang.

important stepping stones in our larger struggle for justice. But the experience of this century has shown that the organic make-up of the profit system inevitably drives it into a cataclysm of economic and social crises that can wipe out the progressive gains of a lifetime. That's the lesson I learned from the triumph of fascism in Germany.

As a Jewish child, I thought fascism gathered without warning, like storm clouds. So when I found a swastika carved into my wooden desktop at school, I feared fascism had arrived and nothing could stop the storm. It's no wonder that I spent so much time studying the real reasons why the Nazis came to power in Germany in the 1930s.

The German economy was in deep decline, and a powerful workers' movement was challenging capitalist rule itself, as were many in the movements of trans people, lesbians, gay men, women, and socialists. Fascism was unleashed to crush this movement, the working class, and all allied organizations. The rise of the Nazis was funded by a segment of the industrialists and bankers. Who paid for the construction of the concentration camps, railroad lines, and ovens? Who profited from the slave labor? Hitler promised to turn around the economy and bring about prosperity, and he delivered. War was still an effective jump start for a stagnant capitalist economy.

War was also "good for business" at the time of the Stonewall Rebellion. But, like any drug, sooner or later quick fixes don't work. When the Pentagon waged war against Iraq, the economy didn't revive. So what does the ultra-right wing have to offer now? They won't deliver jobs. The "leaner, meaner" restructuring, along with the high-tech revolution, has meant more skilled workers are flipping hamburgers for minimum wage.

We are faced with either relinquishing what we and earlier generations won in terms of living and working conditions and political gains – or organizing in a broad counteroffensive.

Looking only at the past, it might seem unrealistic to think that we in the United States could muster a force capable of challenging the ruling class. But looking forward, from the reality of today, as the cities crumble and steel mill furnaces cool, as debts pile up and war production becomes a permanent feature of the economy, as people are faced with hunger and homelessness, as the government underfunds out-of-control epidemics like AIDS and breast cancer, the question that must be asked is: Can such a struggle really be avoided?

Isn't it time for the struggle against capitalism to come out of the closet? Isn't it time to shed old illusions, break with ideologies that justify exploitation and human misery, and, most important of all, isn't it time to have confidence in our own abilities to give birth to a new world?

From the moment I began to even ask this question as a young activist, I was baited as "communist." Well, it's true! I'm not satisfied with removing the laws that determine what clothes I can wear – not when trans youths are sleeping in abandoned cars, or on sidewalks. A banker can afford to waste food served at elegant dinners, while Black and Latina drag queens are forced to turn tricks in order to buy french fries. What you think the solution is to this social crisis depends on, as the old union song said, "Which side are you on?" I believe these deep social crises require thorough-going social solutions.

Red-baiting, in particular, is supposed to frighten us from challenging the existence of an economic system that's not meeting the needs of the majority. In the Middle Ages, we would have been labeled heretics. I grew up feeling the power of anti-communism during the McCarthy era. But red-baiting, like all other divisive weapons, can be defeated. Allan Berubé, a gay, working-class historian, addressed this question in a speech he gave at a lesbian and gay writer's conference in 1995. Berubé explained that the Marine, Cooks and Stewards Union in the 1930s and 1940s, which organized the service personnel on board ocean liners and freighters on the West Coast of the U.S., was a multi-national and left-wing union that included many openly gay transgender workers – drag queens.

One of the organizers of the union, now in his eighties, told Berubé that the communist trade unionists tried to articulate slogans that reflected the composition of the workers. "One of the slogans they came up with in 1936," Berubé told the audience, "was: If you let them red-bait, they'll race-bait; if you let them race-bait, they'll queen-bait. That's why we have to stick together."[2]

That is just one of the important lessons we need to learn from the movements of the past, just as the struggle to battle trans oppression will contribute what it has learned to other movements and to future struggles.

As the deepening general social crisis brought on by the decline of the capitalist system is increasingly felt as an urgent issue by millions, we as trans people should

feel more confident than ever to reach out to our co-workers, neighbors, friends, families, and loved ones and say: They're trying to make us fight each other to keep us from uniting to win real change.

While there is no blueprint for the struggles ahead, we can learn both from engaging a common enemy and from the crystallized experiences of the past. In the last 150 years in particular, the working class has grown to be the key force in society. It is the class responsible for producing all the basic goods and services, and it has become the majority class in most parts of the world.

From the first rudimentary and spontaneous resistance of the cross-gender weavers who called themselves "General Ludd's wives" to today, this class has developed rich revolutionary experience and many, many forms of political organization.

As trans people, we have a history of resistance of which we should be proud. Trans warriors stood up to the slave-owners, the feudal landlords, and the capitalist bosses. Today, as trans warriors we are joining the movement for a just society in greater and greater numbers. By raising the demands of our trans movement within the larger struggle for change, we are educating people about our oppression, winning allies, and shaping the society we're trying to bring into being.

None of us will be free until we have forged an economic system that meets the needs of every working person. As trans people, we will not be free until we fight for and win a society in which no class stands to benefit from fomenting hatred and prejudice, where laws restricting sex and gender and human love will be unthinkable.

Look for us – transgender warriors – in the leadership of the struggle to usher in the dawn of liberation.

LEFT TOP: These Bradford College students, shown here with the author and Professor Peggy Walsh, formed "Students Daring for Diversity" when their college president refused to allow the author to deliver their senior commencement address. Students occupied the main administration building, won the support of their families, faculty, grounds keepers and other staff, alums, and others, and prompted a fax and phone blitz that overwhelmed the president's office. As a result, the author delivered the 1995 commencement speech.

LEFT BOTTOM: A Cuban drag queen at a government-sponsored outdoor performance that included safer-sex education. "Drag shows are highly popular in Cuba today.... from theaters and nightclubs to neighborhoods. I went to a drag show in an open lot, attended by people from that neighborhood, and gays and lesbians from other places in Havana. The people who came ranged in age from infants to elders.... Same-gender couples were dancing, everyone was having a good time. I asked one woman: Why are you here? She said, 'They're so beautiful and so talented and they are my neighbors.' On May Day we saw a group of Afro-Cubans in traditional clothes, playing and singing music that had originated during slavery. A group of drag queens were a lively part of this contingent. " *African-American lesbian author and activist Barbara Smith talking about her trip to Cuba in the spring of 1995.*

THIS PAGE: Genuine family values. The mother's hand-made sign reads: "My child is a transsexual and I love her."

Part Five

"**WITHIN THE WAR**

we are all waging with the forces of death, subtle and otherwise,

conscious or not – I am not only a casualty, I am also a warrior."

AUDRE LORDE

MARSHA "P." JOHNSON *fought back against the police*

during the Stonewall Rebellion. The "P" stood for

"Pay it no mind!" Marsha was photographed by

Warhol and was part of the Hot Peaches Review.

She was a source of strength and pride to me and

many, many others in the drag, transgender, and

lesbian and gay communities. Marsha was found

floating in the Hudson River near the piers in New

York City shortly after the 1992 Pride March. The

police "investigation" reportedly consisted of two

phone calls, and they ruled her death a suicide. A

people's postering campaign dug up reports that

Marsha had been harassed near the piers earlier

that evening.

BRANDON TEENA, *a young white man, moved to a small town in Nebraska in 1993. After a minor brush with the law, the police reportedly exposed the fact that Brandon had been born female. A short time later, Brandon was forcibly stripped at a Christmas party in front of a woman he had dated, and then was kidnapped, beaten, and gang-raped. Yet police refused to pursue charges against the two men Brandon named as his attackers. On New Year's Day, Brandon and two other people were found shot to death; Brandon's body was repeatedly stabbed. While the two men have been convicted, due to public pressure, there has not yet been any investigation of the role of the police in instigating the violence in the first place. Wouldn't Brandon Teena be alive today if the police had allowed him to live and work in dignity and respect?*

QUENTIN CRISP *(far right), has appeared in eight films, and wrote* The Naked Civil Servant *– an autobiography made into a movie in 1975. He was born in 1908.*

Were you feminine as a child?

Why yes, I didn't know any better. You see I was so young when it began that I hadn't been touched by the world. So I swanned about the house saying, "Today I am a beautiful princess."

What was it like to walk through the streets of London in the 1920s and 1930s?

It was very difficult in England for all those years. They stood with their faces here [an inch from his nose] saying, "Who the hell do you think you are?" And I used to say, "Oh dear, you mean I have to be *somebody just to walk down Oxford Street?" The thing the movie didn't show you, because of the expense, was the crowds. I walked along Picadilly and by the time I got to Picadilly Circus the crowd was so big that it flowed out into the street and the police fought their way through it and said "Oh, you again!" turned back to the crowd and said "It's nothing. Go home." And the crowd dissipated. But it was very frightening, because ultimately you get to a place where you can't go any further and then you have to turn back.*

In England I was threatened all the time. You were constantly in danger. You never went past a group of people – you avoided them and went past another way. I lived my life as though I was

in a tunnel and if there was a speck of light at the end of it, I moved toward it. I lived in the digs from which I didn't get evicted, I had the jobs from which I didn't get the sack, I knew the people who could put up with the disgrace.

But the amazing thing is that I didn't get arrested til I was thirty-four. I didn't recognize that the people standing about in the West End were policemen disguised as human beings. [In court] I said it was obvious I was not soliciting anyone in broad daylight because how could anyone speak to me, looking as I did? It just wasn't possible. No one would have spoken to me. No one did speak to me – ever. The magistrate wouldn't say the police were lying, but they let me go.

I didn't know there was any happiness in the world at all until I got here. People say to me "Do you regret anything?" And I say I can't regret anything because there were never any alternatives. I couldn't do otherwise than I did. If I'd endeavored to behave like a man, people would have said "Who does she think she's kidding?"

And I don't know why they were so hostile, except that the English like sex to be tidy, and they couldn't make up their minds whether I was a man or a woman. [There are] words, gestures, clothes, jobs, hobbies, that are suitable for a young man. Then there is another list of things that are suitable for young women. And that gives you an idea that you have a destiny connected with your sex, which of course is not so.

I said to someone, "Your clothes are a way of telling the world who you think you are."

And they said "Who do you think you are?"

And I said "I'm an elderly foreigner of dubious gender."

CRAIG HICKMAN, *poet and performance artist, and author of "Rituals."*

"I'm a Black, gay performance artist – man enough to let his woman shine and woman enough to let his man roar.

"I find that as a cross-gendered artist and person that I have a very big responsibility to myself and to the people who hear or read my work because gender roles stifle and in my opinion are the basis for all oppression. I feel like the world would be liberated if people ignored gender roles.

"I often am seen by people as a 'What's that?' to which I usually respond 'Isn't beautiful enough?' And faces fall and crack and eyebrows may raise and people are left thinking about something that they didn't expect to be thinking about. And so I suppose when I go out into the world I carry it all with me and my very presence is for most people a confrontation."

DEBBIE, *bodybuilder and powerlifter.*

"I was always strong – even when I was little. I was always under the premise of 'Only the strong survive.' I started out mainly as a female bodybuilder. I worked and trained very hard at it. I felt that as hard as I tried, I could never quite be what they were looking for as a bodybuilder and became extremely frustrated.

"As I started training with my best friend, he told me: 'You've got power that's incredible – you just ooze it – you just don't realize it. You have the ability to be a powerlifter.' So I decided, OK, I'll give that a try. I found out powerlifters are very different – very supportive of each other. They seem to accept that if you have power, and you have strength, you've made it there because you're good. You either make your lift or you don't.

"I do have a problem going into the ladies' room. I find it real disheartening. That comes from people not being used to people who look like me. People end up making assumptions on your physical appearance before they really try to get to know you. I just think it's a shame. They judge what they see before they know what it is. Some people go by what they see first; they're not paying attention. I've been in groups where I was wearing earrings and everything, and they still call me 'sir.' Other people take a little extra time to pay attention or maybe they're just a little more progressive – if that's the word.

"I just want people to understand that women can be a rainbow of things and not lose any idea of being a woman. Look at lions and tigers – it's the females who do the hunting, and killing, and feeding – they reek power. Look at their legs – massive and beautiful. I'm taking the extra step – it's something that I've always wanted to do. I'm a small person too – I'm only five foot. I've worked hard to be and to get what I've attained at this point. I am powerful and I can do this."

PAULINE PARK, *Korean-American historian.*

"I did have the usual experience of trying on my mother's clothes, quite furtively, but it wasn't until my teens that I discovered a book in the neighborhood public library on transvestites and transsexuals, that I realized I was not alone. My transvestism has been a part of my life, albeit covertly, for a long time — as long as I can remember. But my acceptance of my own transvestism has been a long time in coming, and it's gone in phases."

MORGAN HOLMES, *holding her son, is intersexual.*

"We live in a binary system that has only two ways of classifying anatomical sex. It is not, therefore, an easy task for most people, feminists included, to understand intersexuality as anything except completely different. *Indeed so different that it qualifies as a medical abnormality. But what many intersexed persons, myself included, have in common with women is that we also live in this world 'as women.' We were raised to be women, to be accorded only whatever rights and privileges women can manage to obtain, within the confines of her race and class in patriarchy.*

"Because of the range in forms that intersexuality takes, there are some for whom it is easier to assume a single sex identity and some for whom it is more difficult, enforced through lifelong medical intervention. What is even more difficult than identifying oneself as a member of the community 'woman' is attempting to define one's identity as an intersex/woman. The task requires taking back an identity which has been made illegitimate by culture and has been stolen through surgery."

PETRIC SMITH, *author of* Long Time Coming *(Crane Hill, 1994).*
Before he transitioned from female to male, Petric (then Elizabeth
H. Cobbs) courageously testified against his uncle, Robert Chamb-
liss, and other Klansmen who stood accused of blowing up the
Birmingham Sixteenth Street Baptist Church that killed four
young African-American girls. Chambliss was convicted. Why did
Smith risk his life to testify?

"I had lived with the fear of the Klan all my life. A part of me
had wanted to stop this man who was my uncle for many, many
years. But I felt helpless – impotent if you will – to do anything
about it. This was an opportunity to stop the things that he was
doing aimed at intimidation of family, and brutality toward his
wife, as well as the larger issue of racist violence.

"I think I started learning not to be a racist as I started meeting
individuals in the Black community – and people of all races – at
work and other situations. I came to know the reality of the cruelty,
the personality that was receiving the cruelty. That was added on
top of this layer of being repulsed by the horror stories that my
uncle would tell over the years. It all became so real to me that it
almost became what life was about to stop him and his kind."

OUTSIDER PRODUCTIONS
SEX
OUTSIDER PRODUCTIONS
SEX
IS...
MARC HUESTIS
Extended by Popular Demand
LUMIERE
THEATRE
California at Polk

MAX WOLF VALERIO, *(preceding page) Blackfoot Confederacy-Kainah (formerly Blood)/Chicano. Max is writing a book about his transition as a transsexual man that will be published in 1996 by William Morrow/Avon.*

"I think most people don't understand how transsexuals feel about our original biological selves. Everyone experiences this discontinuity between identity and body slightly differently, but there's a commonality. For me, it wasn't so much that I hated my body or hated being a woman. First of all, even as I say that I was a woman, that feels as though somehow, it really wasn't true. At some point, I realized that my deepest, most abiding sense of myself was male. When I saw that there was an alternative, that the hormones really work, I knew that I would rather live my life as a man.

"As a man, a more integrated sense of myself began to emerge. Of course, I will never have an intact and completely functional male body, even after surgery. But I am very pleased, ecstatic, with what I do have now.

"My history and consciousness will always have the imprint of my life as a woman. This abiding difference is something to be treasured, not diminished. Transsexuals have been through a powerful transformation that is physical, social, legal, and spiritual, a kind of high-tech initiation rite. Our journey is fraught with paradox and peril. We're agent provocateurs of gender, outside both conservative and politically correct agendas. Intuition and will concretized in the flesh."

JENNIFER MILLER, *bearded woman, performance artist, and juggler.*

Jennifer is a founder and director of Circus Amok, which integrates politics – from budget cuts to the anti-immigrant Proposition 187 – with free outdoor community performances in New York City. Miller refuses to shave.

"If I can't fight the powers when it comes to just this little bit of hair on my face, then what can I do. If I didn't keep my beard, it would be a statement of hopelessness. Women do have facial hair. Keeping secrets requires energy that's debilitating, especially when it's out of shame or fear.

"My beard is a lifelong performance. I live in a very liminal place. 'Liminal' means an 'in-between place.' It means in a doorway, a dawn or a dusk. It's a lovely place. In the theater, it's when the lights go out. And before the performance begins."

LOUIS GRAYDON SULLIVAN *was born Sheila Jean Sullivan in Milwaukee, Wisconsin, in 1951. While working as a secretary in the Slavic Languages Department at the University of Wisconsin in Milwaukee in the early 1970s, Sullivan became active in the campus Gay People's Union and contributed many historical biographical sketches of female-to-male cross-dressers to the GPU News. For several years, Sullivan identified himself as a "heterosexual female transvestite who was sexually attracted to gay men."*

After moving to San Francisco in 1975, however, and starting the process of sex reassignment a few years later, Sullivan began to think of himself as a transsexual gay man. Sullivan was the first FTM peer counselor at the Janus Information Facility, an international clearinghouse of information on transsexuality. As such, he was in contact with FTM and gender-questioning individuals from around the world, and helped lay the foundations for the FTM community that has since emerged. Sullivan organized the first FTM support organization on the West Coast (and only the third in the world) in 1986. He spent his final years involved in a campaign to persuade medical service providers that people like himself who desired a transsexual form of embodiment in order to act on a homosexual desire existed in significant numbers, and often experienced discrimination when seeking health care services.

Shortly before his death from an AIDS-related illness in 1991, Sullivan published his biography of Jack B. Garland, a person with a female body who lived as a man for forty years in early twentieth-century San Francisco. Besides his activism in the transgender community, Sullivan also helped organize the Gay and Lesbian Historical Society of Northern California, where his extensive personal papers are now located.

(This piece on Louis Sullivan was prepared by transsexual researcher Susan Stryker.)

When Lou Sullivan died in March 1991, he left **JAMES GREEN** with
a roll of stamps and a list of about 250 names for the FTM mailing
list. Today James, a transsexual man, is continuing the work that
Lou began. James is the editor of FTM International – with a cir-
culation of over 600 – and a leader of the transsexual men's community. He authored the report to the San Francisco Human Rights
Commission that resulted in San Francisco becoming the fourth city
to win landmark legislation that gives trans people legal protection
and recourse against discrimination.

"I think people are afraid often of people who take great risks.
So they project their own fears onto people who do take risks. Even
though it's a terrible thing for some people to think about people
changing their bodies to the extent that I have, it's important to me
that people understand that I have continuity in my body, and that
if I was worried about other people's judgements of me, I could never
have taken this risk. And had I not taken that risk, I might as well
have shriveled up and died. I just feel so much richer for having
gone through this incredible transition that forced me to talk to so
many people in my life honestly and openly about who I am.

"This is all an issue of basic human rights, very basic human
rights. It's spiritual in nature – it's just about letting people be who
they are.

"In the community of transsexual men, we're still dealing with
individual basic survival. People would like to not fear losing their
job, not have to fear the loss of their social relationships. The loss of
their children. It's just that basic. They're worried about paying for
their surgery, about seeing a doctor, getting good medical care. And
then eventually they start to worry a little bit about being accepted –
especially if they're moving from the lesbian community to the world
of men – they worry about just being accepted as a man. For many,
that means staying in the closet."

SOME OF THE MINNEAPOLIS *trans community members who were in the audience for the keynote speech of the Week of Differently Gendered Lives in the winter of 1995. This week of trans events and education was jointly planned by many communities – on-campus and off – transsexual, drag, transgender, cross-dresser, feminist, lesbian, gay, bi. Hard work by trans activists won an amendment to the Minnesota Human Rights Act (Minnesota State Chapter No. 22, H.F. No. 585), effective August 1, 1993, making it unlawful to discriminate against individuals based on their sexual orientation. For the purposes of the amendment, "perceived as having a self-image or identity not traditionally associated with one's biological maleness or femaleness" is included under the explanation of sexual orientation.*

MARTINE ROTHBLATT, HER SPICE BINA, AND THEIR CHILDREN.

"Our four kids feel they have two women as parents, but they still call me Dad, and we all love each other no less. Before I undertook my transformation I asked each of our kids if they had any objection. None of them did, but each of them reacted differently. Our eighteen-year-old son asked what I was waiting for, since we only live once and time keeps on ticking. Our seventeen-year-old daughter said she learned tolerance for gay, lesbian, bisexual, and transgendered lifestyles in her public school. When someone asked her how she felt about having two mothers, she replied, 'Lots of people have two moms or two dads.' Our eleven-year-old son said he didn't want to lose me as his dad. I promised I would always be his dad, and he remains happy.... Our youngest daughter, age nine, considers being transgendered as just another way people can be."

(From *The Apartheid of Sex: A Manifesto on the Freedom of Gender,* Crown, 1995.)

BO HEADLAM, *a twenty-nine-year-old medical student.*

"I am a Black butch lesbian who wears men's clothing. It is often difficult for me to exist in this manner that is so natural for me. You see, many people in the world (or, at least, the Western world) don't like certain qualities in people. Hence, these individuals do not like me because I am (in no particular order) 1) a woman, 2) Black, 3) a lesbian, and 4) butch. A fifth point of disgust, according to these folks, is that I wear men's clothing, which no woman is supposed to do. But I like myself. I did not in the past. . . . the real reason was that I did not want to fight the world every day. . . . [Today] it felt, and feels, so good to be myself. I find that I now have tremendous amounts of energy. And I no longer consider myself unlovable. I have enough self-love as well as love from others to show me that this simply is not true.

"I confront those who insist that the butch/femme phenomenon is not and has never been important, nor does it exist today. I confront those who think that all Black lesbians are butch studs. I confront other racist remarks. I confront the people who say as I'm walking down the street, 'What is it?' I confront the women in public restrooms who insist that I am a man. I confront anyone else who insists that I am a man. I confront homophobic remarks. And the list goes on and on. You would think that all this confrontation would drain me mentally. But it does not. In fact, I feel stronger each time I confront someone.

"Finally, I am prepared to confront physical violence. Fortunately, I have not experienced much of that. But I have trained to fight since I was in junior high school. Hopefully, I will not have to use any of the skills I have learned. It is so funny for me to think back on how scared I was of myself only a few years ago. I never thought that I would get to a point in my life where I would accept who I am. But I am so glad that I did."

from left to right: **VIRGINIA PRINCE, ARIADNE KANE, & MAXINE MILLER** *in 1981, attending church in Provincetown, Massachusetts, during Fantasia Fair, an annual trans gathering.* **VIRGINIA PRINCE** *published the first known trans magazine in the United States, and created the first social group for cross-dressers. She is regarded as the founding mother of the contemporary U.S. cross-dressing community.* **ARIADNE KANE** *is the director of the Outreach Institute for Gender Studies, and was one of the founders of the Fantasia Fair in 1975.* **MAXINE MILLER** *is an archivist who creates audio and photographic documentation of the Fantasia Fair event every year.*

SKY RENFRO, *of Cree heritage, living in San Francisco.*

"My identity, like everything else in my life, is a journey. It is a process and an adventure that in some ways is bringing me back to myself, back into the grand circle of living. I believe that my life as a two-legged is the same as all other life here, that is, circular. My sense of who I am at any given time is somewhere on that wheel and the place that I occupy there can change depending on the season and life events as well as a number of other influences.

"Trying to envision masculine at one end of a line and feminine on the other, with the rest of us somewhere on that line is a difficult concept for me to grasp. Male and female – they're so close to each other, they sit right next to each other on that wheel. They are not at opposite ends as far as I can tell. In fact, they are so close that they're sometimes not distinguishable.

"I have been able to give my daughter the gift of understanding that what she sees may not be what is under the wrappings. I don't know if I would have been able to do that without walking this path myself.

"I believe that if all of us weren't so afraid of saying, 'Yes, I'm a man, and I also knit,' if we weren't so terrified of what the repercussions would be – we would find out that we are all a little gender variant."

This is a third of a self-portrait triptych by photographer **LOREN CAMERON**. Loren moved to San Francisco in 1979 and participated in the Bay Area's lesbian community for nine years. He began his transition from female to male in 1987. Largely self-taught as a photographer, his exhibition "Our Vision, Our Voices: Transsexual Portraits and Nudes" – from which several photos are included in this book – was Cameron's first body of photographic work. Since then his work has been widely viewed and has received rave reviews. He is currently pursuing other photographic projects dealing with transsexuality.

STORMÉ DELARVERIÉ *joined the Jewel Box Review in 1955 as a male impersonator. Stormé and 25 female impersonators – Black, Asian, Native, and Latina – performed in theaters from Mexico to Canada, in cities large and small, and toured the segregated south during the fifties and early sixties.*

Would you prefer people refer to you as he or she?

I tell people, "Use whatever makes you comfortable."

A sad song doesn't care whose heart it breaks. But there's no use in singing any sad song. [At age fifteen] I got beaten up badly by two gangs – twice. My grandfather told me if I didn't stop running, I'd be running all my life. I stopped running, and I haven't run a day since. I got scars all over my body. My body is 40 miles of bad road. Some of it wasn't at work; it was on the street – like helping some elderly person getting attacked; you can't walk past that. I grew up in the Bayou, and you know we swamp fighters are a lot different than street fighters. I'm like a gator . . . quicker, faster, and unpredictable.

It really doesn't matter whether you're male, female, gay, straight – whatever you want your identity to be – no one has the right to try to take your life or to beat you down for it. They do not have the right. It started with that Stonewall. They call it a riot, a rebellion – it was civil disobedience. They were banged and bruised and some were put in jail. But everybody got tired of being pushed around, of being raided. The cops got the surprise of their lives – those queens were not going to take it any longer. I walked into it. I was coming around the corner and got hit right dead in the eye. I got in a few hot licks against the cops.

I have no regrets. If I did, I wouldn't have lived this long.

Transsexual lesbian performance artist **KATE BORNSTEIN.**

"*My ancestors were performers. In life. The earliest shamanic rituals involved women and men exchanging genders. Old, old rituals. Top-notch performances. Life and death stuff. We're talking cross-cultural here. We're talking rising way way way above being a man or a woman. That's how my ancestors would talk with the goddesses and the gods. Old rituals.*

"*I'd been a performer of one sort or another for over twenty-five years, and now I'm writing plays as well as performing in them. See, I had never seen my story on stage and I was looking. I used to go up to writers I knew. I used to wish they'd write my story. And I'm only just now realizing that they couldn't possibly. . . .*

"*Anyway, I work in theater because I really enjoy working with people, and theater is not an alone art. And current theatrical forms reflect a rigidly bi-polar gender system. They aren't fluid enough for what I want to say, and I feel that form and content in theater as in life should be complementary, not adversarial, so I work on my own gender fluidity and sometimes it works and sometimes it doesn't. And I work on the fluidity of my theatrical style – and sometimes it works and sometimes it doesn't. My life and my theater – my form and my content – sort of do as I say and do as I do. Like my ancestors.*"

(From *Gender Outlaw* by Kate Bornstein, published by Routledge, 1994.)

Below, left to right: **JACOB, MIKEL-JON CARTER, BET POWER**
from the East Coast Female-to-Male Group.

BET POWER: *I started the East Coast Female-to-Male Group (see*
Appendix B) in early 1992 after the death of Lou Sullivan to fill
the tremendous gap in support left me by his loss and to help end
the isolation of FTM's in the eastern states. My first contact with
Lou was in 1986 when he sent his ground-breaking "Information
for the Female-to-Male Crossdresser and Transsexual" to the New
Alexandria Lesbian Library (NALL). Since 1977, I had housed
and directed this national collection, which began in Chicago in
1974 and which I moved to Massachusetts in 1979. Lou thought
that some individuals who visited the collection might want to
read his booklet. Little did he know that the curator who opened
the mail and received his contribution was an FTM. I immedi-
ately flew out West to meet him and we started up a friendship.

On January 1, 1992, I changed the name of NALL to the Sex-
ual Minorities Archives (see Appendix B), reconceptualizing it for
inclusion of materials about all sexual minorities without excep-
tion and with absolutely no censorship – from politics to pornogra-
phy. In particular, we are currently collecting on the
transgendered, sadomasochists, bisexuals, and gay males to aug-
ment the vast lesbian holdings. My dream for the Archives is for it
to be a powerful place of unity where the words and lives of all
queers reside equally, side by side.

SHARON ANN STUART, *a Missouri native, is a bigendered person.*
Sharon, a founding director of the International Conference on
Transgender Law and Employment Policy (ICTLEP) is a spe-
cialist in transgender issues for military personnel and one of
several principal drafters of the International Bill of Gender
Rights (see Appendix A).

"As a bigendered person I present both masculine and femi-
nine identities alternately with equal comfort. I value and
honor both gender roles and spend roughly equal time in each. It
is analogous to being bilingual. To me, gender expression is very
similar to language. For example, some thoughts and feelings
are best expressed in one language as opposed to another. If you
learn English (masculine) as your native language and French
(feminine) as a second language, you will likely speak French
with an accent. Indeed, those who are transgendered typically
retain elements of their native gender identity. Strictly speaking,
no one can be 'all man' or 'all woman.' As a young child, I
acquired the ability to express femininity as well as masculinity.
I regard this as a gift from God."

AVIS PENDAVIS, *mother of the House of Pendavis, and friends outside a drag ball in Harlem. Avis appeared in "Paris Is Burning," a documentary by Jennie Livingston that opened a window for mainstream audiences to see the vast drag network in Harlem that had been rendered invisible for decades.*

Drag balls are part of Harlem's history. The annual Hamilton Lodge Ball, for example – the largest and most famous – dated back to 1869. The majority of the drag queens and kings who attended were working class. As its popularity soared, about 800 guests partied at the 1925 ball and 1,500 in 1926. Attendance peaked at 8,000 in 1937. But a concerted campaign of raids and harassment by the New York City police during the 1930s drove Harlem's drag culture underground.

"**LAURA**, *her husband* **APRIL** *(aka Don), her mother* **EMMA**, *and son* **ARTHUR** *at home in Long Island, New York, in 1994. April's family, friends, neighbors, and co-workers know Don as April and as Don. Even as Don, the never-changing long fingernails and earrings let people know of his transgendered nature.*"

(Mariette Pathy Allen, the photographer who took this picture.)

Right: **KRIS**, *with* **DEBBIE** *in her arms.*

KRIS*: Here in the South, I have trouble passing for female even when I try. Everywhere I hear "Can I help you sir?", "Thank you sir." At first I found it startling. I would correct people with, "that's ma'am." After countless self-conscious and humiliating moments, I do not correct anymore.*

Does the fact that everywhere I go everyone calls me "sir" make me a man? Does the fact that I have breasts and a cunt make me a woman? I have had to think long and hard about the many aspects of gender: social gender, genital gender, emotional gender. Genitally, I am female. But I also have broad shoulders, big hands, a thick frame, and a masculine face. I work in the trades, and I take up space with my movements like men do. In ages past, one's gender was defined greatly by the clothes one wore. If that is the case, then I am most certainly a man. With my girlfriend I am *male and female. I think I am truest with her. She loves me for all the above and more.*

Male, ambiguous, female, male and female. Those are the categories available but they are not adequate to describe who I am. So I have decided that my gender is in the eye of the beholder. I let people place me in whatever gender box that they need to. I know that I am somewhere in between, belonging to a transgender community that is just now beginning to define itself.

From left to right: FRAN, HANNAH, and DAVINA. *Davina Anne Gabriel is the publisher and editor of* TransSisters, *a magazine of transsexual feminism. Davina started the magazine because:* "Transsexual women need feminism as much as do non-transsexual women, probably even more so. Many transsexual women feel that if they can only obtain surgery, then they will have achieved complete liberation to be their true selves. But it is not only the feeling of being 'trapped in the wrong bodies' that imprisons us, it is the patriarchal conditioning we receive and internalize as a result of being born and raised in a patriarchal society. If we only liberate our bodies, we've only half-way liberated ourselves. Liberating our minds is the next step in our liberation process, and only when we do that do we achieve full liberation and selfhood. One of the reasons that I started* TransSisters *was to help us to achieve that."*

Renewing vows of love.

DAN *(Linda), a female-to-male cross-dresser, with* YVONNE, *a male-to-female transgenderist. Love is a many gendered thing.*

Transsexual activist **NANCY NANGERONI**
at Stonewall 25:

"It's time to root out the imposition of gendered
behavior stereotypes from all aspects of our lives.
Ending gender oppression means encouraging
our children to experiment with alternative gender expressions; ending the segregation of boys
from girls; encouraging kids to choose their own
clothes, hairstyles, interests – in short, their own
gender – and supporting their choices.

"We can create a culture where diversity
causes not fear, but pleasure; where men and
women find each other not opaque and threatening, but reasonable and accommodating; where
partnerships yield not disappointment, but ful-
fillment. When our culture no longer imposes
gendered expectations, men will open themselves
up to life's delicate beauty, and women will live
in greater confidence and security.

"It is not gender which causes problems;
rather, it is the imposition of a gender on an individual by another. When the imposition is
removed, polarity of masculine and feminine may
remain, but as personal preference rather than
imposed imperative. Penises, breasts, and vaginas will once again become body parts rather
than regulators of behavior and identity.

"And we'll all breathe a little easier."

in an uninterrupted state of change and development. Time is a measurement of that process. So are revisions.

I originally subtitled this book *Making History from Joan of Arc to RuPaul* in order to breathe recognizable meaning into the word *transgender,* and to convey the sweep of time and cultures in my work. But that was before Dennis Rodman, the greatest rebounder in basketball history, proudly came out as a cross-dresser—and before millions of people of every age and nationality hailed a cross-dressed Dennis Rodman with love and respect.

Many, many thousands—possibly millions—of people of every sexuality in this country cross-dress some of the time or all of the time. Yet fear of violence, humiliation, and harassment has largely driven this self-expression underground. The rise of the transgender liberation movement has opened up space for people like Rodman to emerge as they truly are. In turn, Rodman's bold assertion can only empower others.

Some sports writers immediately accused Rodman of a publicity stunt, comparable to the public cross-dressing of bigot Howard Stern at his book signings. Stern may or may not be a cross-dresser in private. But his public stance—like the burlesque drag acts by upper-class white men in the elite Bohemian Grove Club—is mocking and cruel. Dennis Rodman, already a target of racism, ire, and innuendo, had nothing to gain by coming out as a cross-dresser. He's open about the fact that his gender expression dates back to childhood. He wrote in his bestseller *Bad as I Wanna Be:* "As a kid I would sometimes dress as a girl. You play house, you play doctor—everybody does that, but some people like it more than others. I used to go through the whole routine—dress up, wear makeup, act like a girl."

Reaction from right-wingers ranged from barely concealed baiting to out-and-out foaming at the mouth. Some fumed in the press that Rodman's transgender expression was a "distraction." But while they railed against him in the press boxes, Dennis Rodman played brilliant bare-knuckle ball on the court. His self-expression didn't distract the Chicago Bulls from winning the 1996 NBA championship.

Bulls Coach Phil Jackson remarked to the media that Rodman "reached a heart space with other members of the team I'd never anticipated. Dennis has been a real blessing for us, because he's like a *heyoka*." Jackson explained that among the Lakota people a *heyoka* "was a cross-dresser, a unique person . . . respected because he brought a reality change when you saw him."

When I read Jackson's statement, I wanted to put this book in his hands. And I wanted Rodman to have a copy, as well. *Transgender Warriors* puts Dennis Rodman into the context of a history of transgender people who have helped alter the course of humanity. This book answers the bigoted charges that Dennis Rodman's self-expression—as well as my own—is "not natural." And this book reveals why Rodman, or anyone who is transgender, is a target of reaction.

"It seems that people feel threatened when an athlete does something that is not considered manly," Rodman wrote in his biography. "It's like they've crossed over some imaginary line that nobody thinks should be crossed." I wanted Dennis Rodman to have the information you have just read in *Transgender Warriors* because it reveals when that line was drawn, by whom, and why.

I was *determined* to get copies of this book to Rodman and Jackson. While the media treated Rodman's role in the NBA playoffs like a joke, a vicious attack against his human right to freedom of gender expression was under way. But fans—young and old—tried to express their support for Rodman's self-expression in a society that did not provide any dignified language for such a defense.

I knew that copies of this book, if I had mailed them, would have ended up on a mountain of Bulls' fan letters. So I took the same approach to the task that I apply to my book touring as a whole: I turned to my audiences and asked for their help. I was lucky enough to be in Chicago during the NBA playoffs. During radio interviews and bookstore readings, I talked to audiences about how important it was to defend Dennis Rodman's courage. I asked for their help in getting *Transgender Warriors* into the Bulls' locker room. Sure enough, a serious offer to get the books to Rodman and Jackson materialized.

I don't know if Rodman or Jackson personally received the copies I sent through a system of sympathetic couriers. But my own impassioned defense of Dennis Rodman to audiences, and the individual responses I received to my appeal for their help, illustrate what I love about book signings and speaking tours.

I love getting out on the road. I don't enjoy the musty smell of tobacco in motel rooms guaranteed by the desk clerk to be nonsmoking rooms or the mad races by cab during morning rush hour to an airport. What I love about travel is the people I meet. They teach me about their struggles, and I share mine with them. I've met extraordinary people and received wonderful letters and e-mail. I've been enriched by meeting or corresponding with thousands of trans people from the U.S. and around the world. Others have shared tearfully emotional stories with me about how the complex child or adolescent they once were had been straitjacketed into conformity, and how they miss that person they had wanted to become.

I've received painful letters about the suicide of a masculine woman lover or a feminine brother—grief articulated by those who love them but did not have the words or concepts to defend them. Many have expressed to me how they relate to the struggle for trans liberation because of the discrimination, oppression, belittling, harassment, and humiliation they endured because of their "difference."

I bring all of what I've learned back to my own writing and organizing. My writing is an extension of my activism and helps to develop my commitment to win real change: I'm a person who is part of a historical movement for liberation. I have heartfelt political beliefs born of my life's experience. I am a grass-roots organizer. I stand with everyone I meet in my travels—at every reading, every event, every interaction—who is ready to struggle for change. Together, we are shaping a society that does not yet exist.

After years of travel and discussions on picket lines, at rallies, and at protest marches, I have discovered that I share a profound common cause with people whose oppression is not identical in any way to my own. We are inextricably bound by our deep desire and commitment to win genuine justice and equality.

That's the truth I hope you discovered in these pages. From the hate-filled comments about Dennis Rodman to the murder of a young transgender person in Nebraska whose name you never heard before, your own humanity is under siege and diminished. Whether you are facing layoffs or are one paycheck away from homelessness, whether you are battling bureaucracy to get health care or child care, whether you are confronting racism or anti-Semitism, whether you are standing up for your rights as a woman, defending your sexuality from attack, or fighting as a disabled activist for accessibility—your struggle is tightly bound with ours.

You may have cracked open this book expecting to learn about people you thought you knew nothing about. Yet I hope you realized that we have always been in your life. You may have recognized an old lover, a coworker, or an aunt or uncle that family members whisper about at weddings and funerals.

Or you may have seen yourself mirrored in these pages. And whether or not you identify as a transgender or transsexual or intersexual, you have a stake in our struggle. My right to define and express myself is connected with a thousand threads to your own right to define and express yourself.

I wrote this book for you, and I wrote this book for me. I am so relieved that you are holding this book in your hands. As I reflect today, on my 47th birthday, I realize I have felt driven for most of my adult life to write it. It's a wondrous feeling to have completed such a compelling life task. For so many years I dreamt that the moment the book arrived from the printers I would pack up armfuls and bring them from town to town.

But I have learned an important life lesson in this last year about the frailty of my life and my own physical strength. As I was finishing this manuscript, I fell ill with a catastrophic series of tenacious viral and bacterial infections. At this writing, I am at home tethered to an IV pole from which gravity sucks antibiotics down a tube and into my bloodstream one drop at a time. My battle to regain my health was impeded early on by two obstacles—bigotry and poverty. Like some forty million documented workers in this country, and many millions more undocumented workers, I had no health insurance.

As my temperature spiked dangerously high, I bundled up and traveled through sleet and snowstorms to clinics and hospital emergency rooms. I experienced raw hatred from some health care professionals who refused to care for me solely because I am a masculine female. When I heard doctors and nurses refer to me as a "Martian" or as "It" I was reminded of some hospital staff during the early years of the AIDS epidemic who left food trays on the floor outside my ill friends' rooms. While delirious with fever, I learned once again that my human right to be treated with dignity and respect and caring had to be fought for. Transgender warriors are battling to win health care as a right, not a privilege. That fight has to be waged on two fronts: a struggle to bring affordable health care to all, and a struggle against rampant discrimination.

As you are reading this page, I might still be very ill. Perhaps I was not able to travel to your small town or big city to read to you from this book and to discover more about all that connects us. It is my loss. But I send this book to you.

I am not physically strong enough as a human being—even when healthy—to put *Transgender Warriors* in the hands of each person I want to read it. But I have confidence in *you* as an organizer. If, as you read this book, its ideas resonate as truth, then I know that you will pass it on to a friend, a family member, a coworker, or a neighbor. I am one of many trans voices that are shattering the silence of centuries. We are the harbinger of a mass movement that demands fundamental change.

Transgender Warriors is my voice, my contribution to that movement. This is the work I could produce with my individual strength. I am heartened by my belief that you will lift my work to new heights.

September 1, 1996

Dennis Rodman appeared at a New York City bookstore in
August 1996 to sign copies of his autobiography.

APPENDIX A

International
Bill of Gender Rights

AS ADOPTED JUNE 17, 1995

THE RESTATEMENT OF

the International Bill of Gender Rights (IBGR) was first drafted in
committee and adopted by the International Conference on Transgender Law and Employment Policy, Inc. (ICTLEP) at that organization's
second annual meeting, held in Houston, Texas, August 26–29,
1993.

The IBGR combines and expands from two earlier documents
authored separately by Jo Ann Roberts of Pennsylvania and Sharon
Stuart of New York.

The IBGR strives to express fundamental human and civil rights
from a gender perspective. However, the ten rights enunciated below are
not to be viewed as special rights applicable to a particular interest
group. Nor are these rights limited in application to persons for whom
gender identity and role issues are of paramount concern. All ten parts
of the IBGR are universal rights which can be claimed and exercised by
every human being.

The IBGR is a theoretical expression which has no force of law
absent its adoption by legislative bodies and recognition of its principles
by courts of law, administrative agencies and international bodies such
as the United Nations.

However, individuals are free to adopt the truths and principles
expressed in the IBGR, and to lead their lives accordingly. In this fashion, the truths expressed in the IBGR will liberate and empower
humankind in ways and to an extent beyond the reach of legislators,
judges, officials and diplomats.

When the truths expressed in the IBGR are embraced and given
expression by humankind, the acts of legislatures and pronouncements
of courts and other governing structures will necessarily follow. Thus,
the paths of free expression trodden by millions of human beings seeking
to define and express themselves, and give meaning to their lives, will

ultimately determine the course of governing bodies.

The IBGR is a transformative and revolutionary document, but it is grounded in the bedrock of individual liberty and free expression. As our lives unfold, these kernels of truth are here for all who would claim and exercise them.

This document, though copyrighted, may be reproduced by any means and freely distributed by anyone supporting the principles and statements contained in the International Bill of Gender Rights.

The IBGR remains subject to review and revision by ICTLEP. Proposed revisions to the IBGR and comments should be forwarded to Sharon Stuart, International Bill of Gender Rights Project, P.O. Box 930, Cooperstown, NY 13326, U.S.A. Telephone: (607) 547-4118. E-mail: StuComOne@aol.com

THE RIGHT TO DEFINE GENDER IDENTITY

All human beings carry within themselves an ever-unfolding idea of who they are and what they are capable of achieving. The individual's sense of self is not determined by chromosomal sex, genitalia, assigned birth sex, or initial gender role. Thus, the individual's identity and capabilities cannot be circumscribed by what society deems to be masculine or feminine behavior. It is fundamental that individuals have the right to define, and to redefine as their lives unfold, their own gender identities, without regard to chromosomal sex, genitalia, assigned birth sex, or initial gender role.

Therefore, all human beings have the right to define their own gender identity regardless of chromosomal sex, genitalia, assigned birth sex, or initial gender role; and further, no individual shall be denied Human or Civil Rights by virtue of a self-defined gender identity which is not in accord with chromosomal sex, genitalia, assigned birth sex, or initial gender role.

THE RIGHT TO FREE EXPRESSION OF GENDER IDENTITY

Given the right to define one's own gender identity, all human beings have the corresponding right to free expression of their self-defined gender identity.

Therefore, all human beings have the right to free expression of their self-defined gender identity; and further, no individual shall be denied Human or Civil Rights by virtue of the expression of a self-defined gender identity.

THE RIGHT TO SECURE AND RETAIN EMPLOYMENT
AND TO RECEIVE JUST COMPENSATION

Given the economic structure of modern society, all human beings have a right to train for and to pursue an occupation or profession as a means of providing shelter, sustenance, and the necessities and bounty of life, for themselves and for those dependent upon them, to secure and retain employment, and to receive just compensation for their labor regardless of gender identity, chromosomal sex, genitalia, assigned birth sex, or initial gender role.

Therefore, individuals shall not be denied the right to train for and to pursue an occupation or profession, nor be denied the right to secure and retain employment, nor be denied just compensation for their labor, by virtue of their chromosomal sex, genitalia, assigned birth sex, or initial gender role, or on the basis of a self-defined gender identity or the expression thereof.

THE RIGHT OF ACCESS TO GENDERED SPACE AND PARTICIPATION IN GENDERED ACTIVITY

Given the right to define one's own gender identity and the corresponding right to free expression of a self-defined gender identity, no individual should be denied access to a space or denied participation in an activity by virtue of a self-defined gender identity which is not in accord with chromosomal sex, genitalia, assigned birth sex, or initial gender role.

Therefore, no individual shall be denied access to a space or denied participation in an activity by virtue of a self-defined gender identity which is not in accord with chromosomal sex, genitalia, assigned birth sex, or initial gender role.

THE RIGHT TO CONTROL AND CHANGE ONE'S OWN BODY

All human beings have the right to control their bodies, which includes the right to change their bodies cosmetically, chemically, or surgically, so as to express a self-defined gender identity.

Therefore, individuals shall not be denied the right to change their bodies as a means of expressing a self-defined gender identity; and further, individuals shall not be denied Human or Civil Rights on the basis that they have changed their bodies cosmetically, chemically, or surgically, or desire to do so as a means of expressing a self-defined gender identity.

THE RIGHT TO COMPETENT MEDICAL AND PROFESSIONAL CARE

Given the individual's right to one's own gender identity, and the right to change one's own body as a means of expressing a self-defined gender identity, no individual should be denied access to competent medical or other professional care on the basis of the individual's chromosomal sex, genitalia, assigned birth sex, or initial gender role.

Therefore, individuals shall not be denied the right to competent medical or other professional care when changing their bodies cosmetically, chemically, or surgically, on the basis of chromosomal sex, genitalia, assigned birth sex, or initial gender role.

THE RIGHT TO FREEDOM FROM PSYCHIATRIC DIAGNOSIS OR TREATMENT

Given the right to define one's own gender identity, individuals should not be subject to psychiatric diagnosis or treatment solely on the basis of their gender identity or role.

Therefore, individuals shall not be subject to psychiatric diagnosis or treatment as mentally disordered or diseased solely on the basis of a self-defined gender identity or the expression thereof.

THE RIGHT TO SEXUAL EXPRESSION

Given the right to a self-defined gender identity, every consenting adult has a corresponding right to free sexual expression.

Therefore, no individual's Human or Civil Rights shall be denied on the basis of sexual orientation; and further, no individual shall be denied Human or Civil Rights for expression of a self-defined gender identity through sexual acts between consenting adults.

THE RIGHT TO FORM COMMITTED, LOVING RELATIONSHIPS AND ENTER INTO MARITAL CONTRACTS

Given that all human beings have the right to free expression of self-defined gender identities, and the right to sexual expression as a form of gender expression, all human beings have a corresponding right to form committed, loving relationships with one another, and to enter into marital contracts, regardless of their own or their partner's chromosomal sex, genitalia, assigned birth sex, or initial gender role.

Therefore, individuals shall not be denied the right to form committed, loving relationships with one another or to enter into marital contracts by virtue of their own or their partner's chromosomal sex, genitalia, assigned birth sex, or initial gender role, or on the basis of their expression of a self-defined gender identity.

THE RIGHT TO CONCEIVE, BEAR, OR ADOPT CHILDREN
THE RIGHT TO NURTURE AND HAVE CUSTODY OF CHILDREN AND TO EXERCISE PARENTAL CAPACITY

Given the right to form a committed, loving relationship with another, and to enter into marital contracts, together with the right to express a self-defined gender identity and the right to sexual expression, individuals have a corresponding right to conceive and bear children, to adopt children, to nurture children, to have custody of children, and to exercise parental capacity with respect to children, natural or adopted, without regard to chromosomal sex, genitalia, assigned birth sex, or initial gender role, or by virtue of a self-defined gender identity or the expression thereof.

Therefore, individuals shall not be denied the right to conceive, bear, or adopt children, nor to nurture and have custody of children, nor to exercise parental capacity with respect to children, natural or adopted, on the basis of their own, their partner's, or their children's chromosomal sex, genitalia, assigned birth sex, or initial gender role, or by virtue of a self-defined gender identity or the expression thereof.

Selected Transgender
Organizations

AMERICAN EDUCATIONAL GENDER INFORMATION SERVICE:

Professionally managed support group and national nonprofit clearinghouse for information about gender dysphoria. Referrals to professionals and support groups, and to
individuals, following the Standards of Care; case management; consulting; speakers' service. Publishes *Chrysalis
Quarterly*, transition booklets, bibliographies, J2CP, Janus,
and Erickson Foundation materials.
AEGIS, Box 33724, Decatur, GA 30033-0724.
Tel: 404-939-2128, Help line: 404-939-0244,
Fax: 404-939-1770

THE EAST COAST FEMALE-TO-MALE GROUP:

A peer support network for female-to-male transvestites,
transsexuals, and their partners. Founded in 1992 by Bet
Power, group meets monthly in Northampton, Massachusetts, and draws individuals from throughout New England.
Sunday get-togethers typically include a topic discussion,
video showings, and a potluck dinner or outing to a local
restaurant. Meetings are held in Mr. Power's home, which
also houses the Sexual Minority Archives. ECFTMG meetings and events are open exclusively to FTM's and their
partners. For more information and the group's mailings,
write to: ECFTMG, Box 60585, Florence Station,
Northampton, MA 01060.

EDUCATIONAL TV CHANNEL:

A delightful group of TV's, TS's, SO's, and friends. It is intended as a social, educational group, to meet and to have a good time as well as educate the public. ETVC has an open membership policy with over 400 members and provides a full program of educational and social activities and referrals. ETVC, Box 423602, San Francisco, CA 94142-6486. Hotline: 510-549-2665, Voice-mail: 413-334-3439

FTM INTERNATIONAL:

Monthly support group exclusively for female-to-male cross-dressers, TS's, and their significant others. Publishes quarterly FTM newsletter, FTM Resource Guide. FTM, 5337 College Avenue #142, Oakland, CA 94618

INTERNATIONAL CONFERENCE ON TRANSGENDER LAW AND EMPLOYMENT POLICY:

A nonprofit Texas corporation dedicated to providing education surrounding legal rights and employment, medical, family, and general policy for transgendered persons, and mapping strategies for solutions to problems. Annual conference in Houston each summer. ICTLEP, 5707 Firenza St., Houston, TX 77035-5515. Tel: 713-723-8368

INTERNATIONAL FOUNDATION FOR GENDER EDUCATION:

Educational and service organization designed to serve as an effective communications medium, outreach device, and networking facility for the entire TV/TS community and those affected by that community. Publisher of materials relevant to the TV/TS theme. Sponsors the annual "Coming Together" convention. An international information and referral clearinghouse, speakers' bureau, "drop-in bookstore" for emergency peer counseling, and on-going volunteer work. IFGE., Box 229, Waltham, MA 02154-0229. Tel: 617-894-8340, Fax: 617-899-5703

THE INTERSEX SOCIETY OF NORTH AMERICA:

A peer support, education, and advocacy group founded and operated by and for intersexuals. We who are intersexual are queer because we are born with bodies that defy the cultural notions of male and female. We are also frequently lesbian, gay, and transgendered. ISNA recommends a new paradigm for the management of intersexual children. Our model is based upon avoidance of harmful or unnecessary surgery, qualified professional mental health care for the intersexual child and his/her family, and empowering the intersexual to understand his/her own status and to choose (or reject) any medical intervention

ISNA, Box 31791, San Francisco, CA 94131.

Internet: info@isna.org

METROPOLITAN GENDER NETWORK:

Support, advocacy, and educational group open to all segments of the gender community. Friends and guests welcome. Monthly meetings on the second Sunday, social events, lending library, resource directory, referrals. Brief meeting registration form is sent in response to new inquiries.

MGN, 561 Hudson Street, Box 45, NY, NY 10014.

Tel: 201-794-1665, ext. 332, 718-461-9050

MID-AMERICA GENDER GROUP INFORMATION EXCHANGE:

Coalition of five mid-American gender associations: St. Louis Gender Foundation, Kansas City Cross-dressers and Friends, Iowa Artistry, Wichita Transgender Alliance, and Omaha River City Gender Alliance.

MAGGIE, c/o Jennifer Richards, St. Louis Gender Foundation, Box 9433, St. Louis, MO 63117

MINNESOTA FREEDOM OF GENDER EXPRESSION:

An open service and peer support group for transgendered persons, their significant others, and interested persons.

Services listing for members. Interview required. Newsletter bimonthly.

MFGE, Box 17945, St. Paul, MN 55117. Tel: 612-220-9027

OUTREACH INSTITUTE OF GENDER STUDIES:

Conferences and workshops on gender issues, Gender Attitude Reassessment Program for health care professionals, clinical supervision for sex educators and counselors, Fantasia Fair, speakers' bureau for meetings and conferences, seminars for couples. Publishes *Journal of Gender Studies*, information packets, publications, annotated catalogue.

Outreach Institute, 126 Western Ave., Ste. 246, Augusta, ME 04330. Tel: 207-621-0858

RENAISSANCE EDUCATION ASSOCIATION:

Open group that accepts and helps individuals to grow at their own pace. Monthly meetings with educational programs, Significant Other Support Group, TS Support Group, TV rap groups, and community activities. Speakers' bureau for college, university, radio, and television appearances anywhere in the United States.

Renaissance, Box 60552, King of Prussia, PA 19406. Tel: 610-630-1437 (24 hrs.)

SOCIETY FOR THE SECOND SELF:

Tri-Ess is a nonprofit organization exclusively for heterosexual cross-dressers and their significant others. Tri-Ess provides a correspondence directory, a directory of commercial services, and chapters throughout the United States. Membership and attendance at a local chapter meeting requires an interview with the chapter president or older member to ensure that the applicant is heterosexual, and complies with Tri-Ess code of conduct.

Tri-Ess, c/o Carol Beecroft, Box 194, Tulare CA 93275. Tel: 209-688-9246

TGR! TRANSGENDER RIGHTS!:

A nonprofit advocacy organization defending the human
rights of all transgendered persons. We believe that by supporting the rights of transgendered persons to live freely
and without discrimination, we are benefitting all people,
transgendered and non-transgendered.
TGR! Share Center, Box 892, NY, NY 10009.
Tel: 212–979-8547

THE TRANSSEXUAL MENACE:

A network of transgender activists spanning the country,
working to oppose gender oppression for all people.
The Transsexual Menace, c/o Riki Anne Wilchins, 274 W.
11th St., #4R, NY, NY 10014.

Selected Transgender Publications

The American Boyz
Mailing list for people who were assigned female gender at birth but feel that is not an accurate or adequate description, or do not correspond to the usual expectations of that gender. Transsexual men, f2ms, butch women, boychicks, boss girls, intersexuals (hermaphrodites), and any other gender variant people welcome. Friends, families, significant others, helping professionals, activists and any supportive people are welcome on equal terms. For more info contact: f2m-admin@tantalus.clark.net and ask for the "Welcome & Info article." Or snail mail at American Boyz, Box 1118, Elkton, MD 21922-1118

Chrysalis Quarterly, The Journal of Transgender Issues
The official publication of the American Educational Gender Information Service, Inc. For both consumers and care givers. Theme-related issues explore topics in depth.
AEGIS, Box 33724, Decatur, GA 30033

Cross-Talk
Monthly news, information, commentary, advice columns, national event and hotline listings, make-up and fashion tips, reader letters, humor and more, for cross-dressers and transsexuals, written and published by members of the community.
Box 944, Woodland Hills, CA 91365. Tel: 818-907-3053

FTM International Newsletter
The most widely-circulated newsletter for the female-to-male transgendered. Contains features, photos, reviews,

letters, advice, and networking – all of interest to the female-to-male cross dresser, transsexual, and transgendered. Published quarterly since 1987.

FTM, 5337 College Avenue #142, Oakland, CA 94618

FTM International Website

Information on transitioning, news stories, event listings, personal stories, resources, and more. We are happy to receive articles, event notices, poems, graphics, etc., from or about all ranges of FTMs, to put up on the site.

– The Website can be accessed by any web browser at http://www.ftm-intl.org/

– For people who have net access, but not web access, text files of the site can be obtained by ftp at ftp.yak.net/pub/ftm

– Jamie Walker, self-described "website administrator, coder, and resident arttechnofag," can be reached by e-mail at jamieray@ftm-intl.org

Gendertrash

Devoted to the issues and concerns of transsexuals. Published three to four times a year, it gives a voice to gender described people, who have been discouraged from speaking out and communicating with each other.

Box #500-62, 552 Church St., Toronto, Ontario, Canada M4Y 2E3. Tel: 416-929-2350

Hermaphrodites with Attitude

Published quarterly by the Intersex Society of North America. HWA contains articles about ISNA activities and other news of interest to intersexuals, personal accounts by ISNA members, and guest columns from friends of our community. HWA provides us with a safe space to explore and assert our intersexual identities. Subscription available to all, $12 for four issues ($18 overseas).

Intersex Society of North America, Box 31791, San Francisco, CA 94131. Internet: info@isna.org. Checks and money orders should be made payable to "ISNA."

In Your Face, The Journal of Political Activism Against
Gender Oppression
A complete listing of all subversive trans actions around
the country, with instructions on how to roll your own.
Circulated free of charge as insert to other publications.
c/o Riki Anne Wilchins, 274 W. 11th St., #4R , NY, NY 10014.
Tel: 212-645-1753, Internet: riki@pipeline.com

Journal of Gender Studies
The official publication of the Human Outreach and Achieve-
ment Institute, published twice a year.
Outreach Institute, 405 Western Avenue, Suite 345;
South Portland, ME 04106

Transsexual News Telegraph, The Magazine of
Transsexual Culture
By and for transsexuals, with extensive coverage of issues per-
sonal and political.
TNT, 41 Sutter St., #1124, San Francisco, CA 94104-4903. Tel:
415-703-7161, Internet: gailtnt@aol.com

TransSisters, The Journal of Transsexual Feminism
Nonprofit quarterly magazine on issues of transsexuality from
a feminist perspective. Designed to promote dialog between
the TS and feminist communities and to foster feminist consciousness within the TS community.
c/o Davina Anne Gabriel, 4004 Troost Ave., Kansas City, MO
64110

TV/TS Tapestry Journal
The International Foundation for Gender Education's primary publication and a leading voice in the transgender community. IFGE also publishes and markets a wide variety of
how-to books, presentation transcripts, anthologies of perti-
nent reprints, directories, and other timely material.
IFGE, Box 367, Wayland, MA 01778.
Tel: 617-899-2212, Fax: 617-899-5703

CHAPTER **2.** MY PATH TO CONSCIOUSNESS

1. Richard O. Boyer and Herbert M. Morais, *Labor's Untold Story* (New York: United Electrical, Radio & Machine Workers of America, 1955), 189–91.

2. When asked to describe Workers World Party, leading member and managing newspaper editor Deirdre Griswold wrote: "Workers come in all sizes, colors, shapes, and genders. Unfortunately, there are stereotyped views of what a working-class party is like – most of them fostered by the anti-Communist propaganda of the right wing. Defying stereotypes, **WWP** uses the methods of scientific socialism to chart a course in the modern world toward a society free of class, national, sex, and gender oppression. The WWP strongly believes in militant activism inspired by a Marxist view of history. Humanity can resolve the deadly conflicts of today, says WWP, but only through world socialist revolution and building a society where the wealth produced by working people is shared by all." For more information, phone 212-627-2994, fax 212-675-7869, or telex 6503925801.

3. Frederick Engels, *The Origin of the Family, Private Property and the State*, ed. Eleanor Burke Leacock (New York: International Publishers, 1972).

4. Dorothy Ballan, *Feminism and Marxism* (New York: World View Publishers, 1971).

5. *Workers World* weekly newspaper, 55 West 17 Street, New York, NY 10011; Internet: editor@wwpublish.com. Mention *Transgender Warriors* for a $10 one-year subscription – half the newsstand price. Selected articles are available on the Internet. Contact ww-info@wwpublish.com.

1. Edwin Thompson Denig, *Five Indian Tribes of the Upper Missouri*, ed. John C. Ewers (Norman: University of Oklahoma Press, 1961) 199.

2. Edward Westermarck, "Homosexual Love," *The Origin and Development of Moral Ideas*, 2nd ed., 2 vols. (London: Macmillan, 1917), 2:456.

3. Pedro de Magalhães, *The Histories of Brazil*, trans. John B. Stetson, Jr. (New York: The Cortes Society, 1922) 89–90.

4. Leslie Spier, "Klamath Ethnography," *University of California Publications in American Archaeology and Ethnology* 30 (1930): 51–53.

5. Alvar Núñez Cabeza de Vaca, "Naufragios," *Historiadores primitivos de Indias,* ed. Enrique de Vedia, (Madrid: M. Rivadeneyra, 1852) 538, Vol. 1 of *Biblioteca de autores españoles,* quoted in Jonathan Katz, *Gay American History: Lesbians and Gay Men in the U.S.A.* (New York: Harper & Row, 1976) 285.

6. Jacques Marquette, *Of the First Voyage Made by Father Marquette Toward New Mexico, and How the Idea Thereof Was Conceived,* ed. Reuben Gold Thwaites (Cleveland: Burrows, 1896–1901) 129, Vol. 59 *of The Jesuit and Allied Documents,* quoted in Katz, 287.

7. Joseph François Lafitau, *Moeurs des sauvages ameriquains, comparées aux moeurs des premiers tempts,* 2 vols. (Paris: Saugrain, 1724) 1:52, 603–10, quoted in Katz, 288–89.

8. Francisco Guerra, *The Pre-Columbian Mind* (London: Seminar Press, 1971) 190, cited in Walter Williams, *The Spirit and the Flesh: Sexual Diversity in American Indian Culture* (Boston: Beacon Press, 1986) 137.

9. Cora Dubois, cited in Richard Green, "Historical and Cross-Cultural Survey," *Sexual Identity Conflict in Children and Adults* (New York: Basic Books, 1974) 11.

10. Randy Burns, "Preface," and the Gay American Indian History Project, "North American Tribes with Berdache and Alternative Gender Roles, *"Living the Spirit: A Gay American Indian Anthology,* compiled by Gay American Indians, coordinating ed. Will Roscoe (New York: St. Martin's Press, 1988) 1, see language list on 217–22.

11. Will Roscoe, *The Zuni Man-Woman* (Albuquerque: University of New Mexico Press, 1988) 5.

12. Walter Williams, *The Spirit and the Flesh: Sexual Diversity in American Indian Culture* (Boston: Beacon Press, 1986).

13. Ibid., 137.

14. Ibid., 178.

15. Ibid., 179.

16. S.C. Simms, "Crow Indian Hermaphrodites," *American Anthropologist* ns 5 (1903): 580–81.

17. C. Daryll Forde, "Ethnography of the Yuma Indians," *University of California Publications in American Archaeology and Ethnology* 28.4 (1931): 157, quoted in Williams, *Spirit and Flesh*, 38; Lakota informant as cited in Williams, 112.

18. Williams, *Spirit and Flesh*, 182.

19. Chrystos, telephone interview, 14 March 1995.

20. Ibid.

21. Wesley Thomas, e-mail communication, 5 April 1995.

22. Ibid.

23. Ibid.

24. Spotted Eagle, telephone interview, 16 March 1995.

25. Ibid.

26. Ibid.

27. Ibid.

28. Ibid.

29. Ibid.

30. Chrystos, telephone interview, 14 March 1995.

31. Ibid.

CHAPTER 4. THEY CALLED HER "HOMMASSE"

1. *The Trial of Joan of Arc: Being the verbatim report of the proceedings from the Orleans Manuscript*, trans. W. S. Scott (Westport, CT: Associated Booksellers, 1956) 31.

2. Charles Wayland Lightbody, *The Judgements of Joan: A Study in Cultural History* (Cambridge: Harvard University Press, 1961) 60.

3. Mark Twain (Samuel Clemens*), Personal Recollection of Joan of Arc by the Sieur Louis De Conte* (1896, 1899; San Francisco: Ignatius Press, 1989) 311.

4. Arthur Evans, *Witchcraft and the Gay Counterculture* (Boston: Fag Rag Books, 1978) 5–6; W. P. Barrett, trans., *The Trial of Jeanne d'Arc* (London: George Routledge & Sons, 1931) 154.

5. Sven Stolpe, *The Maid of Orleans*, trans. Eric Lewenhaupt (New York: Pantheon Books, 1956) 200.

6. Margaret Murray, *The God of the Witches* (1931; London: Oxford University Press, 1970) 177; T. Douglas Murray, ed. *Jeanne D'Arc: Being the Story of her Life, her Achievements, and her Death, as attested on Oath and Set forth in the Original Documents* (New York: McClure, Phillips & Co., 1902) 87.

7. M. Murray, *God of Witches*, 177.

8. Ibid., 178.

9. *The Trial of Joan of Arc*, 156.

10. T. D. Murray, *Jeanne D'Arc*, 87.

11. *The Trial of Joan of Arc*, 173; Marina Warner, *Joan of Arc: The Image of Female Heroism* (New York: Knopf, 1981) 140–41.

12. Warner, *Joan of Arc*, 140.

13. *The Trial of Joan of Arc*, 169.

14. Ibid., 173.

15. *A Parisian Journal: 1405–1449 (Journal d'un Bourgeois de Paris)*, trans. Janet Shirley (Oxford: The Clarendon Press, 1968) 263.

16. Evans, *Witchcraft*, 7.

17. M. Murray, *God of Witches*, 187.

CHAPTER 5. OUR SACRED PAST

1. Bob McCubbin, *The Roots of Lesbian and Gay Oppression: A Marxist View* (1976; New York: World View Publishers, 1993).

2. Plutarch, *De Iside et Osiride*, IX, cited by Robert Kellogg and Oliver Steele, eds., *The Faerie Queene: Books I and II*, by Edmund Spenser (New York: The Odyssey Press, 1965) 421, fn. 5.5-9.

3. The *gallae* transsexual priestesses, for example, are well documented. The most authoritative and insightful work on the *gallae* is by a transsexual woman historian, Margaret O'Hartigan. (See note 6 below.) For temple records, see Will Roscoe, *Queer Spirits: A Gay Men's Myth Book* (Boston: Beacon Press, 1995) 101–2, 104.

4. M. Esther Harding, *Woman's Mysteries: Ancient and Modern* (London: Longmans, Green and Co., 1955) 170.

5. Merlin Stone, *When God Was a Woman* (New York: Harcourt Brace Jovanovich, 1976) 149.

6. Margaret Deirdre O'Hartigan, "The *Gallae* of the Magna Mater," *Chrysalis Quarterly* 1:6 (1993): 11–13.

7. David Greenberg, *The Construction of Homosexuality* (Chicago: University of Chicago Press, 1988) 64.

8. Stone, *When God*, 149–50.

9. Jacquetta Hawkes and Sir Leonard Woolley, *Prehistory and the Beginnings of Civilization* (New York: Harper & Row, 1963) 264.

10. Hermann Baumann, *Das Doppelte Geschlecht: Ethnologische Studien zur Bisexualität in Ritus und Mythos* (Berlin: Dietrich Reimer, 1955), as referred to in Randy P. Conner, *Blossom of Bone: Reclaiming the Connections Between Homoeroticism and the Sacred* (San Francisco: HarperCollins, 1993) 38–39. The world maps of Baumann are reproduced as "The Diffusion of Bisexual Mythic Beings and Powers" and "The Ritualistic Permanent Sex Change" in Joseph Campbell, *The Way of the Ani-*

mal Powers (San Francisco: Harper & Row, 1983) 142, 174, vol. 1 of *Historical Atlas of World Mythology*.

11. Greenberg, *Construction of Homosexuality*, 61.

12. Ibid., 56.

13. Maria-Barbara Watson-Franke, "A Woman's Profession in Guajire Culture: Weaving," *Anthropologica* 37 (1974): 24–40, as cited in Greenberg, *Construction of Homosexuality*, 57.

14. John M. Cooper, "The Patagonian and Pampean Hunters," (1944; New York: Cooper Square Publishers, 1963) 159, vol. 1, *The Marginal Tribes*, of *Handbook of South American Indians*, ed. Julian H. Steward.

15. Pauline Park, e-mail communication, 13 June 1995.

16. Justus M. Van der Kroef, "Transvestism and the Religious Hermaphrodite in Indonesia," *Asian Homosexuality*, eds. Wayne R. Dynes and Stephen Donaldson (New York: Garland Publishing, 1992) 89–98, vol. 3 of *Studies in Homosexuality*, cited by Park, 13 June 1995.

17. Serena Nanda, *Neither Man Nor Woman: The Hijras of India* (Belmont, California: Wadsworth Publishing, 1990), cited by Park, 13 June 1995.

18. *A Handbook of Korea*, 5th ed. (Seoul: Korean Overseas Information Service, Ministry of Culture and Information, 1983) 306, cited by Park, 13 June 1995.

19. Wolfram Eberhard, *Local Cultures of South and East China* (Leiden: E. J. Brill, 1968) 306, 46.

20. William P. Lebra, *Okinawan Religion: Belief, Ritual, and Social Structure* (Honolulu: University of Hawaii Press, 1966) 69, 225.

21. Elliott M. Heiman and Cao Van Lê, "Transsexualism in Vietnam," *Archives of Sexual Behavior* 4.1 (1975): 89–95.

22. John Middleton, "Spirit Possession among the Lugbara," *Spirit Mediumship and Society in Africa*, eds. John Beattie and John Middleton (London: Routledge and Kegan Paul, 1969) 224.

23. Franz Boas, *The Eskimo of Baffin Land and Hudson Bay* (New York: American Museum of Natural History, 1901) 199, 130, as cited in Conner, *Blossom of Bone*, 28.

24. Harriet Ngubane, *Body and Mind in Zulu Medicine: An Ethnography of health and disease in Nyuswa-Zulu thought and practice* (London: Academic Press, 1977) 142.

25. Carlos Estermann, *The Ethnography of Southwestern Angola* (New York: Africana Publishing, 1976), 1: 193, 196–97.

26. Walter Williams, *The Spirit and the Flesh: Sexual Diversity in American Indian Culture* (Boston: Beacon Press, 1986), 141.

CHAPTER **6.** WHY BIGOTRY BEGAN

1. Deuteronomy 22:5.

2. Ibid., 23:1.

3. Winston Leyland, ed., *Gay Roots: An Anthology of Gay History, Sex, Politics and Culture* (San Francisco: Gay Sunshine Press, 1993) 2:72.

4. S. R. Driver, *A Critical and Exegetical Comment on Deuteronomy*, 3rd ed. (reprinted; Edinburgh: T. & T. Clark, 1951), 250–51, and L. R. Farnell, *The Cults of the Greek States* (Oxford: The Clarendon Press, 1896) 5:160–61, as cited in Vern L. Bullough and Bonnie Bullough, *Cross Dressing, Sex, and Gender* (Philadelphia: University of Pennsylvania Press, 1993) 40.

5. Bullough, *Cross Dressing*, 40.

6. Meyer Berlin and Shlomo Josef Zeuin, eds. *Encyclopedia Talmudica* (Jerusalem, 1974) 1:386–99.

7. Lewis Henry Morgan, *Ancient Society*, ed. Eleanor Burke Leacock (1877; New York: World Publishing, 1963).

8. Edward I. Margetts, "The Masculine Character of Hatshepsut, Queen of Egypt," *Bulletin of the History of Medicine 25* (1951): 559.

9. Diodorus Siculus, *History*, trans. and ed. C. H. Oldfather (London: William Heinemann, 1933) 2:21, cited in Bullough, *Cross Dressing*, 23.

CHAPTER **7.** BUT THEY HAD SLAVES!

1. Bob McCubbin, *The Roots of Lesbian & Gay Oppression: A Marxist View* (1976; World View Publishers, 1993) 20.

2. Marie Delcourt, "Transvestism in Private and Public Rites," *Hermaphrodite: Myths and Rites of the Bisexual Figure in Classical Antiquity*, trans. Jennifer Nicholson (1956; London: Studio Books, 1961) 1–16.

3. P. M. C. Forbes Irving, *Metamorphosis in Greek Myths* (Oxford: The Clarendon Press, 1990) 149.

4. Irving, *Metamorphosis*, 161.

5. Delcourt, *Hermaphrodite*, 11.

6. Irving, *Metamorphosis*, 193.

7. Pliny the Younger, *Natural History*, 6: 15, 16, 35, 36, quoted in Delcourt, *Hermaphrodite*, 44. See also Emanuel Kanter, *The Amazons: A Marxian Study* (Chicago: Charles H. Kerr & Company Cooperative, 1926).

8. Delcourt, *Hermaphrodite*, 10.

9. Ibid., 23.

10. Anne Fausto-Sterling, e-mail communication, 1 March 1995.

CHAPTER **8.** NATURAL BECOMES "UNNATURAL"

1. Marie Delcourt, *Hermaphrodite: Myths and Rites of the Bisexual Figure in Classical Antiquity,* trans. Jennifer Nicholson (1956; London: Studio Books, 1961) 26–27.

2. Arthur Evans, *The God of Ecstasy: Sex-Roles and the Madness of Dionysos* (New York: St. Martin's Press, 1988) 110–11.

3. Livy, quoted in Burgo Partridge, *A History of Orgies* (New York: Crown, 1960) 54.

4. Evans, *Witchcraft,* 38.

5. Edward Gibbon, *The Decline and Fall of the Roman Empire* (New York: Modern Library) 1:129, referred to in Evans, *Witchcraft,* 39, 41.

6. *Romanarum et Mosaicarum Legum Collatio,* V, 3, trans. and quoted in Eva Cantarella, *Bisexuality in the Ancient World,* trans. Cormac Ó Cuilleanáin (New Haven: Yale University Press, 1992) 177.

7. Cantarella, *Bisexuality,* 180.

8. Vern L. Bullough, *Homosexuality: A History from Ancient Greece to Gay Liberation* (New York: New American Library, 1979) 31–34.

CHAPTER **9.** "HOLY WAR" AGAINST TRANS PEOPLE

1. Frederick Engels, *Socialism: Utopian and Scientific* (1892; Moscow: Progress Publishers, 1970) 18. For specifics of the persecution of minority groups within this context, see Jeffrey Richards, *Sex, Dissidence and Damnation: Minority Groups in the Middle Ages* (New York: Routledge, 1991).

2. Albert Heinrichs, "Greek Maenadism from Olympias to Messalina," *Harvard Studies in Classical Philology* 82 (1978): 158, n. 117, trans. from the Greek and quoted in Arthur Evans, *The God of Ecstasy: Sex-Roles and the Madness of Dionysos* (New York: St. Martin's Press, 1988) 20.

3. Jeffrey Russell, *Witchcraft in the Middle Ages* (Ithaca, NY: Cornell University, 1972) 74, 156–57.

4. Vern L. Bullough, "Transvestites in the Middle Ages: A Sociological Analysis," *American Journal of Sociology* 79.6 (1974): 1384.

5. Marie Delcourt, "Female Saints in Masculine Clothing," *Hermaphrodite: Myths and Rites of the Bisexual Figure in Classical Antiquity,* trans. Jennifer Nicholson (1956; London: Studio Books, 1961) 84–102; Vern L. Bullough and Bonnie Bullough, *Cross Dressing, Sex, and Gender* (Philadelphia: University of Pennsylvania Press, 1993) 51–54.

6. Alexander Cooke, *Pope Joan: A Biography of Pope Joan, 853–855 A.D.* (London: Blunt and Barin, 1610), and Clement

Wood, *The Woman Who Was Pope* (New York: Faro, 1931), referred to in Bullough, *Cross Dressing*, 55–56.

7. H. Usener, *Legends der Heiligen Pelagia* (Bonn: A. Marcus, 1879), as cited in Bullough, *Cross Dressing*, 53.

8. Marina Warner, *Joan of Arc: The Image of Female Heroism* (New York: Knopf, 1981) 152.

9. Bullough, *Cross Dressing*, 61.

10. A. D. Hope, *A Midsummer Eve's Dream* (New York: Viking, 1970) 43, as cited in Evans, *Witchcraft*, 19.

11. Peter Ackroyd, *Dressing Up: Transvestism and Drag* (New York: Simon and Schuster, 1979) 89.

12. Ibid., 90.

13. Harry Brierly, *Transvestism: A Handbook with Case Studies for Psychologists, Psychiatrists and Counselors* (Oxford: Pergamon Press, 1979) 2.

14. Ackroyd, *Dressing Up*, 90.

15. Natalie Zemon Davis, *Society and Culture in Early Modern France: Eight Essays* (Stanford, CA: Stanford University Press, 1975) 97–98.

16. Richard Green, *Sexual Identity Conflict in Children and Adults* (New York: Bantam, 1974) 6.

17. Brierly, *Transvestism*, 3.

CHAPTER 10. LEADING THE CHARGE

1. Pat Molloy, *And They Blessed Rebecca: An Account of the Welsh Toll-gate Riots, 1839–1844* (Llandysul, Wales: Gomer Press, 1983) 1–2. In addition to Molloy, extensive documentation of "Rebecca and her daughters" can be found in David J. V. Jones, *Rebecca's Children: A Study of Rural Society, Crime, and Protest* (Oxford: The Clarendon Press, 1989).

2. Jones, *Rebecca's Children*, 197; see also Molloy, *They Blessed Rebecca*, 37–39, 160–61.

3. Natalie Zemon Davis, "Women on Top: Symbolic Sexual Inversion and Political Disorder in Early Modern Europe," *The Reversible World: Symbolic Inversion in Art and Society*, ed. Barbara A. Babcock (Ithaca, NY: Cornell University Press, 1978) 178.

4. Natalie Zemon Davis, "The Reasons of Misrule," *Society and Culture in Early Modern France: Eight Essays* (Stanford, CA: Stanford University Press, 1975) 98–99.

5. Davis, *The Reversible World*, 167–68.

6. Ibid.

7. Davis, *Society and Culture*, 118–19.

8. Davis, *The Reversible World*, 176, 179.

9. Ibid., 176; see also David J. V. Jones, *Before Rebecca: Popu-*

lar Protests in Wales, 1793–1835 (London: Allen Lane, 1973) 33–34, 47, 66, 203–3.

10. Davis, *The Reversible World*, 178–79.

11. F. R. H. de Boulay, ed. *Documents Illustrative of Medieval Kentish Society* (Ashford, 1964) 254–55.

12. William Edward Hartpole Lecky, *A History of Ireland in the Eighteenth Century*, 2 vols. (1892; New York: AMS Press, 1969) 2: 22–23.

13. Davis, *The Reversible World*, 178.

14. Molloy, *They Blessed Rebecca*, 6.

15. Daniel Wilson, *Memorials of Edinburgh in the Olden Time*, 2nd ed. (Edinburgh, 1891), as cited in Davis, *The Reversible World*, 180.

16. Lecky, *History of Ireland*, 2:22–23. An example from Lecky shows this popular form of resistance co-opted by an Irish Catholic property owner waging a struggle against Protestant English colonialism; see also Lecky, 1:360.

17. Ibid., 2:1–45.

18. Wayne G. Broehl, Jr., *The Molly Maguires* (New York: Vintage, 1964) 25. See also Anthony Bimba, *The Molly Maguires* (New York: International Publishers, 1932), and J. Walter Coleman, *The Molly Maguire Riots: Industrial Conflict in the Pennsylvania Coal Region* (New York: Richmond, Garret and Massie, 1936).

19. Trench's *Realities of Irish Life,* as cited in F. P. Dewees, *The Molly Maguires: The Origin, Growth, and Character of the Organization* (1877; New York: Burt Franklin, 1969) 44, and also in S. B. Liljegren, "The Irish Element in the Valley of Fear," *Irish Essays and Studies VII* (Uppsala: Irish Institute/Uppsala University, 1964) 13. The militant peasants of Ireland who adopted the names and dress of women to fight for justice impacted the United States labor movement. (See Harold W. Aurand, *From the Molly Maguires to the United Mine Workers: The Social Ecology of an Industrial Union, 1869–1897* (Philadelphia: Temple University Press, 1971). Following waves of Irish immigration to this country, the names of the Molly Maguires, White Boys, and Ribbonmen emerge. In his study of the industrial battles in the Pennsylvania Coal Region in the nineteenth Century, Coleman noted that "Organizations known variously as 'Buckshots,' 'Sleepers,' or 'Ribbonmen' made their appearance shortly before and during the Civil War, and took on a legendary as well as a real significance that culminated in the professed belief on the part of employers that these organizations constituted from the very beginning the secret combination known as the *Molly Maguires.*" (*Molly Maguire Riots*, 4)

Irish of all classes at that time belonged to an organization called the Ancient Order of the Hibernians. The former president of the A. O. H. in the United States, Matthew Cummings, described the origin of his group: "The organization has been known in the old land [Ireland] by different names – Confederationists, Whiteboys, and Ribbonmen, and at last became known as the Hibernian Society, as the name of Ribbonmen had been outlawed by the English government." (Bimba, *The Molly Maguires*, 47) But when Irish miners accused of being Molly Maguires were framed by the coal owners in Pennsylvania and faced the gallows, ". . . the national leadership of the A. O. H. joined hands with the hangmen against the anthracite miners. . . . The national organization, with headquarters in New York, was controlled by the Irish bourgeoisie and the Catholic clergy and, therefore, had nothing in common with the real interests of the Irish workers." (Bimba, *The Molly Maguires*, 11) In 1993 and 1994, the New York City branch of the A. O. H. refused to allow Irish lesbians and gay men to march as a contingent in the St. Patrick's Day Parade.

20. O. P. Gilbert, *Women in Men's Guise*, trans. J. Lewis May (London: John Lane The Bodley Head Limited, 1932) 95.

21. Peter Ackroyd, *Dressing Up: Transvestism and Drag* (New York: Simon and Schuster, 1979) 70.

22. Davis, *The Reversible World*, 180.

23. George Rudé, *The Crowd in History: A Study of Popular Disturbances in France and England, 1730–1848* (New York: John Wiley & Sons, 1964) 85.

CHAPTER 11. NOT JUST PASSING

1. O. P. Gilbert, *Women in Men's Guise*, trans. J. Lewis May (London: John Lane The Bodley Head Limited, 1932) 87–91.

2. Vern Bullough, "Transsexualism in History," *Archives of Sexual Behavior* 4.5 (1975) 566–67.

3. Alan Bray, *Homosexuality in Renaissance England* (1982; London: GMP Publishers, 1988) 91.

4. David F. Greenberg, *The Construction of Homosexuality* (Chicago: University of Chicago Press, 1988) 337; Randolph Trumbach, "Sex, Gender, and Sexual Identity in Modern Culture," *Forbidden History: The State, Society, and the Regulation of Sexuality in Modern Europe*, ed. John C. Fout (Chicago: University of Chicago Press, 1992) 92.

5. Bray, *Homosexuality*, 97.

6. Peter Ackroyd, *Dressing Up: Transvestism and Drag* (New York: Simon and Schuster, 1979) 58.

7. Greenberg, *Construction of Homosexuality*, 334. See also

Rictor Norton, *Mother Clap's Molly House: The Gay Subculture in England, 1700–1830* (London: GMP Publishers, 1992).

8. Ackroyd, *Dressing Up*, 60–61.

9. Ibid., 64.

10. Ibid., 84.

CHAPTER **12. FROM GERMANY TO STONEWALL**

1. Philip S. Foner, *Frederick Douglass: Selections from His Writings* (1945; New York: International Publishers, 1964) 10.

2. Ibid., 22.

3. Ibid., 23.

4. Ibid.

5. Warren J. Blumenfeld and Diane Raymond, *Looking at Gay and Lesbian Life* (Boston: Beacon Press, 1993) 196–98.

6. *Codex Theodosius*, IX, 7, 6, trans. and quoted in Eva Cantarella, *Bisexuality in the Ancient World*, trans. Cormac ÓCuilleanáin (New Haven: Yale University Press, 1992) 181.

7. Laurence Senelick, "Boys and Girls Together: Subcultural Origins of Glamour Drag and Male Impersonation on the Nineteenth Century Stage," *Crossing the Stage: Controversies on Cross-Dressing*, ed. Lesley Ferris (New York: Routledge, 1993) 94.

8. Senelick, *Crossing the Stage*, 86. See also Alan Sinfield, *The Wilde Century: Effeminacy, Oscar Wilde and the Queer Moment* (New York: Columbia University Press, 1994).

9. Senelick, *Crossing the Stage*, 88.

10. Vern L. Bullough, *Homosexuality: A History from Ancient Greece to Gay Liberation* (New York: New American Library, 1979) 13, 16, 66–67.

11. Magnus Hirschfeld, *Transvestites*, trans. Michael A. Lombardi-Nash (Buffalo, New York: Prometheus Books, 1991). See also Charlotte Wolff, *Magnus Hirschfeld: A Portrait of a Pioneer in Sexology* (London: Quartet Books, 1986).

12. John Lauritsen and David Thorstad, *The Early Homosexual Rights Movement, 1864–1935* (New York: Times Change Press, 1974) 9, 11. See also James D. Steakley, *The Homosexual Emancipation Movement in Germany* (Salem, New Hampshire: Ayer Publishers, 1975).

13. Lauritsen and Thorstad, *Homosexual Rights*, 46, 50.

14. Ibid., 42.

15. For an oral history of the rebellion, see Martin B. Duberman, *Stonewall* (New York: Dutton, 1993); for a brief history of the movement that followed, see Barry D. Adam, *The Rise of a Gay and Lesbian Movement* (Boston: Twayne Publishers, 1987).

1. Randolph Trumbach, "London's Sapphists: From Three Sexes to Four Genders in the Making of Modern Culture," *Bodyguards: The Cultural Politics of Gender Ambiguity*, eds. Julia Epstein and Kristina Straub (New York: Routledge, 1991) 112–13.

2. *What Is Intersexuality?* (San Francisco: Intersex Society of North America, n. d.).

3. Anne Fausto-Sterling, "The Five Sexes: Why Male and Female Are Not Enough," *The Sciences* March/April 1993: 20–21.

4. Ibid., 23–24.

5. The prevalence of intersexual myths is reflected in documentation as diverse as "Androgyne," *The Woman's Encyclopedia of Myths and Secrets*, ed. Barbara G. Walker (San Francisco: Harper & Row, 1983) 32–34; the Greek *androgyne* of Plato, *The Symposium*, trans. Walter Hamilton (London: Penguin Books, 1951) 58–65; the Japanese *Izanagi/Izanami* unity described in Mircea Eliade, *Myths, Dreams, and Mysteries: The Encounter between Contemporary Faiths and Archaic Realities*, trans. Philip Mairet (1957; New York: Harper & Row, 1975) 179–83; the Yoruban and Dahomean *Mawulisa* and *Seboulisa* of Audre Lorde, *The Black Unicorn* (New York: W. W. Norton, 1978), William Bascom, *The Yoruba of Southwestern Nigeria* (New York: Holt, Rinehart & Winston, 1969), and Melville Herskovits, *Dahomey*, 2 vols. (New York: J. J. Augustin, 1934); the "twofold gods" of Crete, Cyprus, Rome, Greece in Marie Delcourt, *Hermaphrodite: Myths and Rites of the Bisexual Figure in Classical Antiquity*, trans. Jennifer Nicholson (1956; London: Studio Books, 1961) 17–43; and the *Warharmi* of the Kamia of southwestern North America in Walter Williams, *The Spirit and the Flesh: Sexual Diversity in American Indian Culture* (Boston: Beacon Press, 1986) 18. For some information on persecution of hermaphrodites, see the original classical sources referenced in P. M. C. Forbes Irving, *Metamorphosis in Greek Myths* (Oxford: The Clarendon Press, 1990) 149–50, and the French sources in Eugene de Savitsch, *Homosexuality, Transvestism and Change of Sex* (Springfield, IL: Charles C. Thomas, 1958) 30.

6. Cheryl Chase, e-mail communication, 2 February 1995.

7. Sandra Salmans, "Objects and Gender: when an It Evolves into a He or a She," *New York Times* 16 November 1989: B1.

8. Vern L. Bullough and Bonnie Bullough, *Cross Dressing, Sex, and Gender* (Philadelphia: University of Pennsylvania Press, 1993) viii.

9. Ibid.

1. Simone de Beauvoir, as quoted in Monique Wittig, "One Is Not Born A Woman," *The Straight Mind* (Boston: Beacon Press, 1992) 10. See also Simone de Beauvoir, *The Second Sex* (New York: Knopf, 1953).

2. Ann Oakley, *Woman's Work: The Housewife, Past and Present* (New York: Vintage, 1974) 170. For an account of contemporary communal childcare in Vanatinai of Papua New Guinea, based on a matrilineal kinship structure described as *taubwaragha* ("ancient"/"way of the ancestors") by its people, see Maria Lepowsky, "Gender and Power," *Fruit of the Motherland: Gender in an Egalitarian Society* (New York: Columbia University Press, 1993) 281–306. For a brief account, see John Noble Wilford, "Sexes Equal on South Sea Isle," *New York Times* 29 March 1994: C1, 11.

3. Ann Oakley, *Sex, Gender and Society* (New York: Harper & Row, 1972) 134–35.

4. J. H. Driberg, *The Lango: A Nilotic Tribe of Uganda* (London: T. Fisher Unwin, 1923) 210.

5. Alfred L. Koeber, "Handbook of the Indians of California," *Bureau of American Ethnology Bulletin* 78 (1925) 748–49.

6. George Devereux, "Institutionalized Homosexuality of the Mohave Indians," *Human Biology* 9 (1937) 498–527, as cited in Richard Green, *Sexual Identity Conflicts in Children and Adults* (New York: Basic Books, 1974) 10.

7. C. Daryll Forde, "Ethnography of the Yuma Indians," *University of California Publications in American Archaeology and Ethnology* 28 (1931) 157; and Edward Winslow Gifford, "The Cocopa," *University of California Publications in American Archaeology and Ethnology* 31 (1933) 294.

8. This is, of course, a very broad categorization of two currents of women's liberation that often intermingled and overlapped. Both were represented by articles and essays on sex and gender in *Sisterhood Is Powerful: An Anthology of Writings from the Women's Liberation Movement*, ed. Robin Morgan (New York: Vintage Books, 1970). Twenty-five years later, these issues are being revisited by contemporary feminists such as Minnie Bruce Pratt, *S/HE* (Ithaca, NY: Firebrand Books, 1995) and Ann Snitow, "A Gender Diary," *Conflicts in Feminism*, eds. Marianne Hirsch and Evelyn Fox Keller (New York: Routledge, 1990).

CHAPTER **15.** MAKING HISTORY

1. "Big Gap in U.S. Wealth," *New York Times* 17 April 1995, A1.

2. Alan Berubé, presentation in Writing, Class, and Race session, Outwrite: Fifth National Lesbian and Gay Writers Conference, Boston, 5 March 1995.

SELECTED BIBLIOGRAPHY

ACKROYD, PETER. *Dressing Up: Transvestism and Drag*. New York: Simon and Schuster, 1979.

BENNETT, BETTY T. *Mary Diana Dods, A Gentleman and A Scholar*. New York: William Morrow, 1991.

BORNSTEIN, KATE. *Gender Outlaw: On Men, Women and the Rest of Us*. New York: Routledge, 1994.

BRIERLY, HARRY. *Transvestism: A Handbook with Case Studies for Psychologists, Psychiatrists and Counsellors*. Oxford: Pergamon Press, 1979.

BULLOUGH, VERN L. *Homosexuality: A History From Ancient Greece to Gay Liberation*. New York: New American Library, 1979.

_____. "Transsexualism in History." *Archives of Sexual Behavior* 4.5 (1975): 561–71.

_____. "Transvestites in the Middle Ages: A Sociological Analysis." *American Journal of Sociology* 79.6 (1974): 1384.

_____ and Bonnie Bullough. *Cross Dressing, Sex, and Gender*. Philadelphia: University of Pennsylvania Press, 1993.

DAVIS, NATALIE ZEMON. *Society and Culture in Early Modern France: Eight Essays*. Stanford, CA: Stanford University Press, 1975.

_____. "Women on Top: Symbolic Sexual Inversion and Political Disorder in Early Modern Europe." *The Reversible World: Symbolic Inversion in Art and Society*. Ed. Barbara A. Babcock. Ithaca, NY: Cornell University Press, 1978. 147–90.

DEKKER, RUDOLF M. & LOTTE C. VAN DE POL. *The Tradition of Female Transvestism in Early Modern Europe*. New York: St. Martin's Press, 1989.

DENNY, DALLAS. *Current Concepts in Transgender Identity: Towards a New Synthesis*. New York, Garland Publishers, 1996.

_____. *Gender Dysphoria: A Guide to Research*. New York: Garland Publishers, 1994.

_____. *Identity Management in Transsexualism*. King of Prussia, PA: Creative Design Services, 1994.

_____. "The Politics of Diagnosis and a Diagnosis of Politics: The University-Affiliated Gender Clinics, and How They Failed to Meet the Needs of Transsexual People." *Chrysalis Quarterly* 1.3 (1994): 9-20.

ELLMANN, RICHARD. *Oscar Wilde*. New York: Knopf, 1988.

EPSTEIN, JULIA AND KRISTINA STRAUB, eds. *Body Guards: The Cultural Politics of Gender Ambiguity*. New York: Routledge, 1991.

FEINBLOOM, DEBORAH HELLER. *Transvestites and Transsexuals: Mixed Views*. New York: Delta, 1976.

GARBER, MARJORIE. *Vested Interests: Cross-Dressing and Cultural Anxiety*. New York: Routledge, 1992.

GILBERT, O. P. *Men in Women's Guise: Some Historical Instances of Female Impersonation*. Trans. Robert B. Douglas. London: John Lane The Bodley Head Limited, 1926.

_____. *Women in Men's Guise*. Trans. J. Lewis May. London: John Lane The Bodley Head Limited, 1932.

HERDT, GILBERT, ed. *Third Sex, Third Gender: Beyond Sexual Dimorphism in Culture and History*. New York: Zone Books, 1994.

HIRSCHFELD, MAGNUS. *Transvestites*. Trans. Michael A. Lombardi-Nash. Buffalo, New York: Prometheus Books, 1991. A translation from German of *Die Transvestiten*. Leipzig: Max Spohr, 1910.

KESSLER, SUZANNE J. & WENDY MCKENNA. *Gender: An Ethnomethodological Approach*. Chicago: The University of Chicago Press, 1978.

LIVING THE SPIRIT: *A Gay American Indian Anthology*. Compiled by Gay American Indians. Coordinating ed. Will Roscoe. New York: St. Martin's Press, 1988.

LUCAS, R. VALERIE. "*Hic Mulier*: The Female Transvestite in Early Modern England." *Renaissance and Reformation/Renaissance et Réforme* 24.1 (1988): 65–84.

PATHY-ALLEN, MARIETTE. *Transformations: Crossdressers and Those Who Love Them*. New York: E.P. Dutton, Inc., 1989. (Available through the International Foundation for Gender Education.)

PRATT, MINNIE BRUCE. *S/HE.* Ithaca, NY: Firebrand Books, 1995.

ROSCOE, WILL, ed. "Bibliography of Berdache and Alternative Gender Roles Among North American Indians." *Journal of Homosexuality* 14.3-4 (1987).

_____. *The Zuni Man-Woman.* Albuquerque: University of New Mexico Press, 1991.

ROTHBLATT, MARTINE. *The Apartheid of Sex.* New York: Crown Publishers, 1995.

RUBIN, GAYLE. "Thinking Sex: Notes for a Radical Theory of the Politics of Sexuality." *American Feminist Thought at Century's End: A Reader.* Ed. Linda S. Kauffman. Cambridge, MA: Blackwell, 1993.

STONE, SANDY. "The *Empire* Strikes Back: A Posttranssexual Manifesto." *Body Guards: the Cultural Politics of Gender Ambiguity.* Eds. Julia Epstein and Kristina Straub. New York: Routledge, 1991. 208-304

STRYKER, SUSAN. "My Words to Victor Frankenstein above the Village of Chamounix: Performing Transgender Rage." *GLQ: A Journal of Lesbian and Gay Studies* 1.3 (1994): 237-54

_____. "Transsexuality: The Postmodern Body and/as Technology." *Exposure: The Journal of the Society for Photographic Education* 30:1/2 (1995): 38-50.

SULLIVAN, LOUIS. *From Female to Male: The Life of Jack Bee Garland.* Boston: Allyson Publications, 1990.

_____. *Information for the Female to Male Cross Dresser and Transsexual.* (Seattle: Ingersoll Gender Center, 1990).

THOMPSON, C. J. S. *The Mysteries of Sex: Women Who Posed as Men and Men Who Impersonated Women.* New York: Causeway Books, 1974.

TRUMBACH, RANDOLPH. "London's Sapphists: From Three Sexes to Four Genders in the Making of Modern Culture." *Body Guards: The Cultural Politics of Gender Ambiguity.* Eds. Julia Epstein and Kristina Straub. New York: Routledge, 1991. 112–41.

_____. "Sex, Gender, and Sexual Identity in Modern Culture." *Forbidden History: The State, Society, and the Regulation of Sexuality in Modern Europe.* Ed. John C. Fout. Chicago: The University of Chicago Press, 1992. 89–106.

WHEELWRIGHT, JULIE. *Amazons and Military Maids: Women Who Dressed as Men in the Pursuit of Life, Liberty and Happiness.* London: Pandora, 1989.

WILLIAMS, WALTER. *The Spirit and the Flesh.* Boston: Beacon Press, 1986.

page

   4. Personal collection of the author.

   5. TOP: Mariette Pathy Allen; BOTTOM: UPI/Bettmann.

   6. LEFT: UPI/Bettmann; RIGHT: The Bettmann Archive.

   7. The Bettmann Archive.

 10. Lyn Neely.

 19. Bette Spero.

 22. National Anthropological Archives, Smithsonian Institution.

 23. National Museum of the American Indian, Smithsonian Institution, neg. No. 34256.

 24. From T. D. Bonner, ed., *The Life and Adventures of James P. Beckwourth.* (New York: Harper and Bros., 1856).

 25. National Anthropological Archives, Smithsonian Institution, neg. No. 85-8666.

 26. Seaver Center for Western History Research, Natural History Museum of Los Angeles County.

 27. M. P. Schildmeyer.

 29. Rare Books and Manuscripts Division, The New York Public Library, Astor, Lenox and Tilden Foundations.

 32. LEFT: Rouen, Musée de Beaux Arts; RIGHT: Photo by Mary Edith Durham. Reproduced by permission of the Royal Anthropological Institute of Great Britain and Ireland. RAI #2713.

33. LEFT: Copyright British Museum; RIGHT: O. P. Gilbert, *Women in Men's Guises*, The Bodley Head, Limited, London, 1932.

34. TOP: Art and Artifacts Division, Schomburg Center for Research in Black Culture, the New York Public Library, Astor, Lenox and Tilden Foundations; BOTTOM: Fondo Casaola, Fototeca del Instituto Nacional de Anthropologia e Historia.

37. Clarke Historical Library.

40. Mapping Specialists, Inc., based on a map by Gary Wilson.

41. TOP: State Hermitage Museum, St. Petersburg, Russia; BOTTOM: Scala/Art Resource, NY.

42. All photos this page: Pierre Verger.

43. Kevin Bubriski.

44. Andrew Holbrooke.

45. National Anthropological Archives, Smithsonian Institution.

46. Royal Anthropological Institute of Great Britain and Ireland, RAI #3159.

47. Gregory Dunkel

51. The Metropolitan Museum of Art, Rogers Fund and Edward S. Harkness Gift, 1929. (29.3.1).

52. Hulton Deutsch Collection Limited.

56. TOP: Copyright British Museum; BOTTOM: Copyright Cleveland Museum of Art, 1995, Andrew R. and Martha Holden Jennings Fund, 70.16.

57. Nationalmuseum Stockholm.

58. LEFT: Copyright British Museum; RIGHT: Staatliche Museen.

59. Staatliche Museen.

65. The Phoebe A. Hearst Museum of Anthropology, University of California at Berkeley.

69. From "Pope Joan" by Emmanuel D. Rhoides. Trans. by Lawrence Durrell. NY: Overlook Press, 1984, ©1966.

72. Copyright British Museum.

76. Copyright A.C.L.-Brussel, Museum Mayer van den Bergh.

77. Reprinted by permission of the Llyfrgell Genedlaethol Cymru (The National Library of Wales).

78. Reprinted by permission of the Llyfrgell Genedlaethol Cymru (The National Library of Wales).

81. Courtesy of Yamila Azize-Vargas, Puerto Rican feminist writer. The photo is from her personal collection.

84. TOP: The Morning Leader; MIDDLE: Copyright British Museum; BOTTOM: Drawing from the Stockton *Evening Mail*, October 9, 1897.

85. O. P. Gilbert, *Women in Men's Guises,* The Bodley Head Limited, London, 1932.

86. UPI/Bettmann.

87. Courtesy of the Schwartz/Miller collection.

88. TOP AND MIDDLE: Mansell Collection; BOTTOM: The Guildhall Library.

89. Mansell Collection.

92. From the archives of Imperial QUEENS & KINGS of New York, Long Island and New Jersey.

93. Gregory Dunkel.

94. TOP: Robert Giard; MIDDLE: Mariette Pathy Allen; BOTTOM: Andrew Holbrooke.

95. Mariette Pathy Allen.

96. Albert Sanchez.

99. Mariette Pathy Allen.

103. Jhalawar Museum, Rajasthan, India/Art Resource, NY.

105. Department of Library Services, American Museum of Natural History.

106. Kevin Bubriski.

107. Bibliotec Nationale de France.

110. TOP: Rare Books and Manuscripts Division, the New York Public Library, Astor, Lenox and Tilden Foundations; BOTTOM: National Anthropological Archives, Smithson ian Institution, neg. No. 74-662.

111. Library of Congress.

113. Viviane Moos.

114. Alison Bechdel.

117. Loren Cameron.

119. Graphic by author.

123. The Bettmann Archive.

124. Jennie Livingston.

126. Viviane Moos.

128. TOP: Steven Gillis; BOTTOM: Mick Hicks.

129. Mariette Pathy Allen.

131. Andrew Holbrooke.

132. Mariette Pathy Allen.

133. Saskia Scheffer.

135. Marcus Alonso.

136. John Nafpliotis.

138. From the personal collection of Pauline Park.

139. From the personal collection of Morgan Holmes.

140. V. Jon Nivens.

141. Maria Elena Boyd.

143. Dona Ann McAdams.

144. Mariette Pathy Allen.

145. Mariette Pathy Allen.

146. Stephanie Dumaine.

147. From the wallet of Martine Rothblatt.

148. From the personal collection of Bo Headlam.

149. Mariette Pathy Allen, from *Transformations: Crossdressers and Those Who Love Them* (E.P. Dutton, Inc., 1989)

150. Catherine Opie.

152. Loren Cameron.

153. From the personal collection of Stormé DeLarverié.

154. Dona Ann McAdams.

155. Robin Slavin.

156. From the personal collection of Sharon Ann Stuart.

157. Jennie Livingston.

158. Mariette Pathy Allen.

159. From the personal collection of Kris Knutson.

160. Mariette Pathy Allen.

161. Mariette Pathy Allen.

162. Mariette Pathy Allen, from *Transformations: Crossdressers and Those Who Love Them* (E.P. Dutton, Inc., 1989).

163. Mariette Pathy Allen.

169. Copyright Corbis-Bettman.

*Page numbers in **boldface** refer to illustrations.*

Abbeys of Misrule, 76

Abbots of Unreason, 76–77

Abortion, 71, 104–5

Achilles, 56, 58

Ackroyd, Peter, 71

Acoma mojaro with sister and niece, **110**

Affirmative action, 125

Africa, transgender in, 44, 45, **46**, 47

Afro-Mexicana revolutionary, **34**

AIDS, 94, 117, 125, 127, 144

Albright-Knox Art Gallery, 12, 13, 14

Alcatraz, takeover of, 24

Allante, Queen Allyson Ann, **92**, 93

Allen, Mariette Pathy, 158

Amazon River, 22, 58

Amazons, 22, 42, 57–58, 80

American Anthropologist, 25

American Indian movement, 7. *See also* Native Americans

America Online, 102

Amun, 53

Anaconda Copper, 13, 14

Anastasia, Saint, 68

Anatomy, sex, as dichotomy, 103

Androgyny, 58, 114

Anti-Semitism, 11, 15, 49–50

Apache, White Mountain, 28

Aphrodite of Cyprus, 69

Appollinaria, Saint, 68

April (aka Don), 158, **158**

Araucanians, 44, 45

Arcadius, Emperor, 63

Archeholz, Johann Wilhelm von, 88

Ardhanariswara, **103**

Aristotle, 57

Armstrong, King Farrell, **92**, 93

Artemis, 40

Arthur, 158, **158**

Articles of Accusations, 35

Ashtoreth, 40

Ashurbanipal, King, **52**, 53, 85–87

Asia, transgender in, 44–45

Astaroth, 50

Astarte, 40

Atargatis, 40, 50

Athanasia (Alexandria), Saint, 68

Athena, 56, **56**, 57

Attica prisoners, 13, 14, 15

Auffault, Laurie, **94**

"Aunt Nancy Men," 91

Axe, double-edged, 42, 57, 58

Bacchanalia, 63

Bacchus, see Dionysus

Badé, 22, 23, **23**, 25–26

Balboa, Vasco Núñez de, 23, **29**

Ballan, Dorothy, Feminism and Marxism, 17

Barcheeampe (Woman Chief), **24**

Bars, gay, 7–8, 9, 97

Baumann, Hermann, 40

Beauvoir, Simone de, 110

Bechdel, Alison, cartoon by, **114**

Berdache, 21 and n, 22, 25, 45

Berle, Milton, 4

Berubé, Allan, 127

Best, Adele, 87

Bethlehem Steel, 13

Bible, 73, 93

Bigotry, 49–53, 79

Biological determinism, 41, 110–11, 112–13

Birmingham Sixteenth Street Baptist Church, 140

Birth control, 71

Black Elk, 26

Black Liberation movement, 125

Black Panther Party, 7, 123

Blue-for-boys gender assignment, 105–7

"Blues" (NYC), police beatings at, 93

Bo Headlam, 148, **148**

Bohemian Grove, 115

Bonae, 68

Bornstein, Kate, 154, **154**; *Gender Outlaw*, 154

Boulton, Stella (Ernest), 88, **89**, 95

Bowen Collegiate Institute, 111

Bradford college students, **128**, 129

Brandeis, Tala Candra, **117**

Breast(s): of Amazons, 57; cancer, 127; reduction operation, 12–13

Breugel, Pieter, "Dulle Griet" (Mad Margot), **76**, 77

British Daily Telegraph, 59

Brown, Florence Alice Compson, 86, **87**

Brown, John, 110

Brown, Thomas Compson, 86

Brown University, 59

Bry, Theodor de, **29**

Bullough, Bonnie, 50, 69, 106–7

Bullough, Vernon, 50, 69, 106–7

Burns, Randy, 24

Butheric, 64

Cade's Rebellion, 78

Caesarius of Arles, 68

Calancha, Antonio de la, 23

Cameron, Barbara, 24

Cameron, Loren, 117, 152, **152**

Capetillo, Luisa, **81**

Carter, Mikel-Jon, **155**

Castillo, Otto René, 2

Castration, 40, 41, 72

Catholics, Catholic Church, 23, 31, 34–35, 67–68; on belief in fairies, 78; canonization of female-to-male saints by, 68–70, 71; denouncing of transgender expression by, 8, 70; and feudalism, 67, 71–73; transgender liturgical drama in, 70, 71

Cauchon, Pierre (Bishop of Beauvais), 34, 36

Caumont, Jean de, 33

Centaurs, 56

Chambliss, Robert, 140

Charles, King of France, 32–33

Chase, Cheryl, 104

Chevrolet, 13

Chile, military coup in, 14

Chinese Women's Journal, The, 34

Chopin, Frédéric, 87

Christianity, 62, 63, 70

Christina, Queen of Sweden, 80, 87

Chrystos, 26–27, 28–29

Chui Chin, 34

Chumash *joya*, 23

CIA, 14

Circus Amok, 143

Civil Rights movement, 7, 94, 125

Civil War, 37, 125

Clark, Alice, 77, 81

Cleveland, Grover, 25

Cocopa *warhameh*, 23

Code of Theodosius, 93

Colonization, 25, 28–29

Color schemes, gender-based, 105–7

Columbia University, 21

Communalism, 55, 64, 67; overthrow of, 51, 52

Communists, 4–5, 14, 15, 17, 127

Constantine, Emperor, 63

Constitution, 124

Corpus juris civilis, 64

Council of Constantinople, 68

Crazy Horse, 26

Crisp, Quentin, **133**, 133–34; *The Naked Civil Servant,* 133

Cross Dressers International, 94

Crow nation, 22, 24, 25–26; *badé,* 22, 23, **23**, 25–26

Croy, Norma Jean, 24

Cybele, 41, 50

Cyberspace, 102

Dan (Linda), 162, **162**

Darwin, Charles, 51

Davis, Natalie Zemon, 76, 78

Day of Mourning at Plymouth Rock, 24

Dea Syria, 40

Debates, about sexuality/homosexuality, 96

Debbie (bodybuilder and powerlifter), **136**, 137

Debbie (girlfriend of Kris), 158, 159, **159**

Delcourt, Marie, 58

Delarverié, Stormé, 153, **153**

Dengaku, 70

D'Eon, Chevalier (Charles D'Eon), **88**

Deuteronomy, 49, 50, 52, 68, 71

Diana, 40

Dionysus, 56–57, 58, 59, 62–63, 70

Documents, sex categorization on, 61–62, 125

Douglass, Frederick, 91, 99, 120

Drag balls, 157

Drag performance, 115

Drag queen(s), 23, 81; Cuban, **128**, 129

"Dykes to Watch Out For" (cartoon series), 114

East Coast Female-to-Male Group, 155

Effeminacy, Roman edict on male, 63

Egypt, 14, 53

Einstein, Albert, 38

Elagabalus, Emperor, 63

Emma, 158, **158**

Enaree priestess, trans, **41**

Engels, Frederick, 39, 51; *Origin of the Family, Private Property and the State,* 17

England, 78, 79, 80, 88

Erauso, Catalina de, **33**

Eugenia, Saint, 68

Euphrosyne, Saint, 68

Evans, Arthur, 36–37, 63

Fairies, 34, 78–79

Fantasia Fair, 149

Farinelli (Carlo Broschi), **72**

Fascism, 5, 15, 96, 126

Fausto-Sterling, Anne, 59, 103–4

Feast of Fools, 70, 71

Feinberg, Irving, 49

Feinberg, Leslie, **4**, **19**

Female-to-male trans person with husband, **85**

Festivals and carnivals, cross-dressing for, **76**, 76–77, 80, 83

Feudalism, 32, 33, 80, 81, 87; and Catholic Church, 67, 71–73

Field Columbian Museum, 25

Five sexes, 103

Fran, 160, **160**

French Federation of Feminine Sports, 86

FTM International, 145

Gabriel, Davina Anne, 160, **160**

Gainsborough, Thomas, *Blue Boy,* 107

Galla, Saint, 68

Gallae, 41, **41**

Garland, Jack Bee (Elvira Mugarietta), **84**, 144

Garland, Judy, 115

Gay American Indians, 24

Gay and Lesbian Historical Society of Northern California, 144

Gay liberation movement, 8, 97; in Germany, 95–96

Gender-baiting, 98

Gender expression, 8, 12, 16, 92

Gender outlaw, 61, 83, 97

Gender-phobia, 116, 117

General Ludd's wives, 80, 81, 128

Genocide, 21n, 22, 23, 25, 79, 96

Gens, 17, 39, 51

Genuine family values, **129**

German Homosexual Emancipation Movement, 96

Germany, 126; gay liberation movement in, 95–96

Greater New York Gender Alliance, 94

Great Mother, 40–41

Greek antiquity, 55–58

Greek mythology, 56–57, 58

Green, James, 145, **145**

Greenberg, David F., 41

Guajire, 44

Guevara, Che, 16

Guzmán, Nuño de, 25

Haitian march through Brooklyn, NY, **47**

Hall, John (Radcliffe), 87, 94; *Well of Loneliness,* 94

Halloween, 8, 70, 80

Hamilton Lodge Ball, 157

Hannah, 160, **160**

Hatshepsut, King, **51**, 53

Haudenosaunee, 51

Hawkes, Jacquetta, 42–43

Hebrews, 49–51

Hecate, 40

Henry III, King of France, 80

Henry VI, King of England, 34

Heracles, 56, 58, **58**, 59

Heriot, Angus, *The Castrati in Opera,* 72

Hermaphrodites, 23, 26, 40, 91

"He-shes," 97

Heviosso, worshipping, **42**

Hickman, Craig, 135, **135**; "Rituals," 135

Hirschfeld, Magnus, 95, 96

Hitler, Adolf, 126

HIV, 126

Ho Chi Minh, 16

Holmes, Morgan, 139, **139**

Hommasse, 33

Homosexual trans scene, **59**

Hopi illustrations, **22**

Hormones, 104, 105; male, 12, 13, 105; right to affordable, 124

Hot Peaches Review, 131

House of Pendavis, 157

Hundred Years War, 32

Huntington, Henry Edwards, 107

Identification papers, sex categorization on, 61–62, 125

Ihamana, **25**

Imperial Court of New York, 94

Imperial QUEENS & KINGS of New York City, Long Island, and New Jersey, 93

Industrial Revolution, 79, 80

Inquisition, 31, 34, 35, 36, 71–73

International Bill of Gender Rights, 156

International Conference on Transgender Law and Employment Policy (ICTLEP), 156

International Council of Women, 91

International Women's Day, 15

Intersex Society of North America, 103, 104

Intersexual: deity in Nepal, **106**; feeding bird, **56**; statue, Greek, **57**

Intersexuality, 103–4, 139

Iraq, war against, 126

Ireland, 71; White Boys of, 78–79

Iron Age, 59

Iroquois Confederacy, 51

Irving, P. M. C. Forbes, 56–57

Ishtar, 40, 50

Isis, 50

Israel, 14

Ithyphalloi, 56

ITT, 14

Jacob, **155**

Janus Information Facility, 144

Jerome, Saint, 69

Jewel Box Review, 153

Jews, 5, 17, 67, 73, 95; and anti-Semitism, 11, 49–50; and fascism, 126; and military coup in Chile, 14

Joan, Pope (John Anglicus), 68, **69**

Joan of Arc, **32**, 39, 67, 78, 81, 87; cross-dressing by, 31–37, 69–70, 78; execution of, 36, 71; trial of, 34–36; worship of, 36–37

Joe Medicine Crow, 25

Johnson, Lyndon B., 123

Johnson, Marsha "P." ("Pay it no mind!"), **130**, 131

Jones, David J. V., 78

Jorgensen, Christine, 4, **5**, 6–7

Joseph (Hildegund), Saint, 68

Judaism, 49–51, 53

Kaineus (Caeneus), 56

Kane, Ariadne, 149, **149**

Katz, Jonathan Ned, *Gay American History: Lesbians and Gay Men in the U.S.A.,* 22

Klamaths, 22, 25

Kleinhan's Music Hall, 14, 15

Klementi tribe, **32**, 33

Kris, 158–59, **159**

Kroeber, Alfred L., 111–12

Ku Klux Klan, 115, 140

Kumbh Mela festival, male dressed as Hindu deity at, 42, 43

La Branlaire, 77

LaChine, Coco, **94**

Lady Clares, 79

Lady Rocks, 79

Lady Skimmington, 78

Lafitau, Joseph François, 23

Lakota, 26

Lakota Sioux, 24

Lame Deer, 26

Land of the Hermaphrodites, The (painting), 106, **107**

Lange, Jenny Savalette de, 87

Laura, 158, **158**

Lawrence, Sir Thomas, *Pinkie,* 107

Leadership, transgendered, 75–81

Lenin, Nikolai, 18

Lesbian and gay liberation movement, 8

Lesbian Herstory Archives, 94

Lettin It All Hang Out: An Autobiography by RuPaul, 97

Leviticus, 49

Liberté (Angélique Brulon), **33**, 87

Livingston, Jennie, 157

Living the Spirit: A Gay American Indian Anthology (comp. by Gay American Indians; ed., Will Roscoe), 24

Livy, 63

Longest Walk, 24

Lorde, Audre, 131

Lords of Misrule, 76

Lord's Prayer, 73

Luddite Rebellions, 80

Luxemburg, Rosa, 16

McCarthy, Joseph, 4, 5, 127

McCubbin, Bob, 39

Magalhães de Gandavo, Pedro de, 22, 58

Mao Zedong, 16

Mapuche, 45

Mardi Gras, 80

Margarita, Saint, 68

Maricopa *kwiraxame',* 23

Marine, Cooks and Stewards Union, 127

Marinus (Marina), Saint, 68, 69

Marquette, Jacques, 23

Marx, Karl, 51, 90

Marxists, Marxism, 15, 16–17

"Masque Ball," raid on New York City, 4, **5**

Matrilineal societies, 17–18, 51, 56, 68, 70; in early Greece, 55; in Stone Age, 42–43; transsexual priestesses in, 41

Matrona, Saint, 68

Menominee nation, 26

Mére d'Enfance, 76

Mére Folle and her Children, 76, 77, 81

Mére Sotte and her Children, 76

Merrill, Eddy, 16, 18
Merrill, Jeanette, 16, 18
Middle Ages, 67, 68, 70, 76, 79
Midwives, 71
Miller, Jennifer, 143, **143**
Miller, Maxine, 149, **149**
Minnesota Human Rights Act, 146
Mohave, North American, 111–12
Mollies, 87, **88**, 101
Molly houses, 87, 88
Molly Maguires, 79, 81
Montgomery, Josephine, 87
Morgan, Lewis H., 51
Morris, Violette, **86**
Mother Goddess, 51
Mummer's parades, 80
Murray, Margaret A., 37
Museum of the American Indian, 21
Muslims, 67, 73

Nadleeh, concept of, **26**, 27
Nangeroni, Nancy, 163, **163**
Napoleon Bonaparte, 33, 87
Nat dancer, **44**
National Dress Reform Association, 111
National Organization for Women, New
  Jersey (NOW-NJ), resolution passed by,
  119
National Variety Artists Exotic Carnival
  and Ball, arrests at, **123**
Native Americans, 21–29
Navajo, 26, 27
Nazis, Nazism, 5, 96, 126
New Alexandria Lesbian Library (NALL),
  155
New York Times, 122
Nkrumah, Kwame, 16
Noh drama, Japanese, 70
Northern Paiute, 24
Nzinga, King of Angola, **34**

Omphale, Queen, 58
Osh-Tisch, 22, **23**, 25
Outreach Institute for Gender Studies, 149

Paganism, 34, 78
Palestine, 14–15, 50
Papula, Saint, 68
Paragraph 175 (German law), 96
"Paris Is Burning," 124, 157
Park, Fanny (Frederick), 88, **89**, 95
Park, Pauline, 44–45, 138, **138**
Passing, concept of, 70, 83–89
Patriarchy, 17, 42, 51, 56, 68, 70; rise of,
  52–53; and transsexual priestesses, 41
Paula, Saint, 68
Pedone, Monica, **94**
Peithinos, 59
Pelagia, Saint, 68, 69
Peltier, Leonard, 24
Pendavis, Avis, 157, **157**
Phallus, woman carrying, 56, **58**, 59
Pink-for-girls gender assignment, 105–7
Pliny the Younger, 57
Plutarch, 40, 58
Poland, 71
Police raids, 4, 5, 6, 7, 8. *See also* Stonewall
  Rebellion
Porteous Riots, 79
Power, Bet, 155, **155**
Praetorian Guard, 63
Pretty Eagle, 22, 25
Pride March, **94**, 131
Priestesses, transsexual, 40–41, **41**, 43–44,
  50, 58; and Aphrodite, 69; and Catholic
  Church, 71; map showing location of, **40**
Priests, female-to-male, 45
Prince, Virginia, 149, **149**
Proposition 187, 143

"Queer," 92, 98

Racism, institutionalized, 11
"Rebecca and her daughters," 75, 77, **78**, 81
Rebellions, cross-dressing for, 75–76, 77–81
Reconstruction, 125
Renewing vows of love, **161**
Renfro, Sky, **150**, 151
Restrooms, experiences in public,
  116–17, 137

Ribbon Societies, 79
Rockefeller, John D., 110
Rockefeller, Nelson, 13, 14
Rollerarena, 94, **95**
Roman edicts, 62–64
Roman empire, decline of, 64
Roscoe, Will, 24
Ross, Diana, 115
Rothblatt, Martine and Bina, and their children, 147, **147**
RuPaul, **96**, 115; autobiography of, 97

Safer-sex campaign, free condom distribution for, **113**
Saint, Assotto (Yves Lubin), **94**
Saints, canonization of female-to-male, 68–70, 71
Sakpota dancer, **42**
Sand, George, 87
San Francisco Chronicle, 84
San Francisco Human Rights Commission, 145
Scientific Humanitarian Committee (Germany), 95–96
Scotland, 79
Sex-reassignment surgery, 104, 105, 118
Sexual Minorities Archives, 155
Shamans, 25, 41, 44, 45, 47
Shangó, 42, 58
Sharon (Bruno), **126**
"She-males," 97
Simms, S. C., 25–26
Sitting Bull, 26
Slaves, slavery, 52, 62, 71, 80, 91; in Greek antiquity, 55, 57; in Roman empire, 64
Smith, Barbara, 129
Smith, Petric (Elizabeth H. Cobbs), 140, **140**; *Long Time Coming*, 140
Snell, Hannah ("Bill Bobstay the Sailor"), **84**
Societies for the Reformation of Manners, 87
Spier, Leslie, 22
Spotted Eagle, 26, **27**, 28
Stein, Gertrude, 87

Stone, Merlin, 41
Stone Age, 40, 41, 42–43
Stonewall Rebellion, 9, 23, 99, 126, 153; and Marsha "P." Johnson, 131; and mollyhouse raid, 87; significance of, 81, 93, 95, 97, 98, 123
Stryker, Susan, 144
Stuart, Charles Edward ("Bonnie Prince Charlie"), 88
Stuart, Sharon Ann, 156, **156**
Suffrage, women's, 91
Sullivan, Louis Graydon, 144, **144**, 145, 155
Surgery: on intersexual infants, 103, 104; right to affordable, 124; transsexual adult, 104, 105
Synod of Ver, 69
Syria, 14

Taylor, Timothy, 59
Teena, Brandon, 132
Tehuelche, 44
Thatcher, Margaret, 110
Thaw Out Picnic, 8
Theater, 70–71
Theodora, Saint, 68
Theodosius, Emperor, 63, 93
Theseus, 58
Third sex, 96, 101
Thomas, Wesley, 27
Thompson, Franklin (Sarah Emma Edmonds), **37**
Timicuan women, **110**
Tipton, Billy, 83–84
Tommies, 101
Trans-phobia, 116
TransSisters, 160
Transvestite, coining of word, 95
Trumbach, Randolph, *London's Sapphists: From Three Sexes to Four Genders in the Making of Modern Culture*, 101
Truth, Sojourner, 110
Tupinamba, 22, 58
Two-Spirits, **110**
Two-Spirit Tolowa medicine person, 44, **45**
Two-Spirit tradition, 21n, 22–29

Uli figure, **105**
Ulrichs, Karl Heinrich, 96
Usener, Herman, 69

Vaca, Alvar Núñez Cabeza de, 22
Valentinian, Emperor, 63
Valerio, Max Wolf, **141**, 142
Vietnam War, 12, 14; protests against, 7, 12, 123
Vroman, Adam Clark, 26

Wales, 77, 78, 79, 80; toll-gate riots in, 75, 81
Walker, Lynn, **94**
Walker, Mary Edwards, **111**
Walsh, Peggy, **128**, 129
War of the Demoiselles, 78
Wayne, John, 115
Week of Differently Gendered Lives, audience for speech of, 146
Westermarck, Edward, 22
We'Wha, **25**
White, Terry, **94**
White Boys of Ireland, 78–79
White Cindy, 25
White Whale Woman, 45
Wilde, Oscar, 89, 95
Wildfire, Madge, 79, 81
Wilgefortis (Uncumber), Saint, 68
Williams, Walter, 45; *The Spirit and the Flesh*, 25, 26
Wilson, Charley (Catherine Coombes), **84**
Winkte, 26

Winter Solstice, Celt, 70
Wisconsin, University of, 144
Witchcraft, 34, 35, 68, 70, 71
Woman, attempt to define, 109–10, 113
Women, oppression of, 17–18, 53, 83, 85, 87, 113; beginning of, 51; fighting, 119; institutionalized, 110, 116; and trans movement, 118
Women's liberation movement, 7, 12, 17, 62, 102, 116; accomplishments of, 125; and institutionalized oppression of women, 110, 116; and need for trans liberation movement, 109; second wave of, 112–13
Women's Rights convention (Seneca Falls, NY), 91
Workers World Party (WWP), 14, 15–17, 18, 39
World War II, 5
Wounded Knee: massacre at, 14; occupation of, 24

Xtravaganza, Venus, **124**

Yahweh, 50
Yoruba ritual, **42**
Young Lords, 7
Youth Against War and Fascism (YAWF), 15
Yvonne, 162, **162**

Zeus Labrandeus, 58
Zuni, 25